INTERMEDIATE
CORRELATIONAL
METHODS

INTERMEDIATE CORRELATIONAL METHODS

ANDREW R. BAGGALEY

PROFESSOR OF PSYCHOLOGY

TEMPLE UNIVERSITY

JOHN WILEY & SONS, INC.

NEW YORK · LONDON · SYDNEY

Library of Congress Catalog Card Number: 64-23825
Printed in the United States of America

To Arlene, Philip, and Paula

PREFACE

This book is intended chiefly to serve as a textbook for a second-semester course in statistics for students in the behavioral sciences. I have assumed that the reader will have mastered the contents of a first-semester introductory statistics course, including at least the mean and standard deviation, two-variable product-moment correlation, and the basic concepts of sampling theory. Until recent years, the practice in most universities has been to follow such a course with another semester course emphasizing experimental design but including also some material on multiple correlation, reliability, and validity. However, the scope of these topics has been so expanded that it is now very difficult to discuss all of them in one semester except in a superficial manner.

Therefore there has been a tendency in recent years to offer *two* intermediate level statistics courses. The material now available on experimental design is extensive enough to require an entire semester, and so the next level of topics in correlational analysis is treated more fully in a separate course, which often includes an introduction to the increasingly useful technique of factor analysis. Of course, some problems arise when one deals with correlational methods without some discussion of sampling theory. In the present textbook, I present significance tests for use with some of the correlational techniques; however, I make no attempt to develop a rationale for them. In any case, I feel that the demonstration that a correlation coefficient differs significantly from zero (for example) is only the *first* step in establishing the practical utility of a measuring procedure. This point has not been emphasized sufficiently in textbooks on experimental design.

I have tried to be steadfast in my intention to write a *textbook* rather than a *handbook*. The majority of behavioral science students enrolled in statistics courses will not become specialists in statistics or psychometrics! Most authors of textbooks on statistics find it difficult to refrain from inserting into the text extra formulas that they feel the student "might find useful in special situations." However, this procedure often discourages the average student, who is usually quite frightened by a vast array of Greek symbols. I have sought to reserve all such "extra material" for footnotes or the Appendix so that the text itself can be read easily by the *average* behavioral science student. Examples have been taken from various areas in behavioral science in an effort to assure each student that the techniques will be of practical value in his own research problems. I have also made a special attempt to present most of the derivations in more detail than is the case in many textbooks of statistics. A statement like "it can be easily shown that . . ." is often most discouraging to the reader, because the steps that have been omitted are not at all "obvious" to him! Many students with "average mathematical preparation" can be induced to take the necessary time to understand clearly the derivations *if* all the steps are set out for them. If the student can master the concepts developed in this book, he will be prepared to read much of the more advanced material on factor analysis, test score theory, and multivariate statistical analysis.

This manuscript represents an expanded development of class notes for courses that I have taught during the last seven years at Temple University and the University of Wisconsin, Milwaukee. The students in these classes made many suggestions to improve the clarity of exposition. Also I have benefited greatly from the comments by my teaching colleagues, too numerous to list individually unfortunately, who read one or more of the chapters in earlier drafts. I am very grateful to my wife, Arlene, who encouraged me and protected me from external distractions while I worked on these pages.

ANDREW R. BAGGALEY
Wyncote, Pa.
July, 1964

CONTENTS

1

CORRELATIONAL STATISTICS IN BEHAVIORAL SCIENCE

In this textbook we shall be discussing the correlational techniques used in psychology, sociology, anthropology, education, social work, and allied fields. Many of the relationships involved in the basic laws of these disciplines were discovered by correlational analysis.

The distinction between correlational statistics and the group of statistical methods often labeled by the term "analysis of variance" has been used almost synonymously with the distinction between two types of "approaches" to the solution of scientific problems. For example, Cronbach (1957) speaks of "experimental psychology" versus "correlational psychology." However, a more fruitful distinction is that between "experimental" and "nonexperimental" approaches. In the case of the two approaches, the manner of controlling variables is at issue rather than the type of statistical analysis applied to the data. On the one hand, it is possible to use correlational techniques to evaluate the results of experimental treatments. For example, one might correlate dosage level of a drug with speed of an animal traversing a T maze. The usual procedure is to compare a control group with one or more experimental groups by using the statistical technique of analysis of variance. On the other hand, many nonexperimental studies use comparisons between average scores of selected groups of subjects or between the percentages of such groups manifesting a particular response. An example is "criterion keying" (Nunnally, 1959, p. 317) of interest inventories by comparing the percentages of "like" response given to an item by engineers (for example) and "persons in general." However, in point of fact, the correlational methods *have* been the most widely used statistical techniques in nonexperimental investigations.

Since correlational techniques thus are associated mainly with the nonexperimental approach to scientific problems in the behavioral sciences, it will be worth while at this point to list some of the relative advantages of the experimental and nonexperimental approaches. To aid our discussion we shall use, with some modification, a classification scheme devised by Edwards (1960, Chapter 1). The variables used in research in behavioral science can be conveniently classified into three groups—response variables, stimulus variables, and trait variables. Stated symbolically, we seek functional relationships of the general form,

$$R = f(S_1, S_2, S_3, \ldots T_1, T_2, T_3, \ldots)$$

For our purposes, a "stimulus variable" is one that the investigator varies by *physical manipulation*. He may vary the conditions of light, sound, or temperature. He may administer an experimental treatment to one group of animals and treat another group as a "control group." On the other hand, a "trait variable" represents a characteristic of each subject that is assumed to remain relatively constant during the investigation. The most direct example of a trait variable is a physical measurement, such as height, weight, or chronological age. However, as Edwards points out, in behavioral science we often use "response-inferred" trait variables, that is, variables specified by prior observation of response. The famous "IQ" is an example of a response-inferred trait variable. We set up a standard situation (namely, a specified set of test items and test instructions) and "calibrate" each subject by means of his responses to this standard situation. Although there has been much argument about whether the IQ changes over a period of months or years, we assume that it stays constant during the period of hours or days involved in most behavioral science studies.

Using the above vocabulary, we can now define an "experiment" as an investigation that includes *at least one* stimulus variable, that is, a study in which at least one condition is varied by physical manipulation. Thus, if one studied the effect of dimming room illumination on the scores of college students on one mechanical aptitude test, the investigation would qualify as an experiment (although a rather trivial one). On the other hand, a factor analysis of 40 mechanical aptitude tests, which would involve a considerable amount of computation, would be a nonexperimental study because no variable is physically manipulated.

There has been an increasing tendency in recent years to do experiments that include both stimulus and trait variables. To use a simple example, let us suppose that we are interested in the question of whether playing the radio hinders studying. The response variable in such a study might be the score on a standardized achievement test. The stimulus variable would be "radio-on versus radio-off." It is possible that male students are affected in their studying by having the radio on but that this is not so for female students. This would be an example of an "interactive effect." However, such an interactive effect could not be discovered unless both the stimulus variable and the trait variable were studied systematically. This could be done by constituting four groups of subjects—male-radio-on, male-radio-off, female-radio-on, and female-radio-off. Obviously the trait variable must be controlled by selection of subjects rather than by physical manipulation (Brown and Ghiselli, 1955, Chapter 5).

By our foregoing definitions, studies including both stimulus and trait variables fall under the classification of the experimental approach. For many years scientists have tended to prefer use of stimulus variables rather than trait variables because it has been believed that cause-effect relationships can be more validly inferred from their use (Edwards, 1960, pp. 215–217). Certainly the advance of the physical sciences has been accomplished predominantly by the use of the experimental approach. However, are there situations in the behavioral sciences in which a nonexperimental approach is indicated?

In the first place, there are some variables that are impossible to control by physical manipulation. The chronological age of the subject cannot be changed at all by the investigator. The sex of the subject is similarly, for all practical purposes, not under his control! It is usually quite impractical to control the subject's past experience (e.g., years of education) for the purposes of a specific study. Yet all these variables may be highly relevant for predicting behavior. Therefore we often study response variables as a function of these particular trait variables and formulate conclusions on the basis of correlational evidence.

It is possible to manipulate certain other variables, but ethical considerations restrain behavioral scientists from doing so. Social customs in democracies do not allow scientists to inflict conditions on subjects that may result in permanent harm. Brain surgery for experimental purposes is not permitted on human subjects. Similarly, experiments on human breeding are prohibited. To circumvent these limitations, animal subjects are often used, but then there is the problem of generalizing findings between species. Human subjects may volunteer for such experiments, but it is unlikely that these volunteers will be representative of the human species, so again generalization is hazardous. As another example, consider a study of the causes of war. One could hardly expect the United Nations to permit a team of scientists to inflict certain political conditions on an experimental group of countries (as opposed to a matched control group) to test the hypothesis that these political conditions lead to war. In all these situations, the scientist necessarily observes the conditions when they occur naturally and then relates them to his response variables.

In a third type of situation it is possible and socially acceptable to manipulate a variable, but the scientist does not do so because imposing the experimental condition tends to change *the nature of* the response variable being measured. Campbell (1957) has discussed a somewhat more general situation, that involving "reactive measures." He says (pp. 298–299), "A reactive measure is one which modifies the phenomenon under study, which changes the very thing that one is trying to measure. In general, any measurement procedure which makes the subject self-conscious or aware of the fact of the experiment can be suspected of being a reactive measurement. Whenever the measurement process is *not* a part of the normal environment it is probably reactive." If the reactivity is involved in the very process of observation itself, then the difficulty applies to both the experimental and nonexperimental approaches. However, in many problems of behavioral science, imposing an experimental condition is perceived by the subjects as *not* being a part of the normal environment, and therefore their behavior is modified; whereas the same subjects may "act as usual" if the procedures of the nonexperimental approach are applied, that is, the subjects are unobtrusively observed on two or more variables as they go about their normal daily affairs.

Reactive situations (in the narrower sense) seem most likely to occur in the study of motivational and emotional problems and in the study of interactions in social groups. As an example of the first type of problem, consider the analysis of humor. Although little agreement has been reached over the centuries as to what makes people laugh, it is generally agreed that humor is a transient phenomenon. Although a clever experimenter may use a certain amount of ingenuity and deception in manipulating variables, it is likely that observation of "naturalistic" conditions will continue to be the principal source of data in the area of humor.

Similarly, in the area of social group interaction, the limitations of the experimental approach are critical. In recent years many ingenious experiments have been performed using groups of persons assembled only for the purpose of the experiment (Glanzer and Glaser, 1961). Interesting relationships have been established between measures of group behavior and various stimulus variables. However, it is not easy to say whether the findings can be generalized to groups that exist naturally and that have a history of their own, such as families, religious groups, social classes, and political parties.

In summary, experimental manipulation of conditions in behavioral science research can be impossible, unethical, or misleading. However, some of the older sciences (e.g., astronomy, geology, and meteorology) have made considerable progress using mostly the nonexperimental approach.

Whereas the experimenter applies much of his effort to precise control of environmental conditions, the nonexperimental researcher should apply considerable technical skill to the sampling operations in his studies. He should be familiar with survey sampling techniques (Hansen, Hurwitz, and Madow, 1953, Chapters 1–3), and he should pay a great deal of attention to the matter of sampling *situations* as well as sampling people (Brunswik, 1956). If it can be said that a good experimenter collects some precise information about a limited situation, then a good nonexperimental investigator should obtain his somewhat less precise information from a broader and more representative range of situations.

The discussion up to this point has been concerned with the possible use of correlational techniques in the nonexperimental approach to establishing antecedent-consequent relationships, that is, those that might be conceived of as cause-effect relationships. However, another important area for correlational analysis is study of the relationships between response variables. Probability of response, resistance to extinction, amplitude of reaction, quality of response (e.g., "correct" versus "incorrect"), and latency have all been used as response variables. Although, typically, a single response variable is chosen to represent "behavior" in the formulation of behavioral science theories based on experimental results, there is evidence that various response variables actually show rather low intercorrelations (Hilgard and Marquis, 1940, p. 138). Recent research (Pubols, 1960) suggests that incentive magnitude affects "performance" (time-dependent response measures) but not "learning" (time-independent response measures). It is probable that more extensive use of correlational statistics by experimenters would help to explain other situations in which the effect of stimulus variables on behavior is not clear.

The place of correlational statistics in "applied" behavioral science research has been acknowledged more readily than in "basic" research. Yet further consideration leads one to doubt whether some studies can be considered as completely "applied" research. For example, let us consider the development of a formula for predicting freshman grade-point average from a battery of psychological tests. A sample of incoming freshmen is followed through their first collegiate year, and regression weights are calculated (see Chapters 4 and 5). As long as these weights are used merely to obtain the predicted grade-point average for each new incoming freshman, the research can be described only as applied. However, eventually the school counselors will probably wonder why some of the weights are large and others are small and wonder how the test scores are influenced by specific school situations and other personality characteristics. (See also the discussion of "construct validity" in Chapter 6.) If a counselor collects data to answer these questions, then he has moved into the area of basic behavioral science research. Factor analysis, an advanced correlational technique that will be discussed later, was developed to answer some questions of this type.

Although we have touched on the issue above, we shall now concern ourselves directly with the inference of cause-effect relations from correlation. Most introductory textbooks in behavioral science warn that such an inference is *in general* unwarranted, and they cite striking examples to clinch the point. The question that logically follows is "If we cannot infer cause-effect relations from correlations, why calculate correlations at all?" The first answer is that sometimes behavioral scientists are interested in establishing predictable antecedent-consequent sequences, regardless of whether they know the mechanics of how such sequences are mediated. Personnel selection problems in education and industry furnish a good example.

However, for the purposes of "basic research," a second reply is more germane. Suppose, for example, that sociologists assemble 50 hypotheses about what "causes" juvenile delinquency. The most certain answer to this question would have to come from an extensive longitudinal study. But such studies are very expensive. To get some "leverage" on the problem, the sociologists could do a cross-sectional study in which they correlate incidence of delinquency with various demographic and personality variables. The variables that showed correlations not statistically significantly different from zero (see page 20) could be ruled out as possible causal factors in the sense that it is unlikely that they are related to delinquency. However, as with all statistical conclusions, we must consider the possibility of a "Type II error" (Edwards, 1960, p. 19), that is, a particular variable may actually be related to delinquency, but the correlation is near zero because of random sampling variability. Nevertheless, with limited resources the sociologists would be better advised to select the few variables that *do* show significant correlations for further study by carefully controlled experimental designs. In this sense, the non-experimental approach can furnish valuable *negative* evidence toward the solution of research problems.

In this chapter we have discussed some of the general problems involved in the use of correlational statistics in behavioral science, with particular attention being given to comparison of experimental and nonexperimental approaches to research problems.

Problems

1. Why have not correlational techniques been used more frequently to evaluate the results of experimental treatments?

2. A psychologist wishes to study the following presumed factors in paired-associates learning by college students: age, college major, delay in reinforcement, intertrial time interval, length of list, oral versus visual presentation, sex, and socio-economic status of family. Which factors will he probably treat as stimulus variables, and which will he treat as trait variables?

3. What are some of the theoretical and practical problems involved in the use of response-inferred trait variables?

4. In the suggested investigation of whether playing the radio hinders studying, which other stimulus variables could profitably be used in the experiment?

5. Is generalization to human beings from experiments on animal subjects less valid in behavioral science than in biological science? Cite some areas of inquiry to defend your position.

6. "An investigation of the stock market may change the stock market." Is this statement relevant to the discussion of the experimental versus the nonexperimental approach? If so, how?

7. A firm specializing in market research installs a device in the television sets of a selected sample of families within a particular metropolitan area. The device records how long the set is in operation and to which station it is tuned. Comment on this situation from the point of view of reactive variables.

8. A sociologist questions high school students about their sexual practices. Comment on this situation from the point of view of reactive variables.

9. A behavioral scientist wishes to study the effect of desegregation in a large housing project on inter-racial attitudes. Describe a relevant experimental study (including the method of manipulating the stimulus variables) and a nonexperimental study.

10. In the history of medicine, have there been instances in which the study of correlations (broadly defined) between observations has suggested more precise experiments on the factors involved in the causation and prevention of specific diseases? If so, describe some of these.

2

SOME USEFUL
MATHEMATICAL TECHNIQUES

In this chapter we shall consider two mathematical techniques that have proven to be extremely useful in statistics. The first is the concept of linear functions, and the second is a set of three summation laws.

LINEAR FUNCTIONS

Scientific investigations have as one of their most important aims the description of natural phenomena in terms of functional relationships between variables. When it is found that the value of a variable Y depends on the value of another variable X so that for every value of X there is a corresponding value of Y, then Y is said to be a "function of" X. As an example, let us consider the relation between the Fahrenheit and Centigrade scales of temperature. If one is given a temperature value in the Centigrade scale (represented by X), then the corresponding value in the Fahrenheit Scale (represented by Y) can be calculated by the formula

$$Y = 32 + 1.8X \qquad (2.1)$$

If the Centigrade temperature is $10°$, the Fahrenheit temperature is calculated to be

$$Y = 32 + 1.8(10) = 32 + 18 = 50 \qquad (2.2)$$

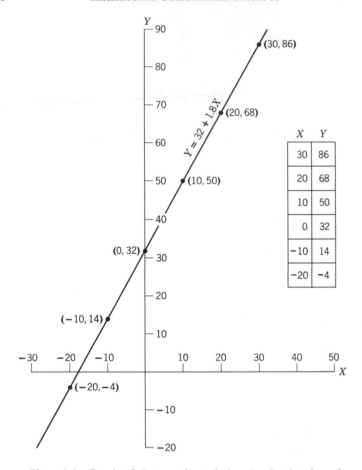

Figure 2.1 Graph of the equation relating the Centigrade and Fahrenheit temperature scales.

Similarly, if the Centigrade temperature is 20°, the Fahrenheit temperature must be

$$Y = 32 + 1.8(20) = 32 + 36 = 68 \qquad (2.3)$$

Let us now plot this relationship on the usual rectangular system of coordinates. First we calculate Centigrade temperatures corresponding to a few more Fahrenheit temperatures and assemble them in a table such as is shown in Figure 2.1. We plot the points corresponding to each pair of numbers and connect them with a line. Note that this procedure gives a straight line.

It will now be stated that *any* equation of the general form, $Y = a + bX$, will generate a straight line on the rectangular system of coordinates. The values a and b represent constants that do not change when the values of X and Y change. Note above in Equations 2.2 and 2.3 that the values 32 and 1.8 appear in both equations, even though X changes from 10 to 20 and Y changes from 50 to 68. Of course, if a new equation is introduced (e.g., the equation for transforming values on the Centigrade scale to values on the Kelvin scale), the a and b values will probably change. Nevertheless, for any calculations made with the new equation, a and b will again remain constant while X and Y change.

It can further be stated that the values of a and b for a particular equation have a definite geometrical representation in the rectangular coordinate system. Note that in Figure 2.1 the equation line crosses the Y axis at the point where Y equals 32. This relationship is represented more generally in Figure 2.2. The Y coordinate of the point where the line crosses the Y axis indicates the "Y intercept," which is always equal to the constant a in the general linear equation. The Y intercept can be negative, in which case the line crosses the Y axis below the "origin" (the intersection of the two coordinate axes). When the line passes directly through the origin, the Y intercept is zero.

The geometrical meaning of b, the other constant in the general linear equation, is a bit more subtle. In Figure 2.3 several lines have been drawn and labeled with their appropriate equations. Note that the lines for the equations $Y = 2 + .5X$ and $Y = 2 + X$ give the same Y intercept, as we would expect because the a value for both is 2. However, they differ in *slope*. The b value in the linear equation represents the slope of the line. The second equation, which has a b value of 1, is steeper in slope than the first equation, which has a b value of .5.

A more exact formulation of this concept of slope is represented in Figure 2.2. If from any point R on the equation line we draw a horizontal line to an arbitrary point S and then draw a vertical line from point S to point T on the equation line, we will have constructed a right triangle. Represent the base of this triangle as distance n and the altitude as distance m. The "slope" is defined as

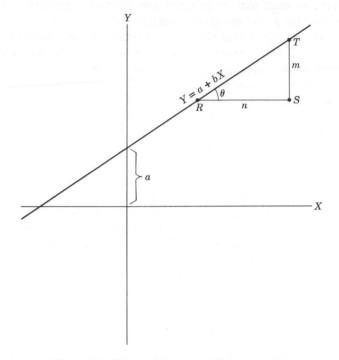

Figure 2.2   Graph of the general linear equation.

the ratio of *m* to *n*. (Readers who know some elementary trigonometry will recognize this ratio as the tangent of the angle θ.)

The important point for our purposes is that, for a given equation, this ratio of *m* to *n* will be constant no matter what the size of the triangle and no matter where along the equation line the triangle is constructed. The particular values of *m* and *n* may change, but their *ratio* will remain constant for all such triangles. Since only two points are needed to define a straight line uniquely, the appropriate line can be drawn directly from inspection of a linear equation. The first point to locate is the point cutting off the *Y* intercept, which is given by the constant *a* in the linear equation. Then another point can be drawn at an arbitrary distance directly to the right of the first point. (It is usually computationally convenient to use 5 or 10 units for this distance.) A third point is drawn directly above the second and at a distance such that the ratio of distances m and n is equal to the constant b in the linear equation. The first and third points are the points through which the line of the equation should be drawn. For example, if the slope of the line were 1.4, the third point could be drawn five units to the right of the first point and seven units above it.

The alert reader will have noticed that, strictly speaking, the above method of drawing the appropriate line for a given linear equation applies only when the b value is positive. However, a simple change covers the situation for negative b values. The second point is drawn to the *left* of the point cutting off the Y intercept. This procedure results in a line that moves *down* as it goes to the right. Such a line, namely that for equation $Y = 1 - .5X$, is shown in Figure 2.3. If b equals zero, the second term in the linear equation vanishes, and

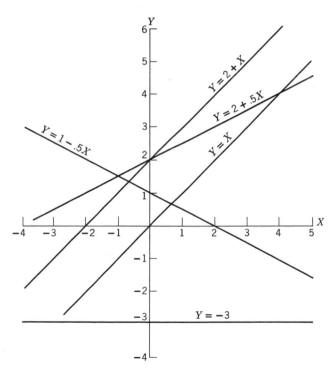

Figure 2.3   Graphs of various linear equations.

the corresponding line lies parallel to the X axis, as is exemplified by the line labeled $Y = -3$ in Figure 2.3.

We shall now apply this concept of the linear equation by showing that the equation for transforming raw scores to z scores (the basic type of standard scores) can be reduced to the linear form. Recall that the basic equation for the z score is

$$z_X \equiv \frac{X - M_X}{\sigma_X} \tag{2.4}$$

First we split the expression on the right side into two fractions:

$$z_X = \frac{X}{\sigma_X} - \frac{M_X}{\sigma_X} \tag{2.5}$$

Next we write the first fraction a bit differently and then reverse the order of the two fractions:

$$z_X = -\frac{M_X}{\sigma_X} + \frac{1}{\sigma_X}(X) \tag{2.6}$$

Let us now consider which of the factors in this expression are constant and which are variable. The mean and standard deviation are constant in that, when the z score for each new person is calculated, the same numbers are put into the formula for M_X and σ_X. On the other hand, for each new person a different X value is substituted, and the z_X is likewise different (except when two consecutive persons have identical scores). Thus it can be seen that, in this formula, the term $-M_X/\sigma_X$ corresponds to a in the general linear equation, and the factor $1/\sigma_X$ corresponds to b.

In Chapter 5 we shall see that another equation that is often used in statistics, the regression equation, can also be transformed into an equation of the linear type. The linear equation, too, is often used to express functional relationships between independent and dependent variables in behavioral science experimentation.

A very useful theorem is that the F ratio of the analysis of variance and the absolute value of the product-moment correlation coefficient are both invariant under any linear transformation of the variables. This means that we can add, subtract, multiply, or divide the raw scores by any number (as long as we do the *same* operation on each raw score) without affecting the magnitude of r or F. In practice, a constant is often subtracted from the raw scores or else they are divided by a constant in order to simplify the computations considerably. The procedure for calculating the correlation coefficient from "coded values" (Guilford, 1956, pp. 143–144) depends on this theorem.

In summary, the linear equation is one of the most useful tools available to behavioral scientists.

THREE SUMMATION LAWS

The second mathematical technique that we shall be using frequently in later chapters is a set of three summation laws. You are already familiar in a general way with the use of the summation sign to indicate that several individual measures of a given variable are to be added together. For example, in calculating the mean score on a spelling test for a fourth-grade class, the individual scores of all the pupils are added together, and their sum is divided by the number of scores.

According to the First Summation Law, the summation sign can be distributed to each term of a series of terms to be added (or subtracted), that is,

$$\sum(X + Y - Z) = \sum X + \sum Y - \sum Z \qquad (2.7)$$

This law can perhaps best be demonstrated by using a small numerical example:

X	Y	Z	$X + Y - Z$
3	7	4	6
2	6	5	3
5	1	8	−2
0	9	4	5
10	23	21	12

Stating the matter somewhat differently, we can say that the grand total of 12 can be reached either by first obtaining the row totals or by first obtaining the column totals. The left side of Equation 2.7 tells us to obtain each value of $X + Y - Z$ (each row total) separately and then to add them. For example, the first row total is $3 + 7 - 4 = 6$. The right side of Equation 2.7 tells us first to obtain the column totals ($\sum X$, $\sum Y$, and $\sum Z$) and then to combine them, that is, $10 + 23 - 21 = 12$.

According to the Second Summation Law, a constant factor can be "taken outside" of the summation sign, that is,

$$\sum kX = k\sum X \tag{2.8}$$

In our numerical example, the number 3 is multiplied by each of a series of X values:

k	X	kX
3	8	24
3	-2	-6
3	5	15
3	0	0
	11	33

Again, we may proceed either by rows or columns. The left side of Equation 2.8 tells us first to multiply each X value by 3 (e.g., $3 \times 8 = 24$) and then to add these products. The right side of the equation says that the same end result can be obtained by first adding the X values and then multiplying *this sum* by the constant 3, that is, $11 \times 3 = 33$.

The Third Summation Law deals with the sum of a constant:

$$\sum k = Nk \tag{2.9}$$

In our numerical example we shall use the constant 7.

k
7
7
7
7
$28 = 4\,(7)$

Here N equals 4, the number of scores, and each score is identically 7.

A more convenient computational form can be derived for many statistical techniques by using these three summation laws, as we shall see in the following chapters.

Problems

1. Change the following equations into linear form and then draw the appropriate line for each on a graph:

(a) $3X = 4Y - 2$
(b) $7 + .4Y = X - 3.8$
(c) $6X - 5 = 2Y - 4$
(d) $3 + Y = 2X + 5 - 2Y$
(e) $12 + 40Y = X - 4.8$

2. Transform the following equations by using the three summation laws:

(a) $\Sigma(S + T^2)$
(b) $\Sigma 27V$
(c) $\Sigma(x^2 + 2xy + y^2)$
(d) $\Sigma(4 + Z)$
(e) $\Sigma(18W^2 - 6cW - 13c^2)$, where c is a constant

3

ALTERNATIVE CORRELATIONAL METHODS

In this chapter we shall consider some techniques that can be used in place of the Pearsonian, product-moment correlation coefficient. These techniques are useful in two types of situations. First, the use that is being made of the data may justify approximate but quicker procedures. For example, if an attitude test of 100 items, each scored on a five-point scale, is being related to some external criterion measure for the purpose of selecting the best items, it hardly seems worth while to calculate 100 product-moment rs. A second type of situation in which these techniques are used occurs when the raw data are presented directly in terms of ranks or in terms of dichotomies.

To illustrate three of these alternative procedures, we shall use the data shown in Table 3.1. Our first concern will be with the columns headed X and Y. Here X represents the scores of students of introductory psychology on a 100-item vocabulary test. The Y variable represents course achievement as measured by two multiple-choice tests. (The fact that X and Y have nearly the same score range is coincidental.) Each row indicates a particular student, whom we shall identify by a letter of the alphabet.

As a point of departure we shall first calculate the product-moment correlation coefficient. A commonly used raw-score formula for this purpose is

$$r_{XY} = \frac{N\sum XY - \sum X(\sum Y)}{\sqrt{N\sum X^2 - (\sum X)^2}\sqrt{N\sum Y^2 - (\sum Y)^2}} \tag{3.1}$$

This formula is a rather difficult one to remember, but fortunately the task can be simplified if we define a new quantity:

$$L_{uv} \equiv N\sum UV - \sum U(\sum V) \qquad (3.2)$$

If for U and V we substitute, successively, X and X, Y and Y, and X and Y, we arrive at these three quantities:

$$L_{xx} = N\sum XX - \sum X(\sum X) = N\sum X^2 - (\sum X)^2 \qquad (3.3)$$

$$L_{yy} = N\sum YY - \sum Y(\sum Y) = N\sum Y^2 - (\sum Y)^2 \qquad (3.4)$$

$$L_{xy} = N\sum XY - \sum X(\sum Y) \qquad (3.5)$$

Table 3.1 *Raw Scores and Transformed Scores for the Example of Vocabulary and Psychology Achievement*

Student	X	Y	X'	Y'	X	Y''	X''	Y''
A	57	62	19	17.5	57	0	0	0
B	58	60	18	20	58	0	0	0
C	68	73	10.5	7	68	1	1	1
D	64	70	12	9.5	64	1	1	1
E	78	62	3.5	17.5	78	0	1	0
F	84	88	2	2	84	1	1	1
G	59	52	17	24	59	0	0	0
H	74	68	6	12	74	1	1	1
I	54	67	21	13	54	0	0	0
J	71	54	7.5	23	71	0	1	0
K	60	75	15	5.5	60	1	0	1
L	55	76	20	4	55	1	0	1
M	45	56	23	22	45	0	0	0
N	68	66	10.5	14	68	0	1	0
O	91	92	1	1	91	1	1	1
P	60	65	15	15	60	0	0	0
Q	78	75	3.5	5.5	78	1	1	1
R	71	78	7.5	3	71	1	1	1
S	60	70	15	9.5	60	1	0	1
T	47	57	22	21	47	0	0	0
U	40	71	24	8	40	1	0	1
V	63	62	13	17.5	63	0	0	0
W	70	62	9	17.5	70	0	1	0
X	76	69	5	11	76	1	1	1

By substituting these three L quantities in Equation 3.1, we obtain

$$r_{XY} = \frac{L_{xy}}{\sqrt{L_{xx}}\sqrt{L_{yy}}} \tag{3.6}$$

For the data in the X and Y columns of Table 3.1, we can calculate $\sum X = 1551$, $\sum Y = 1630$, $\sum X^2 = 103,721$, $\sum Y^2 = 112,924$, $\sum XY = 106,795$, and $N = 24$. (The squares of the numbers from 1 to 1000 are given in Table A in the Appendix.) Putting these figures into Equations 3.3, 3.4, and 3.5, we obtain

$$L_{xx} = 24(103,721) - (1551)^2 = 2,489,304 - 2,405,601 = 83,703$$

$$L_{yy} = 24(112,924) - (1630)^2 = 2,710,176 - 2,656,900 = 53,276$$

$$L_{xy} = 24(106,795) - 1551(1630) = 2,563,080 - 2,528,130 = 34,950$$

$$r_{XY} = \frac{34,950}{\sqrt{83,703}\sqrt{53,276}} = \frac{34,950}{289(231)} = \frac{34,950}{66,759} = .52$$

We can test the hypothesis that the population correlation is zero (the null hypothesis) by reference to Table B in the Appendix. We have only two variables, and the number of degrees of freedom is *two less than* the number of cases (pairs of observations). Since we have 24 cases, a correlation value of .515 is required for significance at the 1 % level and .404 at the 5 % level. Therefore the odds are 99 to 1 that our observed correlation of .52 did *not* arise by random sampling variation from a population in which the correlation is actually zero. From these data we can rather confidently say that there is a nonzero correlation between the vocabulary test and the achievement tests.[1]

However, it should be emphasized at this point that rejection of the null hypothesis is *only the first step* in the establishment of a practically useful prediction procedure. With large samples a statistically significant correlation may be so small in magnitude that it is of little practical utility for prediction (Nunnally, 1960, p. 643). This point will be elaborated on in the succeeding chapters.

[1] The author has assumed that the reader already knows something about basic sampling theory. Since the emphasis in this book is on descriptive rather than inferential statistics (see the Preface), the discussion of the effect of sampling errors on correlational indices has purposely been kept brief. Fuller discussion of this topic can be found in other books, for example, Ezekiel and Fox (1959, Chapter 17), McNemar (1962, Chapter 10).

Now let us rank the scores in the X and Y columns and write the ranks in columns X' and Y', respectively. (The ranks can be thought of as a nonlinear transformation of the raw scores.) Person O scored 91, which is the highest score on the vocabulary test, so we write the number 1 in row O of column X'. Person F's score of 84 is ranked second in a similar fashion. Note that Persons E and Q each scored 78. These two scores should occupy the third and fourth ranks, but we cannot determine which should be which. The solution is to split their total of 7 evenly, so Persons E and Q are each awarded the rank of 3.5. This procedure ensures that the sum of ranks remains invariant, regardless of the number of ties involved. Note carefully that the next rank after these tied ranks is 5 (for Person X), *not* 4!

We find that the same procedure is required for Persons J and R and for Persons C and N. Thus there are two ranks of 7.5 and two ranks of 10.5. A little farther along, however, we find a triple tie among Persons K, P, and S, all of whom scored 60 on the vocabulary test. The sum of the corresponding ranks, 14, 15, and 16, is 45, and an even split gives 15 for each of the three tied scores. Person U made the lowest score, 40, which is assigned the rank 24. The last rank should equal the number of cases, unless it is a tied rank.

The ranking procedure is now repeated for the achievement tests to give column Y'. Again there are some double ties, but we also have a quadruple tie; Persons A, E, V, and W all scored 62. The last previous rank was 15, so we must split the sum of 16, 17, 18, and 19 four ways. Thus all four persons are assigned the rank of 17.5. The alert reader will by now have induced that an *odd* number of tied individuals gives ranks that are integers but that an *even* number of tied individuals gives ranks ending in the decimal .5.

We *could* then use Equation 3.6 directly on these ranks, thus obtaining $\sum X' = 300$, $\sum Y' = 300$, and $\sum (X')^2 = 4896.5$, $\sum (Y')^2 = 4894$, and $\sum X'Y' = 4190.5$, and

$$r_{X'Y'} = \frac{24(4190.5) - 300(300)}{\sqrt{24(4896.5) - (300)^2}\,\sqrt{24(4894) - (300)^2}}$$

$$r_{X'Y'} = \frac{10{,}572}{\sqrt{27{,}516}\,\sqrt{27{,}456}} = \frac{10{,}572}{27{,}556} = .38$$

Table 3.2   *Work Table for Calculating Spearman's rho*

Student	X'	Y'	D +	D −	D^2
A	19	17.5	1.5		2.25
B	18	20		2.0	4.00
C	10.5	7	3.5		12.25
D	12	9.5	2.5		6.25
E	3.5	17.5		14.0	196.00
F	2	2			0.00
G	17	24		7.0	49.00
H	6	12		6.0	36.00
I	21	13	8.0		64.00
J	7.5	23		15.5	240.25
K	15	5.5	9.5		90.25
L	20	4	16.0		256.00
M	23	22	1.0		1.00
N	10.5	14		3.5	12.25
O	1	1			0.00
P	15	15			0.00
Q	3.5	5.5		2.0	4.00
R	7.5	3	4.5		20.25
S	15	9.5	5.5		30.25
T	22	21	1.0		1.00
U	24	8	16.0		256.00
V	13	17.5		4.5	20.25
W	9	17.5		8.5	72.25
X	5	11		6.0	36.00
			69.0	69.0	1,409.50

But there is a shorter method of arriving at almost exactly the same answer. Our X' and Y' columns have been copied from Table 3.1 to Table 3.2. Note that the first step is to subtract Y' from X'. (Which variable is subtracted from which is arbitrary since we shall soon be squaring the differences.) For checking purposes, it is a good idea to write the positive and negative differences in separate columns. The sums of these two columns should be exactly equal; in our example the common sum is 69.0. (This is not a foolproof check, however; certain types of ranking errors will still give equal sums.) The next step is to square the differences, as shown in the last column of Table 3.2. Then the formula for Spearman's rho coefficient[2] can be applied:

$$\rho = 1 - \frac{6\sum D^2}{N(N^2 - 1)} \tag{3.7}$$

For our example

$$\rho = 1 - \frac{6(1409.5)}{24[(24)^2 - 1]} = 1 - \frac{8457}{24(575)}$$

$$= 1 - \frac{8457}{13,800} = 1 - .61 = .39$$

Our present result of .39 differs by only .01 from the value of .38 obtained earlier by applying the product-moment formula to the ranks.[3]

The hypothesis that the population value of ρ is zero can be tested by referring to Table C. According to this table, for 24 cases a ρ of .409 is necessary before we can claim that the odds are 19 to 1 against the ρ appearing by random sampling variation ("chance"). Similarly, the critical value for the 1 % level is .537. Therefore our obtained value of .39 is not significantly different from zero.

At first this conclusion seems to be contradictory in that the product-moment correlation based on the same original data is significant at the 1 % level. However, when we use the procedures discussed in this chapter on data originally measured on a continuous scale, we are "throwing away" much of the available information. The justification is that we want a quick, approximate estimate. However, the price we pay is that more cases are needed to enable us to reject the null hypothesis.

[2] The Greek letter ρ is sometimes used to indicate the population value of the product-moment correlation coefficient.

[3] Although a discrepancy this small *can* arise merely from rounding error, with this formula there is a "real" discrepancy. This is because the procedure for handling ties keeps the means identical but not necessarily the standard deviations. Note that in our example, although $\sum X' = \sum Y'$, $\sum(X')^2$ does not precisely equal $\sum(Y')^2$.

Spearman's ρ has frequently been used as an approximation[4] to the product-moment r. However, if the raw data are presented directly in terms of ranks (e.g., soldiers ranking desserts in order of preference), there are theoretical reasons for preferring a rank-order correlation coefficient developed by Kendall called "tau" (Siegel, 1956, pp. 213–223).

Let us now consider a different type of approximation to r. Suppose that we return to our original scores in the case of the vocabulary test (X, the predictor variable) but *dichotomize* the achievement test scores (Y, the criterion variable). First we locate the median of the Y scores, which is 67.5. Now we transform the Y scores according to the following rule: whenever the person's Y score is 68 or above, the number 1 is written in the corresponding row of the Y'' column of Table 3.1; whenever the person's Y score is 67 or below, the number 0 is written in the Y'' column. In many practical situations the criterion variable is dichotomized (although not necessarily at the median), for example, the number 1 represents "pass" and 0 represents "fail."

We now have two columns of paired numbers (columns X and Y'') that *could* be correlated by the product-moment formula: $\sum X = 1551$, $\sum Y'' = 12$, $\sum X^2 = 103{,}721$, $\sum (Y'')^2 = 12$, $\sum XY'' = 821$, $N = 24$, and

$$r_{XY''} = \frac{24(821) - 1551(12)}{\sqrt{24(103{,}721) - (1551)^2}\,\sqrt{24(12) - (12)^2}}$$

$$r_{XY''} = \frac{1092}{\sqrt{83{,}703}\,\sqrt{144}} = \frac{1092}{289(12)} = .31$$

Note that again there is some repetition of values, for example, the number 12 appears three times in the first equation. Often, in such cases, the alert statistical worker will find that a simpler formula can be derived. The appropriate formula in the present situation is called the "point-biserial correlation coefficient." We need the X mean of the high group, the X mean of the low group, and the standard deviation of the *total* group. The mean of the high group,

[4] The value of ρ is *precisely* equivalent to the product-moment formula *applied to the ranks*. An "approximation" is involved in that the distribution of ranks may give a distorted picture of the distribution of raw scores (Cronbach, 1960, p. 76).

M_p, is obtained by adding all the X values that are adjacent to Y'' values of 1 in Table 3.1 and dividing by the number of them, which is 12. Similarly, the mean of the low group, M_q, is obtained from the X values adjacent to Y'' values of 0. In our example, $M_p = 68.42$ and $M_q = 60.83$.

The standard deviation for the *combined* distribution of X values can be obtained from the formula

$$\sigma_X = \sqrt{\frac{N\sum X^2 - (\sum X)^2}{N^2}} = \sqrt{\frac{L_{xx}}{N^2}} \qquad (3.8)$$

In our example

$$\sigma_X = \sqrt{\frac{83{,}703}{(24)^2}} = \sqrt{\frac{83{,}703}{576}} = \sqrt{145.3} = 12.05$$

To calculate the point-biserial correlation, we need further the quantity $\sqrt{pq}$, where p is the proportion of cases in the high group and $q \equiv 1 - p$. In our example the total sample is split 50–50, so p equals .5 and $\sqrt{pq}$ also equals .5. For other values of p, the corresponding values of $\sqrt{pq}$ can be read from Table D in the Appendix.

Now we are ready to use the point-biserial formula, which is

$$r_{pb} = \frac{M_p - M_q}{\sigma_X} \sqrt{pq} \qquad (3.9)$$

Inserting the numbers calculated above, we have

$$r_{pb} = \frac{68.42 - 60.83}{12.05} \sqrt{.5(.5)} = \frac{7.59(.5)}{12.05} = \frac{3.795}{12.05} = .31$$

If the L_{xx} procedure is used in obtaining the standard deviation, it is somewhat more efficient to define N_p as the number of cases in the high group and N_q as the number of cases in the low group and to use the formula,

$$r_{pb} = \frac{(M_p - M_q)\sqrt{N_p N_q}}{\sqrt{L_{xx}}} \qquad (3.10)$$

To test the null hypothesis for r_{pb}, we can again use Table B in the Appendix. Again entering the table with 22 degrees of freedom, we find that our coefficient of .31 does *not* reach the value of .404 required for significance at the 5% level.

Finally, we can carry the approximation procedure to the next logical step, that is, to dichotomize the predictor as well as the criterion variable. The median of X values is 63.5, and we can use this as a cutoff score to assign 1's and 0's in the X'' column of Table 3.1. Again using Equation 3.6, we could obtain: $\sum X'' = 12$, $\sum Y'' = 12$, $\sum (X'')^2 = 12$, $\sum (Y'')^2 = 12$, $\sum X'' Y'' = 8$, $N = 24$, and

$$r_{X''Y''} = \frac{24(8) - 12(12)}{\sqrt{24(12) - (12)^2}\,\sqrt{24(12) - (12)^2}} = \frac{48}{\sqrt{144}\,\sqrt{144}} = .33$$

Since so many numbers are repeated, it will come as no great surprise that a considerable simplification can be effected. The resulting index, called the "phi coefficient," uses, instead of raw or transformed scores, frequencies. Note in the X'' and Y'' columns of Table 3.1 that there are only four combinations of numbers that can appear in a row: 1 and 1, 0 and 0, 1 and 0, and 0 and 1. The procedure is to count the frequency of each of these combinations and then insert them into the cells of a 2×2 table:

		1	A	B			12	4	8
Y''					$=$				
		0	C	D			12	8	4
			0	1				12	12
				X''					

For example, there are four instances of X'' equaling 0 while Y'' equals 1 (Persons K, L, S, and U), and eight instances of both equaling 1. The numbers to the left and below are "marginal totals," that is, the row and column totals, which in our example are all 12. (In real-life problems, the numbers will seldom come out this symmetrically!) The formula for ϕ is

$$\phi = \frac{BC - AD}{\sqrt{(A + B)(C + D)}\,\sqrt{(A + C)(B + D)}} \tag{3.11}$$

At first this equation looks rather formidable; however, there is a system to it. Note that the four sums in the denominator are the four marginal totals. The numerator is the difference between two products that form the outline of the letter X in the 2×2 table. In our example,

$$\phi = \frac{8(8) - 4(4)}{\sqrt{12(12)}\,\sqrt{12(12)}} = \frac{64 - 16}{12(12)} = \frac{48}{144} = .33$$

To two decimal places, this result is identical with that obtained above using the product-moment procedure on the X'' and Y'' values. A quick test of statistical significance is available by using the relationship,

$$\chi^2 = N\phi^2 \tag{3.12}$$

In our example, $\chi^2 = 24(.33)^2 = 2.61$. For this particular use of χ^2, the numerical value must reach 3.84 for significance at the 5% level and 6.64 for significance at the 1% level. Therefore we accept the null hypothesis that the obtained χ^2 could have arisen by random sampling variation.

When we dichotomize for the purpose of calculating point-biserial rs or phi coefficients, we assign the number 1 to the higher scores and 0 to the lower scores. However, often the data are presented directly in a dichotomous form. Some examples of dichotomous variables are male versus female, experimental group versus control group, yes versus no on a questionnaire item, and Republican versus Democrat. In many such situations there is no logical basis for deciding which group is "high" and which is "low." We then assign 1 and 0 arbitrarily, but when the coefficient is reported, the algebraic sign must be congruent with this assignment. For example, we might assign 1 to extrovert and 0 to introvert. Suppose that for a particular sample, the point-biserial correlation with a scholastic aptitude test turned out to be $-.25$. We could then say that the correlation between scholastic aptitude and extroversion is $-.25$, or we could say that the correlation between scholastic aptitude and introversion is $+.25$. (In factor analysis, this is equivalent to "reflecting a test vector," see page 127.) Often one way of stating the relationship is semantically more convenient than another.

However, the 2×2 table may be presented to the reader in a form other than that shown above. (This particular arrangement was chosen so as to be consistent with the familiar Cartesian co-ordinate system in that the high values are above and to the right.) If so, the reader can either rearrange the table into the form shown above or adjust the algebraic sign in his verbal report. However, the latter procedure is not recommended until the reader has dealt with enough of these approximate correlational procedures that he "has the hang of it."

Many variables in the behavioral sciences are normally distributed

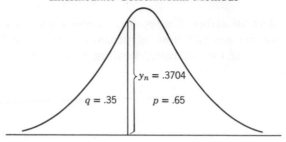

Figure 3.1 Normal ordinate used in calculation of the biserial correlation coefficient.

or approach this distribution rather closely. If it is assumed that the variable underlying a dichotomy is normally distributed, then two further techniques can be used which correspond to the point-biserial and phi coefficients. If one variable is continuous and the other is a dichotomy assumed to represent a normally distributed variable, the formula for the "biserial correlation coefficient" is

$$r_b = \frac{M_p - M_q}{\sigma_X}\left(\frac{pq}{y_n}\right) \qquad (3.13)$$

Comparing this with Equation 3.9, the formula for the point-biserial coefficient, we note a considerable degree of similarity. The new factor, y_n, represents the ordinate for the abscissa of the unit normal curve corresponding to the split between the two groups represented by p and q (see Figure 3.1). For each value of p (or q), the corresponding value of pq/y_n can be read from Table D in the Appendix.

As an illustration of the method, the data from a political survey questionnaire administered a week before the 1960 presidential election will be used. Of 286 college students, 137 expressed a preference for Kennedy, so p equals .48, q equals .52, and pq/y_n equals .626. A special measure of "liberalism" was constructed, and the means for the Kennedy and Nixon supporters on this variable were 4.65 and 3.40, respectively. The standard deviation for all 286 students was 1.84. Substituting in Equation 3.13, we obtain as a measure of correlation between liberalism and preference for Kennedy,

$$r_b = \frac{4.65 - 3.40}{1.84}(.626) = \frac{1.25(.626)}{1.84} = \frac{.7825}{1.84} = .42$$

In using the biserial coefficient here, we are assuming that there was not a sharp separation of preference but that there was an underlying continuum such that many Kennedy supporters would have needed only a slight "push" to make them prefer Nixon and vice versa. Furthermore we are assuming that the "moderates" out-numbered the "extremists" who, for example, would not have voted for Nixon even if he had sprouted a pair of angelic wings just before the election!

Now let us divide Equation 3.9 by 3.13 to obtain

$$\frac{r_{pb}}{r_b} = \frac{y_n}{\sqrt{pq}} \tag{3.14}$$

This equation shows the ratio of the point-biserial to the biserial coefficient *calculated from the same data*. It reaches a maximal value of about .8 when $p = .5 = q$ and decreases as p moves in either direction from .5. Thus it can be seen that the biserial coefficient is always larger than the point-biserial coefficient for the same data but that the two are closest to each other in value when the high and low groups are of equal size.

A corresponding procedure can be used in place of the phi coefficient. If *both* variables are dichotomized, yet assumed to represent an underlying normal distribution, the "tetrachoric correlation" can be computed. The full formula is quite complex, so several approximations to it have been developed. The one we shall use here gives a good approximation as long as the split of the two groups for each variable is not more extreme than 70% to 30%. It employs the same product terms as in the numerator of the phi coefficient formula, BC and AD. However, instead of subtracting, we divide. Then Table E in the Appendix is entered with the quotient, and the magnitude of the tetrachoric correlation is read directly. In order that the size of the table be kept small, we always divide the larger product by the smaller. If BC is larger than AD, the correlation is positive; if BC is smaller than AD, the correlation is negative. (It is assumed that A represents the frequency of 0,1 combinations, B represents the frequency of 1,1 combinations, etc.)

In our political example, dichotomizing also the liberalism variable produces the following 2 × 2 table:

	Conservative	Liberal
Preference for Kennedy	42	95
Preference for Nixon	84	65

For this table, BC is 95(84) = 7980, and AD is 42(65) = 2730. The ratio of BC to AD is 2.92. From Table E we find that the magnitude of the tetrachoric correlation is .40. Since BC exceeds AD, the algebraic sign of the correlation is positive. If AD had exceeded BC, we would have computed the ratio AD/BC and then affixed a negative sign to the tabled value.

Finally, let us consider the relative advantages of the biserial and tetrachoric coefficients, on the one hand, versus the point-biserial and phi coefficients on the other. The distributions assumed to underlie the dichotomies are shown in Figure 3.2. Most variables in the behavioral sciences, except those associated with sex, tend to give unimodal distributions. Of course, if the investigator does the dichotomizing himself, he has from the original data a rather good idea about what the shape of the population distribution is.

In view of the rarity of empirical distributions that approach the point distribution shown in Figure 3.2, it seems preferable to use the biserial or tetrachoric coefficient when a terminal descriptive statistic is desired. However, a disadvantage of these two indices is that their standard error formulas are complex, even approximate formulas (McNemar, 1962, Chapter 12). Furthermore, they involve the assumption that the relationship between the two variables is linear (rectilinear).[5] Finally, if further statistical manipulations are

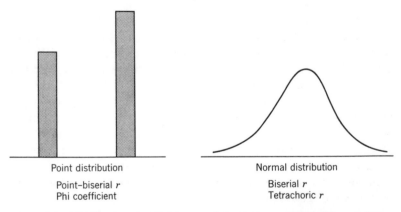

Point distribution   Normal distribution

Point-biserial r Biserial r
Phi coefficient   Tetrachoric r

Figure 3.2 Distributions implied in use of alternative correlational procedures.

[5] For methods of dealing with nonlinear (curvilinear) relationships, see Wert, Neidt, and Ahmann (1954, Ch. 15).

to be made on the data, the point-biserial or phi coefficients are preferable (Comrey and Levonian, 1958).

Problems

1. Heer (1961) compared the marital status of females under 25 years of age between an American second-generation group and a corresponding group in the country of origin. Below are given *ranks* for the percentage never married. Calculate Spearman's ρ for these data.

	Second-Generation	Country of Origin
Austria	3	3
Canada—French	6	7
Canada—Other	10	11
Czechoslovakia	5	8
England and Wales	8	10
Germany	7	4
Ireland	1	1
Italy	2	2
Norway	11	5
Poland	4	9
Sweden	9	6

2. For the *raw scores* given below, calculate (a) Pearson's r and (b) Spearman's ρ. Are they closely comparable for these data? For each coefficient, test the null hypothesis that the population correlation is zero.

X	10	6	4	13	8	1	6	7	12	3
Y	6	7	2	7	11	3	9	3	12	7

3. Heilbrun (1962) compared scores on an adjective check list for various need scales of a "drop-out" group of college females and a "stay" group. Calculate the biserial correlation between each of the six scales and the variable representing "staying power."

Need Scale	Mean for Stay Group (N = 106)	Mean for Drop-Out Group (N = 63)	Over-all Standard Deviation
Achievement	50.38	46.10	11.57
Affiliation	48.87	50.94	10.31
Change	49.91	54.19	9.12
Endurance	50.70	47.69	11.05
Heterosexuality	47.53	50.70	9.70
Order	50.56	47.19	10.50

4. A teacher wishes to correlate a particular test item with scores on the total test of which it is a part. For the 30 students who pass the item, $\Sigma X = 925$ and $\Sigma X^2 = 31,099$. For the 15 students who miss the item, $\Sigma X = 412$ and $\Sigma X^2 = 13,174$. Calculate the biserial correlation and the point-biserial correlation. Which is the more appropriate index of relationship in this situation and why?

5. Suppose that a clinician develops a group of "signs" from a projective test which he thinks can distinguish neurotic from "normal" persons. He administers the test to 7 patients diagnosed as neurotics and 10 normal persons. Below are given scores representing the number of signs for each person. Compute the biserial correlation and the point-biserial correlation between number of signs on this test and "normality." What qualifications might be appropriate if these results were reported?

Neurotic	7	5	8	9	6	3	2			
Normal	8	4	3	2	6	7	4	6	5	4

6. The frequency table below gives the number of married men and the number of unmarried men in an insurance company who are more than and less than 68 inches tall. Calculate the tetrachoric correlation and the phi coefficient and state your results in verbal terms. Which index of relationship is more appropriate in this situation and why?

	Tall	Short
Married	84	58
Unmarried	41	73

7. A sociologist employed at a prison administers the Wechsler Adult Intelligence Scale to 50 prisoners and to 50 other male adults who are matched for age and socio-economic status. For each examinee he notes whether the Verbal IQ is higher than the Performance IQ. From the table of frequencies given below, compute the tetrachoric correlation and state the results verbally in two different ways.

	Control Group	Prisoners
Verbal IQ higher	27	16
Performance IQ higher	23	34

8. Below are given 2×2 tables of frequencies for responses to pairs of items from an attitude scale. "A" means agree, and "D" means disagree. For each table calculate the phi coefficient and test the null hypothesis that its population value is zero. Under what circumstances would it be more appropriate to use these phi coefficients rather than the corresponding tetrachoric correlations for the same data?

	D	A
A	17	24
D	16	11

	D	A
A	27	14
D	11	16

	D	A
A	14	16
D	21	17

	D	A
A	9	21
D	27	11

9. If both X and Y are dichotomous variables, how would the 2×2 table of frequencies look if (a) X is a necessary condition for Y, (b) X is a sufficient condition for Y, (c) X is a necessary and sufficient condition for Y? For further consideration of these relationships, see Francis (1961, pp. 52–53).

4

MULTIPLE CORRELATION:

PART ONE

In the basic correlational procedure, we are concerned with the predictability of one variable from knowledge of another variable. For example, does knowledge of the score of an entering college student on a scholastic aptitude test enable one to predict what his grade-point average will be nine months in the future? To answer this question we obtain test scores from a representative sample of freshmen when they enter college, and then we ascertain the grade-point averages of these *same* students at the completion of their first collegiate year. From these data we can work out a simple "regression formula" that enables us to estimate for each *new* entering freshman his grade-point average at the end of his freshman year. The relative accuracy of our predictions for a *group* of freshmen is expressed by the Pearsonian, product-moment correlation coefficient, which is obtained in the process of working out the formula mentioned above.

If we can secure partial accuracy by using one predictor variable, can the errors of prediction be reduced still further by making use of another predictor variable, say high school rank? The appropriate statistical procedure for accomplishing this aim is called "multiple correlation." In the example under discussion, we have again one "criterion variable," namely, freshmen grade-point average; but we have *two* predictor variables, score on the scholastic aptitude test and high school rank. The number of predictors can be further increased to three, four, or (in theory) any higher number. However, the reader should be warned that "diminishing returns" set in rather quickly and that the gain in predictability resulting from using, say, five rather than four predictor variables rarely compensates for the man-hours involved in obtaining the extra set of measurements.

However, before developing the formulas for multiple correlation, it will be well for us to consider a rigorous derivation of the product-moment procedure for the situation in which only one predictor is available. For this purpose we shall use standard scores (z scores):

$$z_0 \equiv \frac{X_0 - M_0}{\sigma_0} \tag{4.1}$$

$$z_1 \equiv \frac{X_1 - M_1}{\sigma_1} \tag{4.2}$$

It will be noted that, instead of using Y and X as is the usual custom for representing the criterion and predictor variables, respectively, we have employed X_0 and X_1. The reason will become apparent when we consider the topic of multiple correlation.

Before we can apply a regression formula to make actual predictions, we shall need to obtain predictor and criterion scores for a standardization sample of students. In Figure 4.1 each point represents two scores for a particular freshman. The z_1 coordinate of the point represents his scholastic aptitude test score (in standard score units), and the z_0 coordinate represents his freshman grade-point average (also in standard score units). Note that the points are more numerous in the upper-right quadrant (high test score, high grade-point average) and the lower-left quadrant (low test score, low grade-point average). The picture looks hopeful, but we wish to work out an exact formula by fitting a straight line along the general direction of the points. If we can accomplish this aim, then for any *new* freshman we can state an exact value for our prediction. For example, in Figure 4.2, Freshman A makes a score on the z_1 predictor variable indicated by A_1; we then would predict his criterion score to be A_0. Freshman *B* scores below the mean on z_1 (hence a negative standard score), and we predict his z_0 score to be as shown by B_0. It can be seen that, if the new student scores above

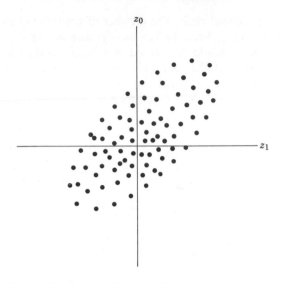

Figure 4.1 Scatter diagram of scholastic aptitude test scores and freshman grade-point averages in z score form.

the mean on the predictor variable, we predict that he will score above the mean on the criterion variable. Analogously a score below the mean on the predictor suggests to us a score below the mean on the criterion.

The alert reader will have noticed that the line would not necessarily have to go through the origin (the intersection of the coordinate axes) as we have drawn it. However, it can be shown (see page 198 of the Appendix) that the line *must* pass through the origin if it is to satisfy the conditions that we are about to impose. Nevertheless, to show this rigorously would require us to start with the raw scores (or deviation scores) rather than the standard scores and to employ the mathematical technique of partial differentiation. For present purposes we shall take the matter on faith; this will simplify our derivation considerably.

However, even if we insist that the regression line pass through the origin, the slope or tilt of the line is yet to be determined. Intuitively, it seems clear that the line should make with the z_1 axis an angle in the range between 0 and 90 degrees. To make an exact determination,

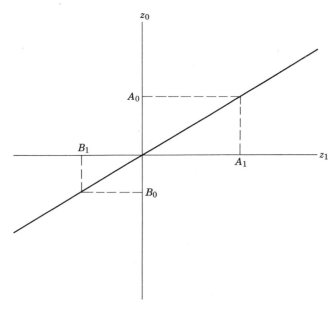

Figure 4.2   Graphic prediction of scores for two particular freshmen.

we use the principle of "least squares." For every point, we note the discrepancy between the observed z_0 value and the z_0 value that would have been predicted from the corresponding z_1 value. In Figure 4.3 this discrepancy is the distance between the large dot and the point on the regression line directly below it, that is, the line segment KL. The discrepancy is called the "error of estimate." If the point lies below the line, the error is negative. (In terms of the scholastic prediction example, students represented by points above the regression line have been called "overachievers"; students whose points fall below the line have been called "underachievers.")

The general aim is to adjust the slope of the line so that the errors, totaled for all points, are as small as possible. For example, the sum of errors would be quite large if the line passed through the upper-left and lower-right quadrants. To avoid the indeterminate outcome of the positive and negative errors canceling each other, we *square* each error of estimate. The least squares criterion requires that we

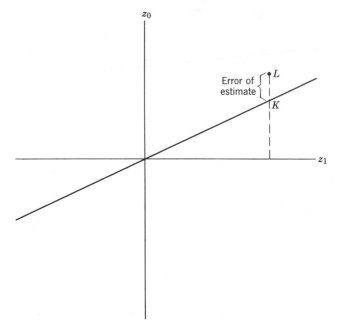

Figure 4.3   A regression line and error of estimate.

minimize the sum of the squares of the errors of estimate, that is, obtain

$$\text{Minimum} \sum (z_0 - \hat{z}_0)^2$$

The letter z with a circumflex above it indicates the predicted value; the unembellished z indicates the value actually observed. We shall use the symbol β_{01} to represent the slope of the regression line.

It will be recalled from Chapter 2 that, in the general formula for a linear equation, $Y = a + bX$, the symbol a represents the Y intercept and b represents the slope of the line. Since our regression line passes through the origin, which has an ordinate (*and* an abscissa) of zero, our regression equation will be

$$\hat{z}_0 = 0 + \beta_{01}z_1 = \beta_{01}z_1 \tag{4.3}$$

The first step in our derivation is to substitute $\beta_{01}z_1$ for $\hat{z}_0$ in the expression for the sum to be minimized, giving

$$\sum(z_0 - \hat{z}_0)^2 = \sum(z_0 - \beta_{01}z_1)^2 \qquad (4.4)$$

Next we square out the expression in parentheses on the right side of Equation 4.4. Just as $(a - b)^2 = a^2 - 2ab + b^2$,

$$(z_0 - \beta_{01}z_1)^2 = z_0{}^2 - 2\beta_{01}z_0z_1 + \beta_{01}{}^2z_1{}^2 \qquad (4.5)$$

Inserting the expansion into the right member of Equation 4.4, we obtain

$$\sum(z_0 - \hat{z}_0)^2 = \sum(z_0{}^2 - 2\beta_{01}z_0z_1 + \beta_{01}{}^2z_1{}^2) \qquad (4.6)$$

Now we apply the First Summation Law, which was discussed in Chapter 2. This law enables us to distribute the summation sign to each of the terms separately, and so now we have

$$\sum(z_0 - \hat{z}_0)^2 = \sum z_0{}^2 - \sum 2\beta_{01}z_0z_1 + \sum \beta_{01}{}^2z_1{}^2 \qquad (4.7)$$

According to the Second Summation Law, the summation of a constant times a variable is equivalent to the constant times the summation of the variable. Which of the factors in the right member of Equation 4.7 are constants? Obviously the number 2 is. The slope β_{01} is also constant because it does not change when we go from one student to another; that is, the slope of the regression line applies equally to *all* the points in the scatter diagram. On the other hand, in general, z_0 and z_1 assume different values for every student. Thus we can take $2\beta_{01}$ outside of its summation sign and likewise $\beta_{01}{}^2$ outside of *its* summation sign. Equation 4.7 then becomes

$$\sum(z_0 - \hat{z}_0)^2 = \sum z_0{}^2 - 2\beta_{01}\sum z_0z_1 + \beta_{01}{}^2\sum z_1{}^2 \qquad (4.8)$$

The next few steps of the derivation require a knowledge of elementary calculus, so readers who are not thus privileged should skip directly to Equation 4.9.

At this point we reverse the roles of the factors in the equations: the constants temporarily become variables, and the variables temporarily become constants. This procedure at first strikes one as quite arbitrary, and an explanation is called for. We assume that the predictor and criterion scores are all in, and that nothing we do now will change them. The die is cast! The points on the scatter diagram are fixed. What we now wish to vary is the slope of the regression line, remembering that it must at the same time pivot on the origin. Thus β_{01} is now a variable, and the three summations involving z_0 and z_1 are constant. (The number 2 of course remains constant.)

The procedure is to find the minimum sum of squares by differentiating the right member of Equation 4.8 with respect to β_{01} and setting it equal to zero. By using the calculus formula $d/dx(cx^n) = cnx^{n-1}$, we obtain

$$0 - 2\sum z_0 z_1 + 2\beta_{01}\sum z_1^2 = 0 \tag{4.9}$$

The strategy of the remainder of the derivation is to solve Equation 4.9 for β_{01}, which then can be calculated for any given standardization sample of students, since all of the z_0 and z_1 values are already known. We collect all terms involving β_{01} on the left side of the equation and all of the other terms on the right side, thus obtaining

$$2\beta_{01}\sum z_1^2 = 2\sum z_0 z_1 \tag{4.10}$$

Now we divide both sides of the equation by $2N$, where N denotes the number of persons in the standardization group, from which we have

$$\beta_{01}\frac{\sum z_1^2}{N} = \frac{\sum z_0 z_1}{N} \tag{4.11}$$

At this juncture we digress to show that the factor $\sum z_1^2/N$ can be greatly simplified. We start from the basic definition of the standard deviation and of a z score:

$$\sigma \equiv \sqrt{\sum x^2/N} \tag{4.12}$$

$$z \equiv \frac{x}{\sigma} \tag{4.13}$$

We square both of these expressions and affix the subscript 1, thus obtaining

$$\sigma_1^2 = \frac{\sum x_1^2}{N} \tag{4.14}$$

$$z_1^2 = \frac{x_1^2}{\sigma_1^2} \tag{4.15}$$

(It is unnecessary to apply the subscript to N because it assumes the same value for the criterion and predictor variables.) Next we take the mean of the $z_1{}^2$ values by summing over all the persons and dividing by the number of them, N. The same operation must then be performed on the right side of Equation 4.15, giving

$$\frac{\sum z_1{}^2}{N} = \frac{\sum (x_1{}^2/\sigma_1{}^2)}{N} \qquad (4.16)$$

Since $\sigma_1{}^2$ is constant, it can come out from the summation sign, giving

$$\frac{\sum z_1{}^2}{N} = \frac{(1/\sigma_1{}^2)\sum x_1{}^2}{N} = \frac{1}{\sigma_1{}^2}\left(\frac{\sum x_1{}^2}{N}\right) \qquad (4.17)$$

Referring back to Equation 4.14 we see that the factor in parentheses is the variance (the standard deviation squared), so that

$$\frac{\sum z_1{}^2}{N} = \frac{1}{\sigma_1{}^2}(\sigma_1{}^2) = 1 \qquad (4.18)$$

In Equations 4.12 through 4.18 we have shown that the mean of squared standard scores is always unity. By using this relationship we can now simplify Equation 4.11 to read

$$\beta_{01} = \frac{\sum z_0 z_1}{N} \qquad (4.19)$$

Thus Equation 4.19 gives a formula for determining the slope of the "best fitting" regression line for predicting z_0 from z_1. (However, this is not the most convenient form for computational purposes.) Many readers will recognize the right member of Equation 4.19 as being a formula for the product-moment correlation coefficient. Thus we see that when (a) only two variables are involved and (b) the raw scores are transformed to standard scores, the regression coefficient is numerically equivalent to the correlation coefficient.

Having derived the two-variable correlation coefficient we are ready to proceed to the more general multiple correlation problem. In the three-variable problem, where there are two predictor variables and one criterion variable, we can again picture the situation, but now we must employ a three-dimensional representation.

Such a plane is shown in Figure 4.4. Again we assume it to pass through the origin. Every pair of scores, X_1 and X_2, obtained by a student in the standardization sample determines a point on the

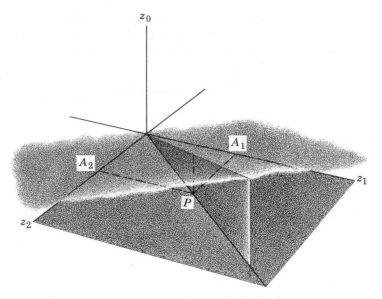

Figure 4.4 A regression plane in three-dimensional space.

plane generated by the z_1 and z_2 axes. For example, in Figure 4.4, we assume that Student A made scores indicated by A_1 and A_2. These two values determine point P. If we had already determined an appropriate regression plane, we would then measure the distance from point P straight up to the plane (i.e., parallel to the z_0 axis), and this would constitute our predicted z_0 value, $\hat{z}_0$.

However, again the slope must be determined by using a standardization sample, that is, following through a group of students and obtaining an X_0 criterion score to correspond to the X_1 and X_2 predictor scores for each student. Then we transform these into standard scores, z_0, z_1, and z_2, and locate a point in our three-dimensional space for each student. If r_{01} and r_{02} are positive and fairly substantial in size, these points will cluster into a figure roughly in the shape of a football tilted in the direction from the origin out toward the reader. Our regression plane will slice about midway through the football. Again the slope is determined by minimizing the sum of squares of the errors of estimate. In this case the geometrical representation of the error of estimate for each student is the vertical distance from his point to the regression plane. If his point is above the regression plane, the error of estimate is positive; if his point is below the regression plane, the error of estimate is negative.

The equation of the regression plane for the three-variable problem is

$$\hat{z}_0 = \beta_{01}z_1 + \beta_{02}z_2 \qquad (4.20)$$

The same principles generalize to the situation involving more than two predictors (although the situation cannot be represented in Euclidean space), for example,

$$\hat{z}_0 = \beta_{01}z_1 + \beta_{02}z_2 + \beta_{03}z_3 + \cdots \qquad (4.21)$$

We see that the predicted z_0 score is a weighted linear combination of the predictor variables in standard form. (It is a *linear* combination because the predictor variables all appear raised only to the first power.) However, in these situations the regression coefficients are *not* necessarily equal to the corresponding correlation coefficients, that is, in general, $\beta_{01} \neq r_{01}$, $\beta_{02} \neq r_{02}$, etc. Henceforth we shall abbreviate β_{01} as β_1, β_{02} as β_2, etc.[1]

By analogy with the two-variable problem (see Equation 4.4), the deviation of a given point from the regression plane is given by the expression

$$z_0 - (\beta_1 z_1 + \beta_2 z_2 + \cdots)$$

We shall merely outline the next few steps; a somewhat more complete treatment can be found in other books, for example, Lewis (1960, pp. 175–176).[2] We square the entire expression and then sum it over all the persons. Now we have not only one variable to differentiate with respect to, but two or more, for example, $\beta_1, \beta_2, \beta_3, \beta_4, \cdots$

The required mathematical technique is partial differentation. We differentiate partially with respect to each predictor variable and set each of the obtained expressions equal to zero. The result is a

---

[1] Strictly speaking, we should write $\beta_{01 \cdot 23}$, $\beta_{02 \cdot 13}$, and $\beta_{03 \cdot 12}$ for a three-predictor problem. The first of these represents the partial regression of z_0 on z_1, with z_2 and z_3 held constant. The $\beta_{01 \cdot 23}$ coefficient for a three-predictor problem would not necessarily equal the β_{01} coefficient for a one-predictor problem.

[2] The derivation for the two-predictor situation is given in the Appendix, page 199.

system of as many equations as there are predictor variables, for example,

$$\begin{bmatrix} \beta_1 + r_{12}\beta_2 + r_{13}\beta_3 = r_{01} \\ r_{12}\beta_1 + \beta_2 + r_{23}\beta_3 = r_{02} \\ r_{13}\beta_1 + r_{23}\beta_2 + \beta_3 = r_{03} \end{bmatrix} \qquad (4.22)$$

The constants in these equations are the correlation coefficients, that is, these values must be computed from the standardization sample before the system of equations can be solved. The rs on the right side of the equations are called "validity coefficients," and the other rs are called "intercorrelations." Several methods are available for solving such a system of equations, and one such method will be described in the next chapter.[3]

Problems

1. Which variables other than high school rank and aptitude test scores might be useful in predicting freshman grades in college?

2. Use Figure 4.4 to locate a score point for a person who scores above the mean on X_0 and above the mean on X_1 but is an "underachiever."

3. By using the summation laws, show that $\Sigma z/N = 0$.

4. If the slope of the regression line is zero, what does the sum of squares of the errors of estimate equal?

[3] These equations can be expressed much more simply in terms of matrix algebra; see Chapter 10 and page 202 of the Appendix.

5

MULTIPLE CORRELATION:
PART TWO

In the previous chapter, the set of equations for obtaining the regression coefficients in multiple correlation was derived. Now we shall consider one of the methods that can be used to solve for the regression coefficients. The method to be described, that of "pivotal condensation" (Aitken, 1937), is not always the shortest in terms of required calculations. However, an important advantage of the method is that it involves only two basic types of arithmetical operations and thus is relatively easy to remember.

As an example of the method, we shall use an actual empirical study of 467 male students entering the University of Georgia in September of 1957 (Franz, Davis, and Garcia, 1958). The relevant data are given in Table 5.1. The criterion, X_0, is the average of

Table 5.1 *Raw Data for the Scholastic Prediction Example*

	X_1	X_2	X_3	X_0	Mean	Standard Deviation
X_1	1.00	.55	.32	.52	394	90
X_2		1.00	.38	.49	435	86
X_3			1.00	.51	24.3	6.4
X_0				1.00	22.0	5.0

first-quarter grades measured on a scale where $A = 40$, $B = 30$, etc. There were three predictor variables:

X_1: Verbal section of the CEEB Scholastic Aptitude Test
X_2: Mathematical section of the CEEB Scholastic Aptitude Test
X_3: High school average in "academic subjects"

For example, the product-moment correlation between the verbal test and high school average, r_{13}, was .32. If we substitute the values from Table 5.1 into Equation 4.22 of the previous chapter, we have the following system of equations to solve:

$$\begin{bmatrix} 1.00\beta_1 + .55\beta_2 + .32\beta_3 = .52 \\ .55\beta_1 + 1.00\beta_2 + .38\beta_3 = .49 \\ .32\beta_1 + .38\beta_2 + 1.00\beta_3 = .51 \end{bmatrix}$$

The first step of the method is to copy the intercorrelations of the predictor variables into the upper-left corner of our work sheet (see Table 5.2). Directly *below* these are written the three validity co-

Table 5.2 *Illustration of the Method of Pivotal Condensation*

						Sum	Check
1.00	.55	.32	−1.00	.00	.00	.87	
.55	1.00	.38	.00	−1.00	.00	.93	
.32	.38	1.00	.00	.00	−1.00	.70	
.52	.49	.51	.00	.00	.00	1.52	
	.698	.204	.550	−1.000	.000	.452	.452
	1.000	.292	.788	−1.433	.000	.647	.648
	.204	.898	.320	.000	−1.000	.422	.422
	.204	.344	.520	.000	.000	1.068	1.068
		.838	.159	.292	−1.000	.289	.290
		1.000	.190	.348	−1.193	.345	.345
		.284	.359	.292	.000	.935	.936
			.305	.193	.339	.837	.837

efficients, r_{01}, r_{02}, and r_{03}, which are the correlations between the criterion and each of the predictors. To the right of the intercorrelations is written a matrix in which the diagonal elements are minus one and all the other elements are zero. (A "matrix" is a rectangular table of numbers, each of which is called an "element" of the matrix, see page 105.) Note that the row containing the validities is extended to the right entirely with zeros. Finally, at the extreme right of the work sheet are written a sum column and a check column. The sums of the first four rows are calculated and written in the sum column, for example, in the second row,

$$.55 + 1.00 + .38 + .00 - 1.00 + .00 = .93$$

The basic operation that we shall be performing is of the form $wx - yz$; however, fortunately w will always assume the value of unity. The four numbers involved in the operation are always at the corners of a rectangle; but the upper-left corner remains stationary within each cycle of the method, hence the word "pivot" in the title. (For many readers it will be helpful actually to visualize a rectangle that changes in height and width.) We start with the first two rows of the table and, initially, the first two columns. The required operation is to multiply the numbers in the upper-left and lower-right corners of the rectangle and from this product to subtract the product of the numbers in the lower-left and upper-right corners. The first calculation for our empirical data is

$$1.00(1.00) - .55(.55) = 1.000 - .302 = .698$$

The value .698 is recorded in the second column of the row directly below the validities. The student should retain *at least* one more decimal place in these calculations than is involved in the original correlations. For the next operation the height of our "rectangle" is kept constant, but the width is increased by one unit. The numbers now at the corners of our rectangle are

$$\begin{matrix} 1.00 & .32 \\ .55 & .38 \end{matrix}$$

Using the same system as before, we calculate

$$1.00(.38) - .55(.32) = .380 - .176 = .204$$

The value .204 is written in the new row and in the column representing the right side of the rectangle, that is, directly to the right of the first calculated value, .698. The next three values in this row are computed in a similar manner:

$$1.00(.00) - .55(-1.00) = .550$$
$$1.00(-1.00) - .55(.00) = -1.000$$
$$1.00(.00) - .55(.00) = .000$$

Now the sum column is treated in exactly the same way as the other columns. The numbers now at the corners of the rectangle are

1.00	.87
.55	.93

The value calculated by the usual method is .452, but it is entered, *not* in the sum column, but in the check column directly to its right. Now the actual sum of the numbers in this row is calculated and written in the *sum* column:

$$.698 + .204 + .550 - 1.000 + .000 = .452$$

In this case the two values check exactly. However, the sum and check values may differ by one or two in the last decimal place because of rounding error. If they differ by more, all the calculations in the row should be performed again. When the sum value is sufficiently close to the check value, we are ready to proceed to the next row.

The next row is calculated in a somewhat different manner. Each number in the row just calculated is *divided by* the first number in that row. The first three computations in our example are

$$.698 / .698 = 1.000$$
$$.204 / .698 = .292$$
$$.550 / .698 = .788$$

(If a desk calculator is available, it is simpler to obtain the reciprocal of .698, which is 1.4327, and lock it in as a constant multiplier.) The entry in the sum column, .452, is likewise divided by .698, and the result, .648, is written *in the check column*. Whenever we deal with numbers in the sum column, the result of the calculation is written in the check column. Note that the actual sum of the row, .647, is not identical to the check value. However, this is due to rounding error, and the discrepancy is sufficiently small.

Now we return to our intercorrelation matrix and deal with the first and third rows. The numbers at the corners of our rectangle are now

$$
\begin{array}{cc}
1.00 & .55 \\
.32 & .38
\end{array}
$$

By the usual method we obtain .204, and this entry is written in the second column of a new row. Then we again keep the height of the rectangle constant but successively increase its width by one unit at a time. For the next operation the numbers at the corners of the rectangle are

$$
\begin{array}{cc}
1.00 & .32 \\
.32 & 1.00
\end{array}
$$

The result with this rectangle is .898, which is written in the third column of the new row. We continue to widen the rectangle and to fill the new row with the resulting calculated values. When we reach the sum column, we write the calculated result in the check column and then obtain the row sum. If the two values are sufficiently close, we move on to the next row of the intercorrelation matrix and continue until the row of validity coefficients is dealt with. This ends the first cycle of computations.

The second cycle is begun by dealing with the sixth and seventh rows of our work sheet. The numbers now at the corners of the rectangle are

$$
\begin{array}{cc}
1.000 & .292 \\
.204 & .898
\end{array}
$$

The calculated result, .838, is written in a new row and in the column representing the right side of the rectangle. Then, as before, the rectangle is successively widened until the sum column is employed to find a check value.

For each new cycle, the first row is obtained by the basic operation, $wx - yz$; however, the *second* row is computed by dividing all the entries in the first row by the first entry in the first row. Then the basic operation is used again until all the rows for the previous cycle are exhausted. Finally, all the columns representing the original intercorrelation matrix are eliminated. The final row contains the regression coefficients that we have been seeking, that is, β_1 is .305,

β_2 is .193, and β_3 is .339. Although we have included checking procedures for all steps in our computational routine, the reader may be interested to make a final verification of the solution by substituting these three β values in each of the three simultaneous equations shown at the beginning of this chapter. Our regression equation for predicting first-quarter college grade averages (see Equation 4.21 of the previous chapter) is

$$\hat{z}_0 = .305z_1 + .193z_2 + .339z_3$$

For each new entering freshman we could multiply his standard score on the Verbal section by .305, add to this the product of his standard score on the Mathematical section by .193, and finally add his high school average in standard score form multiplied by .339. The sum of these three products would give us the "best" prediction (in the "least squares" sense) of the particular freshman's first-quarter grade average in terms of standard scores.

It is interesting to compare the regression coefficients with the corresponding validity coefficients. Note that, although r_{01} is the largest validity coefficient, β_1 is not the largest regression coefficient. The reason why β_3 is larger than β_1 is that X_3 is correlated relatively low with the other two predictors, X_1 and X_2 (see Table 5.1). Thus the X_3 variable can make more of an independent contribution to the predictability of the criterion variable. To a large extent, the Verbal and Mathematical sections of the Scholastic Aptitude Test make overlapping contributions.

The alert reader will have noticed the statement above that we "could" multiply the standard scores by the corresponding regression coefficients to obtain a predicted score for each new entering freshman. However, this is not at all a convenient procedure, because each raw score must first be transformed to a standard score (by subtracting the mean and dividing by the standard deviation) and finally the predicted score for each freshman, $\hat{z}_0$, must be transformed from standard score form back into raw score form. Fortunately, a set of equations can be derived that enable one to deal *directly with the raw scores*.

As an example, we shall consider the three-variable problem and, following the model of Equation 4.21 of the previous chapter, write

$$\hat{z}_0 = \beta_1 z_1 + \beta_2 z_2 \tag{5.1}$$

Each standard score is replaced by the expression that defines it in terms of raw score, mean, and standard deviation, thus giving

$$\frac{\hat{X}_0 - M_0}{\sigma_0} = \beta_1\left(\frac{X_1 - M_1}{\sigma_1}\right) + \beta_2\left(\frac{X_2 - M_2}{\sigma_2}\right) \qquad (5.2)$$

The strategy now is to manipulate this equation until $\hat{X}_0$ is alone on the left side of the equation. First we multiply both sides of the equation by σ_0:

$$\hat{X}_0 - M_0 = \beta_1\frac{\sigma_0}{\sigma_1}(X_1 - M_1) + \beta_2\frac{\sigma_0}{\sigma_2}(X_2 - M_2) \qquad (5.3)$$

At this point it is convenient to define b coefficients, which are simple functions of the corresponding β coefficients and standard deviations,[1] and they are defined thus:

$$b_1 \equiv \beta_1\frac{\sigma_0}{\sigma_1} \qquad (5.4)$$

$$b_2 \equiv \beta_2\frac{\sigma_0}{\sigma_2} \qquad (5.5)$$

These new symbols enable us to write Equation 5.3 more simply as

$$\hat{X}_0 - M_0 = b_1(X_1 - M_1) + b_2(X_2 - M_2) \qquad (5.6)$$

Next we multiply out on the right side of the equation to obtain

$$\hat{X}_0 - M_0 = b_1X_1 - b_1M_1 + b_2X_2 - b_2M_2 \qquad (5.7)$$

Now we add M_0 to both sides and then rearrange the terms on the right side to obtain

$$\hat{X}_0 = (M_0 - b_1M_1 - b_2M_2) + b_1X_1 + b_2X_2 \qquad (5.8)$$

The expression in parentheses can be defined as a:

$$a \equiv M_0 - b_1M_1 - b_2M_2 \qquad (5.9)$$

By substituting a in Equation 5.8, we obtain the final raw score equation,

$$\hat{X}_0 = a + b_1X_1 + b_2X_2 \qquad (5.10)$$

In a four-variable problem there would be another term on the

---

[1] Recall that, in the two-variable problem, $\beta_1 = r_{01}$ (see page 41).

right side of the equation, b_3X_3, and so on for problems involving a larger number of predictor variables. Note that a and the bs are constant for a given problem. This means that they can be calculated at once from the means, standard deviations, and regression coefficients and then used repeatedly for each new freshman. The X_1 and X_2 values change from person to person, but a, b_1, and b_2 remain the same. The predicted criterion score is a linear function of the scores on the predictor variables.

Let us now apply the technique to obtain a regression equation for the scholastic prediction example discussed above. The three β values calculated above and the means and standard deviations from Table 5.1 are inserted into equations analogous to Equations 5.4, 5.5, and 5.9:

$$b_1 = .305\left(\frac{5.0}{90}\right) = \frac{1.525}{90} = .017$$

$$b_2 = .193\left(\frac{5.0}{86}\right) = \frac{.965}{86} = .011$$

$$b_3 = .339\left(\frac{5.0}{6.4}\right) = \frac{1.695}{6.4} = .265$$

$$a = 22.00 - .017(394) - .011(435) - .265(24.3)$$

$$a = 22.00 - 6.70 - 4.78 - 6.44$$

$$a = 4.08$$

Therefore the appropriate regression equation is

$$\hat{X}_0 = 4.08 + .017X_1 + .011X_2 + .265X_3$$

Suppose that a new student makes the following raw scores on the three predictor variables: 423, 478, and 19.3. His predicted first-quarter average grade would be obtained as follows:

$$\hat{X}_0 = 4.08 + .017(423) + .011(478) + .265(19.3)$$
$$\hat{X}_0 = 4.08 + 7.19 + 5.26 + 5.11$$
$$\hat{X}_0 = 21.6$$

Now suppose that we were to calculate a predicted score, $\hat{X}_0$, for each student *in the original standardization group* and correlate these scores with the criterion scores actually earned by the same persons, X_0. Such a correlation is called the "multiple correlation coefficient." Just as the two-variable, simple correlation coefficient gives an index of the degree of predictability from *one* predictor to the criterion, the multiple correlation coefficient gives an index of degree of predictability from *more than one* predictor to the criterion. Fortunately, we need not actually obtain all the separate predicted scores but can use the formula,

$$R = \sqrt{\beta_1 r_{01} + \beta_2 r_{02} + \beta_3 r_{03} + \cdots} \qquad (5.11)$$

Each validity coefficient is multiplied by its corresponding regression coefficient, the products are added, and then the square root is taken. The multiple correlation coefficient is always taken to be positive. Using the values obtained above, for our example we calculate the multiple correlation to be

$$R^2 = .305(.52) + .193(.49) + .339(.51)$$
$$R^2 = .1586 + .0946 + .1729$$
$$R^2 = .4261$$
$$R = .65$$

To get a more empirical idea of how the multiple correlation coefficient is affected by addition of new predictors to a battery, consider Table 5.3. It shows Rs from differing numbers of predictor

Table 5.3 *Multiple Correlation Coefficients for Various Problems in which the Validity Coefficients Are All .30**

Number of Predictor Variables	Intercorrelations			
	.00	.10	.30	.60
1	(.30)	(.30)	(.30)	(.30)
2	.42	.40	.37	.34
3	.52	.47	.41	.35
4	.60	.53	.44	.36
9	.90	.67	.48	.37

* Adapted from R. L. Thorndike, *Research Problems and Techniques*, No. 3 in the AAF series, Washington, D.C., U.S. Government Printing Office, 1947.

variables, each correlating .30 with the criterion variable, but with varying intercorrelations. It can be seen that a considerable increase in multiple correlation takes place when a new predictor variable is added if the new predictor correlates low with the existing predictors (see the column with .00 at the top). Even here, however, "diminishing returns" set in rather early in that, for example, the fourth predictor does not add as much predictability to an existing battery of three predictors as the third predictor adds to an existing battery of two. On the other hand, note the situation when each new predictor correlates .60 with existing predictors. Nine predictor variables correlate only .37 with the criterion. The resulting increase in predictability would hardly compensate for the computational labor involved in obtaining the nine b coefficients. Unfortunately, most tests of aptitude and achievement do show rather large intercorrelations. Therefore there is little to gain in the typical prediction situation with such tests by using more than four or five predictors *unless* the new predictor is quite different in content or process from its predecessors. In fact, one of the principal motives for using factor analysis (discussed in Chapters 8 to 13 of this book) is to aid in the discovery of new tests that will show low correlations with existing tests. The situation with personality tests, which show many near-zero and negative intercorrelations, is more complex.

An interesting exception to the above principles is the "suppressant variable," of which the K scale of the Minnesota Multiphasic Personality Inventory is an example (Meehl and Hathaway, 1946.) Even though this type of variable correlates low with the criterion, it still improves prediction because it correlates high with the other predictors, thus reversing the usual principles. The theory of suppressant variables has been developed elsewhere (McNemar, 1962, pp. 186–187).

Another reason why it is usually not practical to employ more than four or five predictor variables is the fact that the sampling variabilities of the separate correlations that enter into the calculation of the multiple correlation tend to be compounded. This is especially true with small samples. Some authors, for example, Guilford (1956, pp. 398–399), present a formula for the multiple correlation corrected for "shrinkage." However, the correction represented by this formula is usually considerably less than the decrease in R that actually occurs with fresh samples.

When only two predictor variables are used, the β coefficients can be obtained directly from the following equations:

$$\beta_1 = \frac{r_{01} - r_{02}r_{12}}{1 - r_{12}^2} \tag{5.12}$$

$$\beta_2 = \frac{r_{02} - r_{01}r_{12}}{1 - r_{12}^2} \tag{5.13}$$

A corresponding equation for the multiple correlation coefficient can be derived by substituting Equations 5.12 and 5.13 in Equation 5.11 (the steps are left to the reader as an exercise), thus obtaining

$$R = \sqrt{\frac{r_{01}^2 + r_{02}^2 - 2r_{01}r_{02}r_{12}}{1 - r_{12}^2}} \tag{5.14}$$

The analogous equations for the three-predictor problem are considerably more complex (Lewis, 1960, p. 178). With more than three predictors, the pivotal condensation method described above can be used.

Let us now return to Equation 5.11, the equation for the multiple correlation coefficient. If we square the right member, we will have an expression for R^2, which is called the "coefficient of multiple determination" and which has an interesting interpretation:

$$R^2 = \beta_1 r_{01} + \beta_2 r_{02} + \beta_3 r_{03} + \cdots \tag{5.15}$$

In Figure 4.3 of the previous chapter we represented an error of estimate for z scores. However, to demonstrate certain further relationships, we shall have to use raw scores. An example of a regression line for raw scores is given in Figure 5.1. To keep the diagram relatively simple, we are representing only one predictor variable; however, the principles can be generalized easily to the situation of multiple correlation. Note that this particular regression line does *not* necessarily pass through the origin of the raw scores. However, it does pass through the intersection of the lines indicating the level of the two means. (This point is precisely the origin of the corresponding z scores.)

The error of estimate for raw scores can be obtained by subtracting from the actually observed score on the criterion variable (line segment *GL*) the criterion score that would be predicted from know-

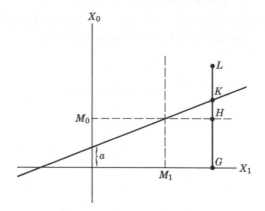

Figure 5.1   A regression line for raw scores.

ledge of the person's score on the predictor variable (line segment
GK). The difference (line segment *KL*) represents the error of estimate.

If we were to calculate the standard deviation of the errors of
estimate for all persons in the sample, we would obtain a quantity
called the "standard error of estimate," and *its* square, which is the
variance of the errors of estimate, is called the "variance error of
estimate." Fortunately, we need not go to the trouble of actually
computing the variance of the N errors of estimate but can use the
formula,

$$\sigma_{est}^2 = \sigma_0{}^2(1 - R^2) \tag{5.16}$$

If we were to calculate the variance of the observed criterion scores,
this process would essentially involve squaring the deviation of
each score from the mean of these scores. In Figure 5.1 the deviation
score is represented by line segment *HL*. This particular line segment
consists of the parts *KL* and *HK*. In terms of an algebraic identity,

$$(HL) \quad = \quad (KL) \quad + \quad (HK)$$
$$X_0 - M_0 = (X_0 - \hat{X}_0) + (\hat{X}_0 - M_0) \tag{5.17}$$

The two parts, *KL* and *HK*, are statistically independent of each
other, so the variance of *HL* equals the variance of *KL* plus the
variance of *HK* (see page 77). Since the variance of *KL* is the variance of *errors* of estimate, we can think of it as being the "non-

predicted variance." By analogy, the variance of *HK* is the "predicted variance." The relationship between the three types of variance is indicated by the formula,

Total variance = Nonpredicted variance + Predicted variance

$$\sigma_0{}^2 \quad = \quad (1 - R^2)\sigma_0{}^2 \quad + \quad R^2\sigma_0{}^2 \qquad (5.18)$$

Note that this formula is an algebraic identity. Thus R^2, the coefficient of multiple determination, gives the *proportion* of the total variance that is predicted by the predictor variables that have been employed. In the practical problem of predicting grades of college freshmen with which we dealt above, the multiple correlation coefficient was .65; therefore 43 % of the variance of freshman grades was predicted by the combination of high school average and the two SAT scores. The higher the multiple correlation, the higher the percentage of variance that has been "accounted for." The discrepancy between the obtained R^2 and a perfect R^2 of 1.00 represents a challenge to behavioral scientists to find other predictors that will account for more of the criterion variance.

In practice, the statistical hypothesis in which we are most interested is the "null hypothesis," the hypothesis that the multiple correlation in the population is zero. The 5 % and 1 % levels for values of *R* are shown in Table B of the Appendix. The appropriate column of the table is indicated by the total number of variables, including the criterion variable. In our example there were three predictors and one criterion, so we look in the column headed by the number 4. The "degrees of freedom" are given by the number of cases (467 persons in our example) minus the number of variables. There is no row in Table B for 463 degrees of freedom, so we employ the conservative procedure of using the next lower number given in the table, which is 400. Even so, our multiple correlation of .65 is well above the value of .167 required for significance at the 1 % level. Thus we can reject the null hypothesis with considerable confidence.

For readers who have some knowledge of the basic theory of analysis of variance, in the Appendix (page 200) an explanation is given of how this test is essentially a type of variance-ratio test. Also another variance-ratio test is described for the very practical situation of deciding whether addition of a new predictor variable results in a significant increase in the multiple correlation over that obtainable with the existing battery of predictors. Whether a "significant increase" also has practical utility is discussed below (see page 87).

A procedure that is closely related to multiple correlation is Fisher's "discriminant function" (Baggaley, 1947). The two procedures are alike in that both involve two or more predictor variables, each measured on a continuous scale. However, the discriminant function involves a dichotomous criterion variable. For example, a researcher might be interested in determining which weighted linear combination of scores on the Guilford-Zimmerman Temperament Survey most clearly differentiates sales engineers from mechanical engineers. An extension to more than two criterion groups, called the "multiple-group discriminant function," has been accomplished by Bryan (1951) and Rao (1952); however, the required computations are considerably more complex than in the situation where only two criterion groups are contrasted.

The procedure for Fisher's discriminant function also differs from multiple correlation in that the cross products involve deviations from the means of the two criterion groups taken separately, rather than from the general mean. However, Wert, Neidt, and Ahmann (1954, pp. 263–271) have worked out a technique more closely comparable to multiple correlation, which they claim is more appropriate to "selection" of personnel, as opposed to "classification" (see page 87). They also give a computational example of the more traditional discriminant function procedure (1954, pp. 366–370).

Problems

1. What does the fact that, in our example, the high school grades correlated higher with the Verbal than the Mathematical section of the Scholastic Aptitude Test imply about the nature of our high school curriculum?

2. Suppose that, in a two-variable problem, for $X_1 = 27$ we find that $\hat{X}_0 = 33$. Under what special circumstances would it also be true that, for $X_0 = 33$, $\hat{X}_1 = 27$?

3. When the multiple correlation is zero, what happens to the standard error of estimate and the predicted variance. Demonstrate, using Equations 5.16 and 5.18. Do the same for the situation when $R = +1.00$.

4. Lewis (1962) obtained the following matrix of intercorrelations and validities for 1158 male students at Southern Illinois University. Compute the β coefficients and the multiple correlation.

	X_2	X_3	X_4	X_0
X_1: School and College Abilities Test	.61	.61	.33	.41
X_2: Cooperative English Grammar Test		.42	.29	.34
X_3: Illinois Mathematics Placement Test			.38	.33
X_4: High school rank				.32
X_0: College grade-point average				

5. Ogburn and Talbot (1929) were concerned with predicting (actually "postdicting") the percentage voting for Smith in the 1928 presidential election in 173 counties in 8 states. They also calculated for the same counties the percentage voting for Cox in 1920 and for the "wet" position in liquor referenda and also the percentage of the population that was urban, Catholic, and foreign-born. The correlations between these variables are shown below. Calculate the β coefficients and the multiple correlation.

	X_2	X_3	X_4	X_5	X_0
X_1: Foreign-born	.44	.44	−.38	.34	.33
X_2: Catholic		.39	−.18	.37	.47
X_3: Wet vote			−.03	.34	.65
X_4: Cox vote				.07	.11
X_5: Urban					.16
X_0: Smith vote					

6. Given the following data, perform the calculations to obtain the values of a, b_1, and b_2 in the raw-score regression formula for predicting X_0 from X_1 and X_2: $M_1 = 6.43$, $\sigma_1 = 1.38$, $\beta_1 = .28$, $r_{01} = .41$, $M_2 = 5.76$, $\sigma_2 = .87$, $\beta_2 = .34$, $r_{02} = .45$, $M_0 = 5.43$, and $\sigma_0 = 1.54$. Also calculate the multiple correlation and the standard error of estimate.

7. Look up in Table 5.3 the values of R for the first two rows of the correlations below. Then compute the appropriate β weights and R for the third row, using Equations 5.12, 5.13, and 5.14, and compare the values of R for the three rows.

$$r_{01} = .30, \quad r_{02} = .30, \quad r_{12} = .00$$
$$r_{01} = .30, \quad r_{02} = .30, \quad r_{12} = .60$$
$$r_{01} = .30, \quad r_{02} = .00, \quad r_{12} = .60$$

Note the algebraic sign of the β_2 value for the third row. Here X_2 is functioning as a suppressant variable.

6

RELIABILITY AND VALIDITY
OF MEASUREMENTS: PART ONE

In the next two chapters we shall discuss some of the technical criteria that are used in deciding which particular behavioral science measuring instruments should be used in a given practical situation. The focus of our discussion will be on the criteria traditionally included under the labels "reliability" and "validity." Other criteria, such as cost and time of testing, availability of parallel forms, and availability of norms for various populations, are discussed in books more specifically oriented to surveying types of tests and other forms of evaluation, for example, those by Anastasi (1961), Cronbach (1960), and Thorndike and Hagen (1961).

Traditionally it has been said that reliability concerns the question "How consistently does a test measure?" and validity concerns the question "Does the test measure what it is supposed to measure?" However, over the years it has been found that these simple sounding questions encompass rather complex matters. For example, "consistency" of measurement can mean internal consistency or consistency over time. Therefore there has been a growing tendency to subdivide the terms "reliability" and "validity" by prefixing adjectives, for example, "predictive validity" and "content validity." In 1954 a joint committee of the American Psychological Association, American Educational Research Association, and National Council of Measurements Used in Education prepared a pamphlet entitled

Technical Recommendations for Psychological Tests and Diagnostic Techniques, in which an attempt was made to standardize these subclassifications. In the discussion below, the outline proposed by the committee will be used, with some modification. It is probable that the terms "reliability" and "validity" will eventually be superseded by more definitive terms, as is discussed below.

At the outset it may be useful to present a skeletal outline of the system which will be described.

Reliability
> Temporal (retest)
> Interobserver agreement
> Internal consistency
>> Equivalence
>> Split-halves procedures
>> Kuder-Richardson formulas

Validity
> Practical
>> Concurrent
>> Predictive
> Construct
> Content

RELIABILITY

One often used procedure for estimating the reliability of a measuring instrument is to administer it at one time and then again after an interval of time. The two sets of scores are then correlated. By now it seems evident that the quality of the test thus being assessed may be quite different in nature from that assessed by, for example, an odd-even reliability coefficient. In fact, there are some measurements, such as physiological measurements (blood pressure, galvanic skin response), which we expect to change for a group of subjects, even over periods of time as short as hours or minutes. Even with measures of "traits" more properly falling within the sphere of behavioral science, our general theory allows us to contemplate the possibility that a subject's "intelligence" (for example) may "really" change over a period of six months, that is, this change may not be merely a fault of the measuring instrument. Such changes are some-times called "function fluctuations." There is no completely ob-jective technique for distinguishing the two types of changes; we must depend on our general knowledge of the area of behaviors that the test samples.

Thus, if the time interval is too *long*, a retest may not measure "the same thing" as the original test; on the other hand, if the time interval is too *short*, other difficulties may complicate interpretation of retest coefficients. The subjects may remember specific item content, or fatigue or warmup effects may occur. For these reasons it is probably better that the time interval for estimation of retest reliability be not shorter than a week but not longer than six months. In any event, the time interval should be reported along with the coefficient.

It should be remembered that, if these effects are constant for all subjects, the correlation coefficient remains invariant because a linear transformation of the variables is involved (see page 14). In the above discussion, it was assumed that the effects differ between subjects, for example, one person remembers specific item content but another person does not.

Tests involving selective ("objective") items (multiple-choice, true-false) can be scored equally well by any person with a certain minimum of clerical and computational ability. However, behavioral scientists often assess traits by more subjective means and then assign trait ratings to individuals. This suggests the second category of reliability, interobserver agreement, as another important aspect of "consistency of measurement." Although we shall do no more than mention this category in the present discussion, Ebel (1951) showed how the techniques of analysis of variance can be applied to assess the agreement of sets of ratings of the same subjects made by different judges. If the ratings are in the form of rankings, Kendall's coefficient of concordance can be used (Siegel, 1956, pp. 229–238).

The most widely useful types of reliability estimates are those involving internal consistency. Here no time interval is in-volved, and only one person is needed to score the subjects' per-formances. However, their use demands that the test consist of experimentally independent parts (e.g., test items) from which a total score is obtained by summing part scores, weighted either equally or differentially.

To examine internal consistency let us suppose that a test of vocabulary is desired for 10-year-old boys, and 200 words have been selected as representative of the universe of content (see "content validity" below). Suppose further that an estimate of "reliability" of measurement is desired. One procedure would be to construct two 100-item tests of approximately equal average item difficulty, administer them to a representative sample of 10-year-old boys, and correlate the two sets of scores. This type of reliability is usually called "equivalence reliability," and the separate tests are called "parallel tests" or "parallel forms of a test." If *three* parallel forms are constructed, a statistical test of their equivalence is available (Gulliksen, 1950, Chapter 14). It should be mentioned parenthetically that there are practical advantages in having more than one form of a test in addition to that of enabling calculation of a reliability coefficient. For example, an examiner who has given an individual intelligence test may feel that the subject was handicapped by unusual emotional stresses during a particular testing session and wish to obtain another measurement.

Instead of constructing two separate 100-item test forms, a behavioral scientist may administer all 200 items at one sitting but score them as though they constituted two separate test forms ("split halves"). In order to control the effects of warmup, fatigue, etc., the scorer usually counts the odd-numbered items separately from the even-numbered items. Then the two sets of numbers are correlated; one set represents the scores on items 1, 3, 5, . . ., 199, and the other set represents the scores on items 2, 4, 6, . . ., 200. This procedure gives the reliability of a test of this nature consisting of only 100 items, whereas what is desired is the reliability of a 200-item test. A formula is used to "correct" the coefficient upward; however, consideration of this formula is better postponed until the next chapter, where it will be seen that the correction is a special case of the general formula showing reliability as a function of test length (page 80).

Kuder and Richardson (1937) developed a series of reliability formulas that were derived from a more general theoretical approach. Cronbach (1951) showed that one of these formulas gives the mean of the correlations resulting from all possible ways of splitting a given test into two halves and that it gives the proportion of first-factor variance extracted from the intercorrelations of the test items (see Chapter 13). He suggested that the Greek letter alpha be used to designate this particular index instead of "Kuder-Richardson formula number 20," but unfortunately this suggestion has not been generally adopted. Two raw-score formulas for "coefficient α" are

$$
\begin{aligned}
\alpha &= \frac{n}{n-1}\left[\frac{N\sum X^2 - (\sum X)^2 + \sum I^2 - N\sum I}{N\sum X^2 - (\sum X)^2}\right] \\
&= \frac{n}{n-1}\left[\frac{L_{xx} - (N\sum I - \sum I^2)}{L_{xx}}\right]
\end{aligned}
\tag{6.1}
$$

$N \equiv$ the number of persons
$n \equiv$ the number of test items
$X \equiv$ the number of items answered correctly by a
      particular person (person score)
$I \equiv$ the number of persons giving the correct answer to a
      particular item (item score)

To calculate coefficient α for a particular problem it is convenient to assemble a person-item matrix (see Table 6.1). If a particular person answered a particular item correctly, a value of "1" is entered in the corresponding cell of the matrix. If he missed the item, a value of "0" is entered. The X column gives the ten row sums, which are the person scores; the I row gives the eight column sums, which are the item scores. The numbers in the X column should be added, which in our example gives the result 50; the sum of the values in the I row then serves as a check. The X^2 and I^2 values are needed in the formula; however, note especially that the sum of the X^2 values does *not*, in general, equal the sum of the I^2 values. The remaining calculations are shown in detail in the table.[1] (However, the numbers do not have to be arranged so that the values of X and I are in descending order, as has been done for Table 6.1.)

---

[1] Ferguson (1951) extended this approach to reliability to situations where the items have more than two categories of response.

Table 6.1 *Calculation of coefficient alpha (Kuder-Richardson formula 20)*

Person	A	B	C	D	E	F	G	H	X	X^2
1	1	1	1	1	1	1	1	1	8	64
2	1	1	1	1	1	1	1	0	7	49
3	1	1	1	1	1	1	0	0	6	36
4	1	1	1	1	1	0	1	0	6	36
5	1	1	1	1	1	0	0	0	5	25
6	1	1	1	0	1	0	0	1	5	25
7	1	1	1	1	0	1	0	0	5	25
8	1	0	0	1	0	1	1	0	4	16
9	1	1	0	0	0	0	0	1	3	9
10	1	0	0	0	0	0	0	0	1	1
I	10	8	7	7	6	5	4	3	50	
I^2	100	64	49	49	36	25	16	9		

$$\Sigma X^2 = 286, \quad \Sigma I^2 = 348, \quad N = 10, \quad n = 8$$

$$a = \frac{8}{8-1}\left[\frac{10(286) - (50)^2 + 348 - 10(50)}{10(286) - (50)^2}\right]$$

$$a = \frac{8}{7}\left[\frac{2860 - 2500 + 348 - 500}{2860 - 2500}\right]$$

$$a = \frac{8}{7}\left[\frac{208}{360}\right] = \frac{1664}{2520} = .66$$

The value of .66 for a reliability coefficient may seem surprisingly low; however, note that this test is only eight items long. A formula is given later (see page 79) to estimate how much the reliability would be expected to increase for a longer test of the same general content.

An important qualification to be made at this point is that the split-halves and Kuder-Richardson formulas should *not* be calculated for "speeded" tests. If we use the somewhat arbitrary definition that a "power" test is one in which at least 80% of the subjects can attempt to answer all the items (Thorndike and Hagen, 1961, p. 39), then all other tests are considered speeded tests. The rationale for this admonition is best explained by considering the extreme example of a test in which no subject ever misses or omits any of the items. With such a test, the subject's score is simply the number of items he manages to reach. With an odd-even procedure, every subject's two scores will either be identical or the score on the odd items will exceed the score on the even items by one point. If there is any appreciable variability between subjects in total score, this means that the correlation between odd and even items will inevitably be quite close to a perfect positive relationship. In more general terms, the fact that a test is highly speeded introduces a spuriously high correlation between the items. Although over the years there has been an increasing tendency to give generous time limits for pencil-and-paper tests of aptitude and achievement, it seems that some traits involve speed even in their theoretical conception, for example, tests of perceptual speed or arithmetical operations. With such tests, in order to obtain a theoretically appropriate estimate of internal consistency reliability, it is necessary to give part-tests separately timed, which means that one is essentially obtaining a measure of "equivalence."

VALIDITY

One of the most straightforward theoretical approaches to answering the question "Does the test measure what it is supposed to measure?" is to find out whether it correlates with some "criterion performance." The "criterion," as defined technically, refers to some socially important outcome, for example, grades in a training course, supervisors' ratings, recidivism of prisoners, etc. This involves "practical validity," which is the type of validity that makes most sense to the person mainly concerned with test application. From this point of view, a test has not just one validity coefficient but as many validity coefficients as there are criteria for it to predict. Thus a mathematical reasoning test might be valid for predicting grades in physics but invalid for predicting grades in literature. A test for supervisors might predict success at the Jones Company but not at the Smith Company.

The major difficulty with the approach of practical validity is that competent authorities often disagree about the appropriate criterion variable to use. How does one identify the most "successful" physicians? Which criterion measurement should be used—income, number of patients, mortality rate of patients, number of scholarly papers read at scientific meetings? All the foregoing can be criticized as unjustly favoring some physicians over others. Furthermore, such "ultimate" criterion data take a long time to collect. The upshot of the matter is that the criterion variable most often used in vocational test validation is grades in the relevant training course, even though many legitimate objections can be raised against this procedure. Hopefully, additional criterion data can be collected later as the trainees move out of the schools and on to the jobs.

It may even turn out that a test is valid for predicting one aspect of job performance, but not another, for example, production, but not supervisors' ratings. Of course, there is a practical limit to this process of fractionation; no behavioral scientist is going to calculate separate correlations for every combination of test, job, and aspect of job performance! He must assume that there is some generality between similar situations. Nevertheless, he should realize that a gamble is always involved in such generalizations, and he should apply practical checks whenever it is feasible to do so.

The report of the committee mentioned previously recommended that what we have called practical validity be subdivided into the categories of "concurrent validity" and "predictive validity." The two differ in that, in concurrent validity, the criterion information is available at the same time as (or even before) the test is administered. Predictive validity coefficients tend to be lower than concurrent validities because, with the passage of time, a person's life is cumulatively influenced by an increasing number of relatively fortuitous variables, which no single test or set of measurements could be expected to predict.

An example of the distinction from the field of vocational prediction is a comparison of the "present-employee" and "follow-up" methods of test validation (Tiffin and McCormick, 1958, pp. 82–89). In the former method, criterion information is available on present employees during the general period of time when the test is being administered; thus *concurrent* validity is involved. In the follow-up method, job applicants are tested, the test is *not* then used as a device for selection, and criterion information on the subjects is collected after they have learned the job; thus *predictive* validity is involved.

Tiffin and McCormick discuss the relative advantages of the two procedures.

If either a predictor variable or the criterion variable consists of ratings, it is important that the raters have no knowledge of scores on the other variable until they have finished making their ratings. Otherwise the validity coefficients will tend to be spuriously high, a situation that is called "contamination of criteria" (Cronbach, 1960, pp. 352–353).

A more theoretical objection that has been raised to the general procedure of evaluating a test by correlating it with an admittedly fallible criterion is that the test, from many points of view, can often be thought of as a better measure of a particular quality than the criterion (Ebel, 1961, p. 644). Therefore, it is argued, it is hardly fair to discard the test because it does not agree with the "inferior" criterion. Considerations of this sort led to formulation of the controversial concept of "construct validity." Among those who find little use for this concept is Bechtoldt (1959), who presented a report entitled "The Construct Validity of Construct Validity," in which he implied that it has no "construct validity"!

Construct validity is the concept that most closely involves an attempt to answer the question "What does the test 'really' measure?" Thus it is the type of validity that is most closely tied to behavioral science theories. One approach to construct validity is to check the test against other tests (not criteria) about which we have more knowledge. The most systematic procedure for doing this is factor analysis (see Chapters 8 to 13). New tests about which we know little are put in a battery together with old tests about which we know more. For the purposes of construct validity, finding out the variables that correlate *low* with a particular test is as important as learning the variables that correlate high with the test (Campbell and Fiske, 1959). (Although the term "test" has been used in much of the discussion in this chapter, most of the principles apply equally well to other behavioral science measurements, such as ratings and crime records.)

An example of the type of problem falling under the heading of construct validity is the question of whether a particular intelligence test is "fair" to culturally deprived groups. In comparing the intelligence of whites and Negroes, a behavioral scientist may attempt to control such variables as years of education and length of residence in the city where tested. Whether such techniques provide a fair comparison is a controversial question, but the point being made here is simply that the test scores are not considered to be operationally valid in themselves; rather, an attempt is made to learn what they "really" represent. Thus one technique for studying construct validity is comparison of scores between sociologically defined groups, varying on such variables as sex, age, occupation, place of residence, and amount of education.

Another approach in studying the construct validity of a measuring device is to compare scores before and after an experimental treatment. For example, Alexander and Husek (1962) administered a semantic differential questionnaire before and after the showing of a color film of a surgical operation on the frontal sinus of a human patient, which presumably aroused "anxiety" within the subjects. Items that showed significant differences were assembled to constitute a questionnaire measure of anxiety.

Thus we see that the establishment of the construct validity of a measuring device depends on the accumulation of a variety of bits of evidence over a period of time. Even from the standpoint of a practitioner, construct validity is useful because it gives him better grounds for deciding whether a test that has shown practical validity in one situation will continue to be valid in a somewhat different situation. For example, suppose that a battery of tests has proved to be valid over a period of years for selecting men to repair a particular machine. Suppose further that the design of the machine is changed rather radically. The practitioner can make a more intelligent decision on which tests to take out of the selection battery and which tests to put in (assuming limited testing time) if some evidence is available on their construct validity. Of course, he will want to check his hunches by collecting later criterion information and calculating predictive validities, but the decision on how to revise the battery (if at all) must often occur now rather than later!

The fourth kind of validity distinguished by the committee is "content validity." In this conception it is assumed that there is a "universe of content" which can be closely defined. (However, as Thorndike and Hagen, 1961, p. 162, remark, the word "content" should also be understood to include "process.") If the universe can be broken down into more or less equivalent and independent units, then sampling procedures can be applied to it. For example, if the ability to add two one-digit numbers is under consideration, the universe by definition consists of 100 possible problems. To construct a test for this ability, one might then take a random sample of 25 of these 100 problems. Of course, this example is atypical in that seldom are we able to define the universe of content with such precision. However, procedures such as the Q sort (Stephenson, 1953) and the critical incident technique (Flanagan, 1954) involve varying kinds of selection from defined universes.

The area of application in which content validity is particularly relevant is achievement testing. Thorndike and Hagen (1961, pp. 29–34) describe a "test blueprint" procedure whereby a classroom teacher can gain some confidence that her tests are measuring the teaching objectives as well as the course content that she is attempting to stress in her teaching activities. It is not easy to envision a statistical index that would indicate how much content validity a test possesses; however, the promoter of a test should make some attempt to specify the procedures that were used in selecting test content.

GENERAL REMARKS ON RELIABILITY AND VALIDITY

By this time the reader has probably concluded that there are rather complex relationships between the various procedures discussed above. Some of these relationships cut across the distinction between "reliability" and "validity." Factor analysis is used in connection with both internal consistency reliability and construct validity. Sampling from a universe of content is involved in both equivalence reliability and content validity. A lapse of time is involved in both temporal reliability and predictive validity. Thus, over a period of years, the meaning of the terms "reliability" and "validity" has become increasingly vague, and they may eventually be dropped from the technical vocabulary and replaced by more uniquely descriptive terms.[2] For a discussion of this question from a somewhat different point of view, see Campbell and Fiske (1959, p. 83).

In actual test development there is usually a kind of reciprocal interweaving of the procedures discussed above. In their article on

---

[2] Unfortunately, the word "reliability" is occasionally used in the completely different sense of "sampling invariance," for example, Guilford (1956, Ch. 9).

construct validity, Cronbach and Meehl (1955, pp. 286–287) ingeniously illustrate this process by comparing the development of the Binet intelligence test with the "validation" of a thermometer. Before "intelligence" could be measured at all, Binet had to have at least a rough conception of the relevant content from which to select the tasks to be included in his initial test (content validity). If this initial test had not agreed *at least partially* with teachers' judgments (concurrent validity), it would have been discarded along with the tasks previously tried by Cattell and Wissler a few years before. However, in the intervening years, the Binet test has been found to show high correlations with many other tests presumed to measure "intelligence" (one approach to construct validity). Furthermore, the test is an excellent predictor of future success in school (predictive validity). For these and other reasons, if today a teacher's evaluation of a pupil's intelligence disagrees markedly with the pupil's tested Binet IQ score, we are more likely to trust the test than the teacher. Thus we see that all four types of validity have been involved in the process of "validating" the Binet test over a period of years.

Problems

1. Tests of "intelligence" given during the first three years of life do not show very high correlations with the Stanford-Binet test given to the same persons during adolescence (Bayley, 1949). Comment on this situation from the point of view of reliability of intelligence measurement.

2. How could one establish the reliability of the judgment of who have been the five greatest Presidents of the United States?

3. Can the internal consistency of the Rorschach test be measured? If so, how?

4. Discuss some advantages in clinical, educational, and industrial situations of having available two or more parallel forms of a test.

5. Describe a visual pattern of 1's and 0's that would tend to give a higher value of α than that shown in Table 6.1. Also describe a pattern that would give a lower value. What is the relevance of Guttman's "coefficient of reproducibility" (Edwards, 1957, Ch. 7) for describing these patterns?

6. Which of the meanings of "reliability" discussed in this chapter corresponds most closely with the use of the term by physical scientists and engineers?

7. Suggest some criterion measurements that you would use to measure the "success" of (a) college teachers, (b) morticians, (c) lawyers, (d) experts in labor relations, (e) claim adjusters for insurance companies, (f) Congressmen.

8. Discuss the problem of test motivation in the present-employee and follow-up methods of test validation.

9. Which variables would have to be controlled in order to afford a "fair comparison" between the intelligence of whites and Negroes?

10. Suppose that a group of sailors rated a set of photographs of college girls on physical beauty (a) while the sailors were at sea and (b) after the sailors had been stationed at a port for a month. Would the difference in ratings have construct validity as a measure of sexual drive?

11. Briefly outline a universe of content for measuring achievement in a course in (a) American history, (b) creative writing, (c) automobile driving, (d) human relations.

12. Cronbach (1960, pp. 602–604) uses the concepts of "bandwidth" and "fidelity" in his discussion of testing. Are these concepts related to reliability and validity, and if so, how?

13. For the person-item matrix given below, calculate the α coefficient of reliability.

Item

Person	A	B	C	D	E	F	G	H
1	1	1	1	1	0	1	1	1
2	1	1	1	1	1	1	0	1
3	1	1	1	1	1	0	1	0
4	1	1	1	1	1	1	0	0
5	1	0	1	1	0	1	0	1
6	1	1	0	1	1	0	1	0
7	1	0	1	0	0	1	1	1
8	1	1	1	0	1	0	0	0
9	1	1	0	0	1	0	0	0
10	0	0	0	1	0	1	0	0

7
RELIABILITY AND VALIDITY
OF MEASUREMENTS: PART TWO

In the previous chapter we undertook a general discussion of the concepts that have been subsumed under the heading of the terms "reliability" and "validity." We concluded that these terms, as presently used, are rather ambiguous. Nevertheless, over the period of half a century, a system of mathematical theory has been developed involving reliability and validity. This system has proved very useful in describing various characteristics of behavioral science measurements and in predicting how they will change with changes in conditions such as variability of population and length of test.

The body of theory we shall be discussing has sometimes been called "classical test score theory." It probably originated in the work of the British psychologist, Spearman (1904). Although this particular approach to reliability and validity has been the most popular one, it should be noted that there are alternative approaches, for example, Gulliksen, (1950, Chapter 3), Guttman (1953) and Tryon (1957). Several of the working formulas derived from these alternative approaches are identical with those we are to discuss; they were simply arrived at by a different route.

The basic notion is that any observed measurement is contaminated by an "error of measurement." Thorndike (1951, p. 568) and Cronbach (1960, p. 128) have attempted to classify these errors exhaustively. Their system involves the two dimensions of lasting versus temporary characteristics of the individual and general versus specific characteristics of the individual. According to this system, temporary-specific characteristics are always regarded as "error," but whether lasting-specific characteristics or temporary-general characteristics are considered to be error depends on whether one is thinking of reliability in the internal consistency sense or in the temporal (retest) sense, respectively. Classical test score theory seems to follow more logically from the former assumption. Therefore it should be assumed in this chapter that the reliability coefficients being discussed are measures of internal consistency and that the validity coefficients involve practical validity, that is, correlation with an external criterion. It should further be emphasized at the outset that we shall *not* be talking about errors due to drawing a sample from a larger population of individuals (e.g., persons, animals). Sampling errors are essentially independent of errors of measurement.

Classical test score theory began in the field of ability testing and is still easiest to describe if it is assumed that the score involves a summing of more or less independent parts; for instance, responses to "items" on an intelligence test (Baggaley, 1960b). We then make the basic assumption that an observed score X can be divided into two additive components, a "true score" T and an "error score" E, that is,

$$X = T + E \tag{7.1}$$

We further assume that these errors are not constant errors (e.g., errors arising from repeated measurements by a yardstick that is a little too short) but can be considered "random." From an intuitive notion of the concept of randomness, two important consequences can be deduced. First, the mean of these errors, averaged over a large number of measurements (usually this implies different persons measured), will be zero:

$$M_E = 0 \tag{7.2}$$

In other words, the positive and negative discrepancies will tend to balance out. Furthermore, if the errors are random, they should logically be independent of the true scores, which supposedly measure a general and/or lasting characteristic of the person being measured.

If the true and error scores are independent, then they are uncorrelated, that is,

$$r_{TE} = 0 \tag{7.3}$$

In the discussion of internal consistency reliability in the previous chapter, the concept of parallel forms of a test was introduced. If the errors on two forms of a test are random, then these errors are similarly uncorrelated. This leads to our final basic assumption, which is that

$$r_{E_g E_h} = 0 \tag{7.4}$$

The sub-subscripts, g and h, refer to two forms of the test.

Armed with this set of postulates, we are now ready to undertake our derivations. First, we shall demonstrate a theorem dealing with observed, true, and error variances. We sum Equation 7.1 over the sample of measurements (usually persons) and obtain

$$\sum X = \sum (T + E) \tag{7.5}$$

According to the First Summation Law (see Chapter 2) we can distribute the summation sign on the right side of the equation, which leads to

$$\sum X = \sum T + \sum E \tag{7.6}$$

Now we divide both sides of Equation 7.6 by N, the number of measurements, to obtain

$$\frac{\sum X}{N} = \frac{\sum T + \sum E}{N} = \frac{\sum T}{N} + \frac{\sum E}{N} \tag{7.7}$$

From the basic definition of the arithmetic mean, Equation 7.7 is equivalent to

$$M_X = M_T + M_E \tag{7.8}$$

The next step is to subtract Equation 7.8 from Equation 7.1, which gives

$$\begin{aligned} X - M_X &= (T + E) - (M_T + M_E) \\ &= (T - M_T) + (E - M_E) \end{aligned} \tag{7.9}$$

The three terms of Equation 7.9 are all basically deviation scores, so we can write the equation as

$$x = t + e \tag{7.10}$$

Now we take the defining equation for the variance and apply it successively to the observed, true, and error scores by affixing appropriate subscripts:

$$\sigma_X{}^2 = \frac{\sum x^2}{N} \tag{7.11}$$

$$\sigma_T{}^2 = \frac{\sum t^2}{N} \tag{7.12}$$

$$\sigma_E{}^2 = \frac{\sum e^2}{N} \tag{7.13}$$

Substituting Equation 7.10 in the numerator of Equation 7.11 gives

$$\sigma_X{}^2 = \frac{\sum (t + e)^2}{N} \tag{7.14}$$

Now we expand the expression in parentheses, which leads to

$$\sigma_X{}^2 = \frac{\sum (t^2 + 2te + e^2)}{N} \tag{7.15}$$

By means of the First and Second Summation Laws, we can distribute the summation sign to the three terms and then take the constant "2" outside the second term, which gives us

$$\sigma_X{}^2 = \frac{\sum t^2 + 2\sum te + \sum e^2}{N} \tag{7.16}$$

Now we split the right member of Equation 7.16 into three fractions:

$$\sigma_X{}^2 = \frac{\sum t^2}{N} + \frac{2\sum te}{N} + \frac{\sum e^2}{N} \tag{7.17}$$

In preceding pages we wrote in Equation 7.3 that the true and error scores are uncorrelated. In terms of one of the formulas for the product-moment correlation coefficient, the correlation between true and error scores is

$$r_{TE} = \frac{\sum te}{N\sigma_T\sigma_E} \tag{7.18}$$

Combining Equations 7.3 and 7.18, we have

$$\frac{\sum te}{N\sigma_T\sigma_E} = 0 \tag{7.19}$$

Multiplying by $2\sigma_T\sigma_E$ gives

$$\frac{2\sum te}{N} = 0 \tag{7.20}$$

Substituting Equation 7.20 in Equation 7.17 gives

$$\sigma_X{}^2 = \frac{\sum t^2}{N} + 0 + \frac{\sum e^2}{N} \tag{7.21}$$

Finally, substitution of Equations 7.12 and 7.13 in Equation 7.21 gives

$$\sigma_X{}^2 = \sigma_T{}^2 + \sigma_E{}^2 \tag{7.22}$$

Stated verbally, this theorem says that the variance of observed scores equals the sum of the true variance and error variance. It is a special case of a more general theorem, which is basic to the statistical techniques called "analysis of variance;" namely, the variance of the sum of *independent* measures equals the sum of the variances of the measures taken separately.

We shall now define the "reliability coefficient," r_{gh}, of a measuring device as the correlation between two parallel forms of the device. Using this definition and the foregoing assumptions, it can be shown (Gulliksen, 1950, pp. 13–14) that the reliability is the proportion of true variance in the observed scores,[1] that is,

$$r_{gh} = \frac{\sigma_T{}^2}{\sigma_X{}^2} \tag{7.23}$$

From Equation 7.22, we can obtain

$$\sigma_T{}^2 = \sigma_X{}^2 - \sigma_E{}^2 \tag{7.24}$$

Therefore,

$$r_{gh} = \frac{\sigma_X{}^2 - \sigma_E{}^2}{\sigma_X{}^2} = 1 - \frac{\sigma_E{}^2}{\sigma_X{}^2} \tag{7.25}$$

[1] The third basic assumption, identified above as Equation 7.4, is used in this demonstration.

From this relationship we can see that the more that error of measurement contributes to the variability of a measuring device, the less reliable the device will be. This conclusion is congruent with our intuitive notions of "error" and "reliability."

Our next task is to develop a formula for estimating how much scores will tend to vary because of unreliability of the testing device. First, we multiply Equation 7.23 by σ_X^2 and reverse the order, thus obtaining

$$\sigma_T^2 = r_{gh}\sigma_X^2 \tag{7.26}$$

Now Equation 7.26 is substituted in Equation 7.22 to give

$$\sigma_X^2 = r_{gh}\sigma_X^2 + \sigma_E^2 \tag{7.27}$$

Next we subtract $r_{gh}\sigma_X^2$ from both sides of Equation 7.27 and reverse the order to obtain

$$\sigma_E^2 = \sigma_X^2 - r_{gh}\sigma_X^2 \tag{7.28}$$

Factoring the right member gives

$$\sigma_E^2 = \sigma_X^2(1 - r_{gh}) \tag{7.29}$$

Finally we take the square root and obtain

$$\sigma_E = \sigma_X\sqrt{1 - r_{gh}} \tag{7.30}$$

This expression is called the "standard error of measurement." It is expressed on the same scale of measurement as the raw scores, for example, if the raw scores are in yards, the standard error of measurement will also be in yards. For comparing the reliability of different measuring devices, this fact is a disadvantage. However, it is advantageous when a person's score on a single test is being interpreted.

The mode of interpretation is analogous to the process of establishing a confidence interval for a population mean (Underwood et al., 1954, pp. 114–117). However, because of basic sampling theory, we must make our statement of interpretation in a somewhat unique manner. It will be noted that, in the derivation of the standard error of measurement, no assumption was made about the shape of the frequency distribution of errors. However, to make a probability statement we must now make some such assumption, and it is usually assumed that the errors of measurement are normally distributed.

For persons with a particular observed score, X_i, we can make the following statement:

$$(X_i - k\sigma_E) < T_i < (X_i + k\sigma_E)$$

This statement sets limits within which the true score for these persons probably lies. The interval thus delimited is called a "confidence interval." The probability of our statement being correct depends on k, which is specified by the level of confidence we choose to work with. (Usually k is taken to be 2, which corresponds approximately to the "5% level.") Suppose that the standard error of measurement of a test is 5. For persons obtaining a score of 43, we state that their true score probably lies between 33 and 53, that is,

$$[43 - 2(5)] < T_i < [43 + 2(5)]$$
$$33 < T_i < 53.$$

It can be seen that the greater the standard error of measurement, the greater is the distance between the limits. Although this manner of reporting test results to the general public would at present seem unfamiliar, its use should be strongly encouraged.[2] The result would be that the public would view behavioral science measurements in a less "absolute" manner, would be less disappointed by errors in prediction, and would therefore be less sceptical in the long run of results reported by behavioral scientists.

An important formula in test score theory is the general Spearman-Brown formula, which is used to estimate how much the reliability of a test will change when its length changes:

$$r_{GH} = \frac{Kr_{gh}}{1 + (K - 1)r_{gh}} \tag{7.31}$$

r_{GH} represents the reliability of a test K times as long as a test whose reliability is r_{gh}. It is derived (Gulliksen, 1950, pp. 74–79) by assuming that each successive increase in total length is accomplished by adding what could be considered a "parallel test" to the original test. For example, if a test consists of 100 vocabulary words,

---

[2] For reporting scores on their SCAT and STEP tests, the test authors of the Educational Testing Service provide for plotting of "score bands" rather than score points.

tripling it would mean adding 200 more words of similar content and difficulty level, and K would equal 3. It is further assumed that such factors as warmup and fatigue do not complicate the issue.

In the previous chapter, the split-halves procedure for calculating the internal consistency reliability of a test was described, and it was mentioned that the obtained value should be corrected upward because it represents the reliability of a test only one-half as long as the original test. Since this correction represents a doubling of the length of the half-test, we can substitute 2 for K in Equation 7.31, giving

$$r_{GH} = \frac{2r_{gh}}{1 + (2 - 1)r_{gh}} = \frac{2r_{gh}}{1 + r_{gh}} \tag{7.32}$$

For example, if the value obtained by the split-halves procedure were .73, the corrected reliability coefficient would be

$$r_{GH} = \frac{2(.73)}{1 + .73} = \frac{1.46}{1.73} = .84$$

Table F in the Appendix gives corrected values corresponding to uncorrected values at intervals of .01. The relationship represented by Equation 7.32 is shown graphically in Figure 7.1. If there were no correction, the points would all fall on the diagonal line from the lower-left to the upper-right corners of the graph, that is, each corrected value would equal the uncorrected value. The vertical distance of the actual curve of the equation above the diagonal line represents the extent of correction. It can be noted that, at the higher levels, "diminishing returns" set in. For example, the corrected value corresponding to an uncorrected value of .83 is .91; here the correction involves an increase of only .08 as opposed to the increase of .11 in the example above.

Equation 7.31 can also be used with values less than one; this situation would mean a correction *downward* for a shortened test. It is of particular interest to discover what would happen to the reliability if the test were made infinitely long.[3] First, we multiply out in the denominator of Equation 7.31 to obtain

$$r_{GH} = \frac{Kr_{gh}}{1 + Kr_{gh} - r_{gh}} \tag{7.33}$$

[3] This particular method of derivation was suggested to the author by Kenneth Perchonok.

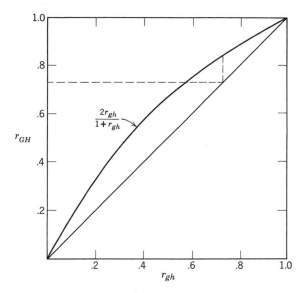

Figure 7.1 Graph of the Spearman-Brown formula for $K = 2$.

Next each term in the numerator and denominator of the right member is divided by K, which gives

$$r_{GH} = \frac{r_{gh}}{1/K + r_{gh} - r_{gh}/K} \tag{7.34}$$

Now we let K approach infinity:

$$r_{GH} \rightarrow \frac{r_{gh}}{0 + r_{gh} - 0} = \frac{r_{gh}}{r_{gh}} \tag{7.35}$$

Thus, if r_{gh} is greater than zero, the reliability of an infinitely long test would be unity, that is, perfect reliability.

By making various additional assumptions, we can show (Gulliksen, 1950, pp. 98–99) that, if a test is lengthened by a factor K and a criterion measure is lengthened by a factor L, the correlation between the two lengthened measures can be estimated as

$$r_{KL} = \frac{r_{XY}}{\sqrt{1/K + (1 - 1/K)r_{XX}} \sqrt{1/L + (1 - 1/L)r_{YY}}} \tag{7.36}$$

r_{XX} and r_{YY} are the reliabilities of the test and criterion, respectively, and r_{XY} is the original correlation between them, that is, the uncorrected validity coefficient. Now let both K and L approach infinity. Most of the quantities vanish, leaving

$$r_{KL} \to r_{\infty\infty} = \frac{r_{XY}}{\sqrt{r_{XX}r_{YY}}} \tag{7.37}$$

This formula is called the "correction for attenuation." It is an estimate of the correlation between an infinitely long test and an infinitely long criterion. In the preceding material we showed that an infinitely long test would be perfectly reliable; by analogous reasoning, an infinitely long criterion would likewise be perfectly reliable. Therefore this formula is also an estimate of the correlation between a perfectly reliable test and a perfectly reliable criterion. To examine it further, let us split the right member into three factors:

$$r_{\infty\infty} = r_{XY}\left(\frac{1}{\sqrt{r_{XX}}}\right)\left(\frac{1}{\sqrt{r_{YY}}}\right) \tag{7.38}$$

Obviously no one will ever administer an infinitely long test or measure an infinitely long criterion! However, suppose that a test constructor gives a test and obtains an r_{XY} value of .54. The contracting agency (e.g., a medical school) protests that this validity coefficient is too low. Suppose also that the test has a reliability of .81. This means that the highest validity that could be obtained *by lengthening the test* would be only .60, which is obtained by multiplying .54 by the reciprocal of the square root of .81. At this point the astute test constructor should inquire into the reliability of the *criterion*. If it is only .36 (which is not uncommon), then the optimal validity obtainable *by lengthening the criterion* is .90 (.54 multiplied by the reciprocal of the square root of .36). Therefore the test constructor would suggest that research resources should then be applied to improving the criterion. Thus the correction for attenuation should not be reported with the implication that the higher coefficient has already been attained. Rather, it should be used to indicate the most profitable direction for future validation research.

The foregoing remarks apply when we are concerned with *practical* validity. However, the situation is somewhat different when we are concerned with *construct* validity. Suppose that we are exploring a general area (e.g., measures of extroversion) and wish to determine whether two different measures are "conceptually equivalent" (Block, 1963). For this problem, use of the correction for attenuation is quite appropriate, and it may lead to a considerable saving of time and money in test development. However, if we reach the point of using a particular test of a given length to predict a particular practical criterion, the uncorrected validity coefficient is more meaningful to tell us how successful our predictions actually are at that period of time.

Correlation coefficients vary not only with the length of the measures being correlated but also with the heterogeneity of the population with respect to these measures. Thus if a test is standardized on a relatively homogeneous group (e.g., college students), we may expect an increase in *both* reliability and validity when it is applied to a more heterogeneous group (e.g., soldiers). In Figure 7.2 the points representing pairs of scores for college students would tend to cluster in the shaded area, but the points for soldiers would scatter more widely within the elliptical figure.

The formulas given below depend on certain assumptions; and, of course, if these assumptions are seriously violated in practice,

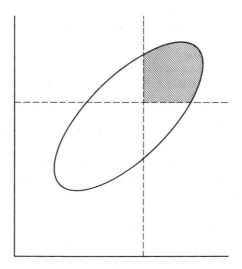

Figure 7.2 Correlation as a function of group heterogeneity.

the formulas will give misleading predictions. However, there is empirical evidence from Air Force studies (Guilford, 1956, p. 322) that the correlations *do* behave about as the formulas predict, so the assumptions made in deriving them seem to be rather realistic.

If the standard error of *measurement* is assumed to remain constant over the score range, it can be shown (Gulliksen, 1950, pp. 110–111) that the reliability of a test in group X is given by

$$r_{XX} = 1 - \left[\frac{\sigma_x^2}{\sigma_X^2}(1 - r_{xx}) \right] \tag{7.39}$$

σ_X^2 is the test variance in group X, and σ_x^2 and r_{xx} are the test variance and reliability, respectively, in group x. The lower-case letter represents the group for whom the reliability coefficient is known, independently of whether this group has the greater or lesser score variability. It can be seen that, if σ_X^2 exceeds σ_x^2, then r_{XX} exceeds r_{xx}, which confirms what was said above about greater reliability resulting from greater variability of scores (i.e., more heterogeneity).

As an example, let us now estimate the reliability of a test in a new group, when the following information is available:

r_{xx}, the reliability of the test in the original group, is .70;
σ_x^2, the variance of the test in the original group, is 10; and
σ_X^2, the variance of the test in the new group, is 25.

In this example, since σ_X^2 exceeds σ_x^2, the new group is more heterogeneous than the original group; hence we expect an increase in the reliability. Substituting in Equation 7.39, we have

$$r_{XX} = 1 - \tfrac{10}{25}(1 - .7) = 1 - .4(.3) = 1 - .12 = .88$$

Thus we anticipate an increase of reliability from .70 to .88 in the more heterogeneous group.

Parenthetically it should be mentioned that any measurement involves an interaction of several factors, such as the trait structure of the individual, the nature of the measuring device (e.g., the difficulty of the test), and the conditions of testing (e.g., absence of noise, fatigue). The variability of scores for a group of persons can be affected by a change in any of these; hence it is unrealistic to think of "*the* reliability" as being an absolute characteristic of a measuring device, even when differences due to the variability of the population have been taken into consideration.

Similar reasoning can be applied to validity coefficients. If the standard error of *estimate* is assumed to remain constant over the score range, it can be shown (Gulliksen, 1950, pp. 131–138) that the correlation between a test and a criterion in group XY can be estimated by one of two formulas:

$$r_{XY} = \frac{\sigma_X r_{xy}}{\sqrt{\sigma_x^2(1 - r_{xy}^2) + \sigma_X^2 r_{xy}^2}} \tag{7.40}$$

$$r_{XY} = \sqrt{1 - \left[\frac{\sigma_y^2}{\sigma_Y^2}(1 - r_{xy}^2)\right]} \tag{7.41}$$

σ_Y^2 is the criterion variance in group XY, and σ_y^2 and r_{xy} are the criterion variance and the validity, respectively, in group xy. Again the lower-case letters indicate the group for which the correlation is known. To use either formula, one must know r_{xy}. However, Equation 7.40 further involves the variabilities of the two groups with respect to the *test* (or other predictor variable), whereas Equation 7.41 involves the variabilities of the two groups with respect to the *criterion* variable. Therefore the choice of formula depends on which information is available.

As an example of the first situation, suppose that we use the figures given above for the variabilities of the two groups (i.e., $\sigma_x^2 = 10$ and $\sigma_X^2 = 25$) and suppose further that the validity in the original group is .40. Substituting these values in Equation 7.40, we have

$$r_{XY} = \frac{5(.40)}{\sqrt{10[1 - (.40)^2] + 25(.40)^2}} = \frac{2}{\sqrt{10(.84) + 25(.16)}}$$

$$= \frac{2}{\sqrt{8.4 + 4}} = \frac{2}{\sqrt{12.4}} = \frac{2}{3.52} = .57$$

Just as we estimated a higher reliability for the test in the more heterogeneous group, we estimate that the validity will also increase, that is, from .40 to .57.

To illustrate the second situation, suppose that a validity of .63 has been found for an aptitude test for predicting college grade-point average and that we wish to use the same test with graduate students. Since graduate students represent a more select group than college students, we know that their grades will show less variability (assuming that the same grading scale is used to mark both groups). Suppose that the standard deviation of grades for college students is .6 and for graduate students is .5. How much validity can we expect the test to show in the graduate school group? Substituting in Equation 7.41, we have

$$r_{XY} = \sqrt{1 - \left\{ \frac{(.6)^2}{(.5)^2}[1 - (.63)^2] \right\}} = \sqrt{1 - \frac{.36}{.25}(1 - .3969)}$$

$$r_{XY} = \sqrt{1 - 1.44(.6031)} = \sqrt{1 - .8685} = \sqrt{.1315} = .36$$

Thus we estimate that the validity of the test will fall from .63 to .36. Whether we still may decide to use the test depends on other factors, some of which are discussed below.

Michael, Jones, Gaddis, and Kaiser (1962) have presented "abacs" with which one may estimate graphically the quantities involved in Equations 7.40 and 7.41.

A more general problem is the estimation of how the correlation between two variables will change when the variability of the subjects with respect to one or more *other* variables is altered. Thurstone (1947, pp. 443–450) formulated this problem in terms of matrix algebra and vector geometry. Suppose that the variability of a particular variable is completely curtailed, that is, the variable is held constant. The estimated correlation between the two original variables is called the "partial correlation." The general formula is

$$r_{12.3} = \frac{r_{12} - r_{13}r_{23}}{\sqrt{1 - r_{13}{}^2}\sqrt{1 - r_{23}{}^2}} \qquad (7.42)$$

The subscript 3 indicates the variable being held constant. The partial correlation can also be thought of as a kind of average of the rs in groups of individuals classified on the basis of X_3 (Snedecor, 1946, p. 357). Other formulas are available for "higher-order partial correlation," which involves holding more than one variable constant. However, partial correlation is of relatively little practical interest, because practitioners will not often deal with groups of persons completely homogeneous with respect to a particular continuous variable. Some exceptional situations are discussed and illustrated with computational examples in other books, for example, Guilford (1956, pp. 316–318). If there is theoretical interest in the general structural relationships between a number of variables, a better procedure is to apply the techniques of factor analysis, which are discussed in the remaining chapters of this book.

In this chapter we have discussed some of the consequences of using semireliable measuring devices. However, only a bare beginning has been feasible, and it is recommended that the student read Gulliksen's (1950) excellent treatise, which has been referred to so frequently in the preceding pages.

APPLICATION IN PERSONNEL SELECTION

In the remainder of the chapter we shall discuss briefly the interpretation of validity coefficients in personnel selection work, with which many psychologists and educators are concerned. First, we shall distinguish "selection" from the closely related procedures of "guidance" and "classification":

>Selection involves many persons and one position.
>Guidance involves one person and many positions.
>Classification involves many persons and many positions.

The term "position" should be interpreted broadly to include job openings, vacancies in the freshman class of a medical school, etc. The statistical theory for classification has only been sketched out on broad lines (H. E. Brogden, 1959; Horst, 1960). In addition, the theory for guidance has not been developed very extensively, although the development of the multiple-group discriminant function, which was mentioned at the end of Chapter 5, promises to effect a "breakthrough" (Hall, 1957; Maxwell, 1961).

In selection procedures, the question often arises whether a new selective device should be added to the existing battery of devices. The first thing to find out is whether the multiple correlation coefficient is increased significantly (see page 201). As we saw above, this in turn depends on the validity of the new device *and* its intercorrelation with the devices already in use. Let us suppose that the increase does exceed the minimum required for statistical significance. It still may not be practical to employ the device because factors other than validity affect the decision.

The utility of a selective device depends also on the "selection ratio" (i.e., the proportion of all applicants examined who are selected) and the "success ratio" (i.e., the proportion of all applicants examined who would have been successful at the criterion performance if selected). The scope of this book does not allow us to examine in detail the relationships, which are rather complex (Guilford, 1956, pp. 380–384). However, much information can be summarized in the statement that a low selection ratio and/or a low success ratio tend to compensate for a low validity coefficient. Some meaning can be attached to this statement by considering a couple of extreme possibilities. If a "tight labor market" exists and *all* job applicants are hired, it would obviously be a waste of time to give any tests or other selective devices. Here the selection ratio is 1.00, and even a test of very high validity is useless. At the other extreme, consider a scholarship competition in which one winner is to be selected from a hundred applicants. Here a test of low validity may still be quite useful, in the sense of increasing the success ratio considerably over what it would have been had the test not been used. The personnel worker rarely can manipulate the selection ratio or the success ratio himself, but he should use this information to help decide whether a new device is worth adding to his selection battery.

Cost factors also enter into the decision. If the cost of testing is low (e.g., the test is a short paper-and-pencil device that can be administered and scored routinely by a clerk), even a test of low validity may be worth while. On the other hand, if the cost of testing is high (e.g., a projective device that requires the services of a $50/hour psychoanalyst), the increase in multiple correlation should be considerable to warrant use of the test. Balanced against the cost of testing is the cost of training. The cost of training a bomber pilot is quite high, and a great saving can be effected even if only a few of the applicants who would have "washed out" of the program are selected out. Thus a test of low validity may pay high dividends. On the other hand, for a very routine job involving a short period of training, administration of selection tests may be a waste of time, because a replacement for an unsatisfactory worker is so easy to obtain and train.

In summary, a test of low validity may still be a useful addition to a selection battery if it intercorrelates low with existing predictors, if the selection ratio and success ratio are low, if the cost of testing is low, and if the cost of training is high. A test of high validity may still *not* be useful if it intercorrelates high with existing predictors, if the selection ratio and success ratio are high, if the cost of testing is high, and if the cost of training is low. Cronbach and Gleser (1957) have attempted to use decision theory to integrate many of the above factors; however, it is too early to evaluate the fruitfulness of this approach.

Some authorities, for example, Cronbach (1960, pp. 342–344), believe that a "multiple-cutoff" procedure is often preferable to the weighted composite of scores used in, for example, multiple correlation as discussed in Chapters 4 and 5. They argue that the composite procedure depends on the "compensation hypothesis," namely, that a person may compensate for a low score on one variable by obtaining a high score on another variable of the composite. In some cases, this assumption may be quite unrealistic. Symphonic conductors should have good pitch discrimination and should also be intelligent. However, if an applicant's pitch discrimination is poor, he will not succeed as a symphonic conductor, no matter how high his IQ. In the multiple-cutoff procedure, critical scores are set for each variable, and the variables successively screen the applicants. To be accepted, an applicant must exceed all of the critical scores.

However, the multiple-cutoff procedure has several disadvantages of its own. Lord (1962) showed that the composite procedure is considerably more efficient than the multiple-cutoff procedure in selection unless the predictor variables are unusually reliable. In practice, the best solution is probably to set low cutting scores on the variables and then to apply a weighted-composite formula to the scores of all applicants who survive the initial screening.

Problems

1. Describe a set of circumstances in educational testing for which the assumption involved in Equation 7.4 would *not* be tenable.

2. A spelling test has a standard deviation of 7.34 and a reliability of .87. Calculate its standard error of measurement.

3. A pupil earns a score of 26 on the spelling test mentioned in Problem 2. Make a probability statement about his true score, using the 5% level of confidence.

4. An industrial psychologist wishes to be able to use a 5% confidence interval of 15 units' width. If the standard deviation of his measuring device is 13.8, how reliable must it be?

5. A history teacher has available a standardized test of 120 questions, with a reliability of .84. He is pressed for testing time and would like to administer only every third question of the test. What would one predict the reliability of this procedure to be?

6. A psychologist has developed a questionnaire measure of dominance consisting of 20 items, which has a reliability of .77. How many items of similar content would he have to *add* to the test to obtain a reliability of .90?

7. A scholastic aptitude test of reliability .79 correlates .57 with an achievement test, which has a reliability of .86. Compute the correlation of the two tests corrected for attenuation.

8. Becker (1961) reports the correlation between the C and O factors of the 16 Personality Factor Questionnaire to be −.61 and their reliabilities to be .56 and .74, respectively. Comment on this situation from the point of view of conceptual equivalence.

9. An educational counselor has found that, in the high school where he has been employed, a particular aptitude test with a standard deviation of 8 has a reliability of .84 and a validity of .52 for predicting college freshman grades. He accepts a position at a select preparatory school and finds that the standard deviation of the test at this school is only 5. How much reliability and validity should he expect the test to have at the prep school?

10. During a period of increased demand, a company accepts job applicants of lower ability, and the standard deviation of supervisors' ratings of their proficiency increases by 25%. A trade test had previously correlated .27 with the criterion of supervisors' ratings. How much validity could be expected in the new situation?

11. Describe some conditions under which a personnel manager should not hire all applicants, even when they are fewer than the number of job openings.

12. For each of these situations, discuss the factors that enter into the decision of whether to do further testing: (a) a college student is being considered for referral to a part-time consulting psychiatrist; (b) a large corporation is selecting a manager for a new plant that will employ 2000 workers; (c) nursing students are being considered for vacancies in a hospital; (d) a parole is being considered for a well-known prisoner in a state penitentiary; (e) graduates of a teachers' college are being selected for vacancies in the school system of a large city.

13. For each of the following jobs, list levels of particular traits that would be quite necessary for an applicant to possess before he could be further evaluated: (a) lawyer, (b) truck driver, (c) receptionist, (d) airplane pilot, (e) bank teller.

8

FACTOR ANALYSIS
IN BEHAVIORAL SCIENCE

The final topic that we shall consider in this book is factor analysis. In a very general sense, factor analysis is a set of methods for analyzing a table of intercorrelations. Usually it is concluded on the basis of such an analysis that the intercorrelations can be "explained" by one or more theoretical constructs which Thurstone (1947) called "functional unities." Whether these functional unities should be conceived of as "intervening variables" or "hypothetical constructs" in the MacCorquodale-Meehl (1948) sense has been the subject of considerable controversy.[1] This controversy is related to another on whether the functional unities found by behavioral scientists are determined by heredity or environment. Yet the technical aspects and many of the practical applications of factor analysis do not depend on final resolution of either of these controversies. Nevertheless, some of the broader and more philosophical questions in behavioral science are involved here, so in this chapter we shall spend some time discussing the rationale for applying factor analytic techniques in the attack on problems of behavioral science.

[1] See Henrysson (1957, Chapter 4) for a useful summary of this controversy as related to factor analysis.

CRITERIA FOR THEORIES IN SCIENCE

At the outset we shall address ourselves to the very general problem of what are the basic criteria for application of theoretical frameworks to explain the data of empirical science. The author's reflections have convinced him that there are five basic criteria: (1) internal consistency, (2) verifiability, (3) comprehensiveness, (4) closeness of fit to the data, and (5) parsimony.

Internal consistency is probably the most general of these criteria because it is applicable to any theoretical framework applied to any data. This requirement simply states that the relationships between the theoretical constructs must involve no *logical* contradictions. Here we are *not* referring to instances in which the data refute one of the hypotheses of the framework. The requirement applies before any observations at all have been made. An example of such a logical contradiction is involved in the following sequence of propositions: $A > B$, $B > C$, and $C > A$. This framework is inconsistent, regardless of what A, B, and C represent empirically. In view of the importance of this criterion, it would seem mandatory for any theoretician to check his theory for internal consistency *before* applying it to any data.

Verifiability is a criterion that has been brought to the attention of the scientific audience by the logical positivists (Carnap, 1936). This criterion applies to the translation between theoretical constructs and empirical data. The key phrase here is "operational definition." It has been pointed out that behavioral scientists can hardly hope to establish valid scientific laws if they do not even agree on the definition of the basic terms being used. Unfortunately behavioral science has inherited from the common parlance many terms with rather vague meanings, for example, habit, instinct, purpose, role, and status. This has meant that, in many cases a particular researcher has had to specify rather precisely in which sense he is using a particular term in his investigation. For instance, if an experimenter compares a "high anxiety" and a "low anxiety" group with respect to some performance, he should specify whether "anxiety" here refers to score on the Taylor test of Manifest Anxiety (Taylor, 1953), to whether the subject has or has not been electrically shocked, or to some other "operation." Over a period of time a gradual community of agreement seems to arise on how a given term shall be defined. Sometimes new words are coined so as to avoid the excess literary connotations adhering to existing terms. For example, to describe the characteristics of a group as a whole, Cattell(1957, p. 415) uses the word "syntality", that is, syntality: group = personality: person.

However, the argument for use of operational definitions can be overstated. In the exploratory stages of any science, there are times when progress would be hindered if scientists demanded too precise specification of their terms. Underwood (1957, p. 54) suggested that "literary definitions" may usefully precede operational definitions. Even Watson (1930, p. 15) pointed out that his use of "response" should not be limited to "the recording of minute muscular responses" but should involve a wide range of human adjustive behavior. Nevertheless, behavioral science will probably proceed more efficiently and fruitfully if its cohorts work *toward* operational definitions of the phenomena that they observe.

Beyond the requirements of internal consistency and verifiability, there is still a wide range of choice of competing theoretical explanations that can account for given empirical data. The remaining criteria of comprehensiveness, closeness of fit to the data, and parsimony should be considered in close conjunction because, as we shall see, it is a rare situation when they can simultaneously be satisfied, at least satisfied completely. *Comprehensiveness* refers to the range of phenomena that the theoretical framework attempts to encompass. A theory that covers a wide range of phenomena is ordinarily more intellectually satisfying than a theory that is restricted to a small domain of observations, other things being equal. An important reason why Newton's laws of motion held such great excitement for his contemporaries was because they encompassed types of phenomena that previously had demanded separate explanations. However, about 200 years later, Einstein found that a range of phenomena that Newton could not have observed because of instrumental limitations demanded an elaboration of Newton's laws. Thus scientists tend to seek increasingly general theories to explain their observations.

Closeness of fit to the data is a rather obvious criterion; however, it is only in recent years that efficient statistical techniques for measuring closeness of fit have been devised. Generally speaking, the more comprehensive a theory is, the less likely it is to give a close fit to the data.

The final criterion we shall discuss is *parsimony*, which gives us another reason why Newton's theory was so exciting. He succeeded in accomplishing with three laws what had previously demanded a variety of special assumptions, for example, the theory of "epicycles" (Frank, 1949, Chapter 13). Other things being equal, a simpler theory holds more appeal for scientists and laymen alike than a complex theory. Thurstone (1947, p. 52) expressed the idea thus.

The convincingness of a hypothesis can be gauged inversely by the ratio of its number of degrees of freedom to that of the phenomena which it has demonstrably covered. It is in the nature of science that no scientific law can ever be proved to be right. It can only be shown to be plausible. The laws of science are not immutable. They are only human efforts toward parsimony in the comprehension of nature.

Parsimony is often accomplished at the expense of comprehensiveness and/or closeness of fit to the data, however. A theoretician can easily be parsimonious if he attempts to explain only a narrow range of observations. Furthermore, if he is willing to tolerate large errors of fit of the data to the theoretical concepts, it is not difficult for him to be parsimonious. Thus we see that any scientific theory involves some compromise between the conflicting criteria of comprehensiveness, closeness of fit to the data, and parsimony.

As an example, let us consider the field of human motivation. We shall hold constant the variable of comprehensiveness. One of the reasons why McDougall's (1908) theory of instincts fell into disrepute was that the list of instincts tended to grow so long they began to appear to be merely *ad hoc* hypotheses. At the other extreme, Freud (1905) tended to regard most human behavior as being motivated by a single motive, sex. Even he, however, defined "libido" more broadly than in the traditional conception of the sexual motive, and later Freud (1920) found it necessary to add aggressive motives, that is, "life instinct" versus "death instinct." In any case, many scientists have felt that Freud's (1930) attempted explanation of not only neurotic behavior but also religion, beauty, social organization, communism, anti-Semitism, etc. leaves much to be desired with respect to closeness of fit to the data. Yet these same scientists would probably not want to return to McDougall's extensive list of instincts. On the other hand, they might agree with Freud's use of libido to explain neurotic behavior without accepting extension of his theory to further realms. In this case, parsimony would be saved at the expense of comprehensiveness.

Thus we conclude that the decision about whether to accept a new scientific theory depends on a consideration of the interaction of comprehensiveness, closeness of fit to the data, and parsimony.

FACTORS AND PHILOSOPHY OF SCIENCE

Now what does the foregoing discussion of issues in philosophy of science have to do with factor analysis? The issues of comprehensiveness, goodness of fit, and parsimony are relevant to the practical problem of how many factors to extract from a given correlation matrix. Spearman (1904) preferred one "general factor" plus a "specific factor" for each variable, but Thurstone (1947) and others speak of "group factors," which are involved in *several but not all* of the variables. Which point of view is "correct"? By now it is generally agreed that there is no over-all answer to this question; the answer depends on the practical use that is to be made of the analysis. Many contemporary psychometrists agree with Burt's (1941, pp. 164–168) hierarchical conception, which involves all three—general, group, and specific factors. However, as Nunnally (1959, pp. 173–174) points out, the factor analyst's problem here is similar to that of a cartographer who must decide how finely differences in elevation will be shown in the contour lines of his map, that is, the solution must ultimately be justified on pragmatic grounds. After we have developed some theoretical equations in later chapters, we shall return to this question of parsimony with respect to the number of factors extracted.

In regard to techniques for advancing behavioral science, factor analysis has sometimes been compared with analysis of variance. At this point, it is useful to consider Tucker's (1955, p. 210) distinction between "exploratory factor analyses" and "confirmatory factor analyses." If analysis of variance is compared with confirmatory factor analyses in regard to efficiency of *testing* hypotheses, the advantage seems presently to lie with analysis of variance. This is particularly true for "experiments" (as defined in Chapter 1), although it is possible to use factor analytic methods when some of the variables are physically manipulated (Cattell, 1957, Chapter 15).

However, it is as a method of *discovery* that factor analysis plays a unique role. The old canard that one gets out of a factor analysis only what one puts into it is valid *only* in the sense that it is also valid for *any* scientific investigation. On the other hand, a factor analysis that refutes the researcher's tentative *a priori* hypotheses may also suggest *new* hypotheses to be investigated in further studies.[2] A good example of this use of factor analysis is the series of studies of the structure of intellect by Guilford and his students (Wilson, Guilford, Christensen, and Lewis, 1954). Although factor analytic procedures do often throw new light on scientific areas about which little is already known, it should be emphasized that the researcher has no advance guarantee that this will happen. Thus the investigator who merely throws a heterogeneous lot of variables into "the factor analytic pot" with no guiding principles at all is likely to be disappointed in his quest. We shall have more to say about the topic of choice of variables for a factor analysis in Chapter 13.

A final philosophical point to be considered is the alleged reification of factors. It has been said that factor analysis is a return to the discredited "faculty psychology." The critical difference here is that the factors are discovered and justified by the same empirical and mathematical techniques used in other areas of modern behavioral science rather than by "armchair speculation." The "verbal comprehension factor" and the "perceptual speed factor" have the same logical status as "ego," "habit strength," "cognitive map," "population of stimulus elements," "role," and "cognitive dissonance." All these constructs represent man-made attempts to bring order into the natural phenomena observed by behavioral scientists. Their justification is ultimately pragmatic; do they or do they not aid in the development of scientific laws? Factors that represent effects of training and experience may be just as useful as factors representing genetic, endocrinological, or central nervous system effects.

Having completed this short inquiry into some of the philosophical problems suggested by factor analysis, we next turn to a development of the basic equations.

---

[2] Strictly speaking, it is also true of studies with analysis of variance that "unsuccessful experiments" sometimes suggest new leads. However, factor analysis does this more efficiently.

Problems

1. "Intelligence is whatever is measured by intelligence tests." To what extent is this a useful definition in behavioral science research?

2. Ellis (1956) attempted to reformulate the basic Freudian hypotheses in more operational terms. Has he preserved the "essence" of the original ideas?

3. Comment on current theories of learning (e.g., Hilgard, 1956) from the point of view of comprehensiveness, closeness of fit to the data, and parsimony. Do the same for current theories of personality (e.g., Hall and Lindzey, 1957).

4. Is it more parsimonious to attempt to explain behavior in biochemical terms than in psychological or sociological terms?

5. "No two clients who appear for counseling are ever exactly alike." Is this statement of any aid in the formulation of laws of behavioral science?

6. Give an example of an aptitude factor that might appear as a group factor in one investigation but as a general factor in another investigation.

7. How does the use of the term "factor" in "factorial experiment" (Edwards, 1960, Chapter 12) differ from its use in "factor analysis"?

8. Before the invention of factor analysis, were there any systematic "methods of discovery" used by scientists to discover new laws?

9

FUNDAMENTAL THEOREMS
OF FACTOR ANALYSIS

In Chapter 7 it was shown that a number of interesting developments pertaining to the use of tests are possible when it is assumed that an observed test score can be divided into two additive components, a true score and an error score. In factor analysis it is assumed that the true score can be further subdivided into additive components due to various *common* factors and a factor *specific* to each test. In addition, it is assumed that the common factors, the specific factors, and the error factors are independent and therefore uncorrelated with each other.

Perhaps these abstract statements will gain more meaning if a particular example is described. Consider a test of Mechanical Principles. In such a test the examinee may be shown diagrams with pulleys, gears, wheels, etc.; and he is asked in which direction and how fast a given part is moving. It seems likely that success in such a task would be determined to a great extent by an ability to visualize the movement of objects in two- or three-dimensional space. Let us call such an ability "spatial ability." However, since the directions in each problem of such a test are presented in words and offer some difficulty in themselves, it is further likely that "verbal ability" is a partial determiner of success in Mechanical Principles. In addition, there are probably certain elements of difficulty in this particular test that would differ from those in other tests similarly requiring spatial and verbal ability. Thus we additionally postulate a "specific factor." If we continue to accept the basic assumption in Chapter 7, we must add an "error of measurement." The relationships can be expressed by a linear equation:

$$z_j = a_j z_a + b_j z_b + s_j z_{sj} + e_j z_{ej} \tag{9.1}$$

Note that the scores are represented in standard form; hence the recurrence of the symbol z. The score on test j (in our example, the Mechanical Principles test) has been transformed to standard form by subtracting the mean and dividing by the standard deviation; therefore the expression z_j is used. The scores of a given examinee on the various factors have similarly been transformed to standard form, for instance, z_a is the standard score on factor A. However, we cannot immediately calculate the numerical value of z_a for a given subject because the factors at this point are still hypothetical.

The symbols a_j, b_j, s_j, and e_j are called "factor loadings."[1] They indicate the extent to which each factor participates in the test. Let factor A be the spatial factor and factor B the verbal factor. If a_j exceeds b_j, the spatial factor is more important in determining success on the Mechanical Principles test than the verbal factor. However, an examinee whose spatial ability is rather poor might still do well on the test because of good verbal ability, that is, a very high z_b score would compensate for the low z_a score. An analogous interpretation can be made for the factor loadings of the specific and error factors. In this respect factor loadings resemble the β coefficients of multiple correlation (see Chapter 5).

Let us now analyze another test standard score, z_k, into *its* components and assume that the spatial and verbal factors are also involved in this second test. (The adjective "common" indicates that the factor must be involved in at least two tests.) The standard score on test k can be broken down as follows:

$$z_k = a_k z_a + b_k z_b + s_k z_{sk} + e_k z_{ek} \tag{9.2}$$

Note particularly the way in which this equation differs from Equation 9.1. The subscripts of the factor loadings have changed from j to k. Similarly, the standard score subscripts for the test itself and for the *specific* and *error* factors have changed correspondingly.

---

[1] In an "oblique simple structure" (see page 145), technically speaking, they are "reference vector correlations"; see Harman (1960, Chapter 13).

However, z_a and z_b remain the same because the same two *common* factors are involved in test k as in test j.

Now we are about to derive the fundamental theorem of factor analysis.[2] We wish to express the correlation between two tests, j and k, in terms of factor analytic constructs. We begin with one of the defining equations of the product-moment correlation coefficient,

$$r_{jk} \equiv \frac{\sum z_j z_k}{N} \qquad (9.3)$$

Verbally this equation indicates that the correlation coefficient equals the mean "inner product" of standard scores. However, in the preceding material we have analyzed z_j and z_k into polynomial expressions. Therefore we first multiply Equation 9.1 by Equation 9.2, thus obtaining the 16-term polynomial,

$$
\begin{aligned}
z_j z_k = \; & a_j a_k z_a{}^2 && + a_j b_k z_a z_b && + a_j s_k z_a z_{sk} && + a_j e_k z_a z_{ek} \\
+ \; & b_j a_k z_b z_a && + b_j b_k z_b{}^2 && + b_j s_k z_b z_{sk} && + b_j e_k z_b z_{ek} \\
+ \; & s_j a_k z_{sj} z_a && + s_j b_k z_{sj} z_b && + s_j s_k z_{sj} z_{sk} && + s_j e_k z_{sj} z_{ek} \\
+ \; & e_j a_k z_{ej} z_a && + e_j b_k z_{ej} z_b && + e_j s_k z_{ej} z_{sk} && + e_j e_k z_{ej} z_{ek} \qquad (9.4)
\end{aligned}
$$

At first Equation 9.4 strikes one as being quite formidable, but the reader should take heart because it can be greatly simplified. According to Equation 9.3, we must next sum the entire expression on the right side of Equation 9.4 and then divide it by N. However, we may distribute the summation sign (according to the First Summation Law; see Chapter 2) and the N to each of the 16 terms. Taking for a moment only the first of the 16 terms, we can then bring the factor loadings, which are constant over persons, outside of the summation according to the Second Summation Law:

$$\frac{\sum a_j a_k z_a{}^2}{N} = a_j a_k \frac{\sum z_a{}^2}{N} \qquad (9.5)$$

Thus the first four terms corresponding to the terms of the right member of Equation 9.4 can be written:

$$a_j a_k \frac{\sum z_a{}^2}{N} + a_j b_k \frac{\sum z_a z_b}{N} + a_j s_k \frac{\sum z_a z_{sk}}{N} + a_j e_k \frac{\sum z_a z_{ek}}{N}$$

[2] The factor analytic model with which we shall be dealing is that formulated by Thurstone (1947). However, the fundamental equations of several other factor analytic models are similar in form.

Now note that the factor $\sum z_a^2/N$ in the first term is the mean of squared standard scores. In Chapter 4, pages 40-41, it was shown that the mean of squared standard scores always equals unity. Thus the first term can be simplified to $a_j a_k$. Similarly, the term corresponding to the *sixth* term of the right member of Equation 9.4 is simplified to $b_j b_k$. If the reader will now compare the factor behind the summation sign of the other terms with Equation 9.3, he will see that *all* the other 14 terms involve a correlation! For example,

$$a_j b_k \frac{\sum z_a z_b}{N} = a_j b_k r_{ab} \tag{9.6}$$

Now we shall again collect all 16 terms into one equation, which gives

$$
\begin{aligned}
r_{jk} = a_j a_k \quad &+ a_j b_k r_{ab} \; + a_j s_k r_{a,sk} \; + a_j e_k r_{a,ek} \\
+ b_j a_k r_{ba} \; &+ b_j b_k \quad\;\; + b_j s_k r_{b,sk} \; + b_j e_k r_{b,ek} \\
+ s_j a_k r_{sj,a} \; &+ s_j b_k r_{sj,b} \; + s_j s_k r_{sj,sk} \; + s_j e_k r_{sj,ek} \\
+ e_j a_k r_{ej,a} \; &+ e_j b_k r_{ej,b} \; + e_j s_k r_{ej,sk} \; + e_j e_k r_{ej,ek} \tag{9.7}
\end{aligned}
$$

The symbolization in some of the above terms may be at first confusing. The symbol $r_{sj,ek}$, for example, is intended to indicate the correlation between the factor specific to test j and the error factor of test k.

However, at the outset it was assumed that the common, specific, and error factors are mutually uncorrelated. This means that all the correlations in Equation 9.7 equal zero and therefore that 14 of the 16 terms of the right member vanish, leaving

$$r_{jk} = a_j a_k + b_j b_k \tag{9.8}$$

This, the most basic theorem of factor analysis, states that the correlation between any two tests equals the inner product of their *common* factor loadings. It generalizes to any number of common factors. For example, if we had four common factors, we could write

$$r_{jk} = a_j a_k + b_j b_k + c_j c_k + d_j d_k \tag{9.9}$$

Note especially that the specific and error factors do *not* contribute to the *correlation* between two tests. However, we shall soon see that they *do* contribute to the test *variance*.

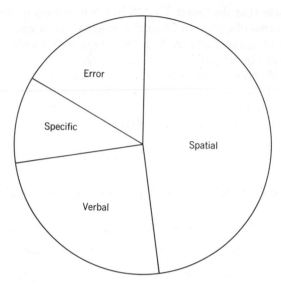

Figure 9.1   Partition of the variance of the Mechanical Principles test.

Another important relationship can be shown in a manner analogous to the development above. We square Equation 9.1, sum both sides, divide by N, simplify as above, and then obtain (the details are left to the student as an exercise):

$$\frac{\sum z_j^2}{N} = a_j^2 + b_j^2 + s_j^2 + e_j^2 \tag{9.10}$$

Since the left member is a mean of squared standard scores, we can also write

$$1 = a_j^2 + b_j^2 + s_j^2 + e_j^2 \tag{9.11}$$

Now Equation 11 is multiplied by σ_j^2, the variance of test j, giving

$$\sigma_j^2 = a_j^2\sigma_j^2 + b_j^2\sigma_j^2 + s_j^2\sigma_j^2 + e_j^2\sigma_j^2 \tag{9.12}$$

Let us now write some numerical values into Equation 9.1:

$$z_j = .70z_a + .50z_b + .32z_{sj} + .40z_{ej} \tag{9.13}$$

Inserting the values of the factor loadings into Equation 9.12, we have

$$\sigma_j{}^2 = .49\sigma_j{}^2 + .25\sigma_j{}^2 + .10\sigma_j{}^2 + .16\sigma_j{}^2 \qquad (9.14)$$

Thus the total variance of a test can be broken down into additive components, and the *square* of each factor loading indicates the *proportion* of variance due to that particular factor. A visual representation is given by the "pie diagram" of Figure 9.1. In this sense, we can say that success in the Mechanical Principles test is "49% determined by the spatial factor," and so forth for the other factors. However, it should be kept in mind that the factor loadings are not available until the factor analysis is complete; what one has at first are merely the intercorrelations of the tests.

It has been found convenient to use special terms to represent various composite portions of the total test variance (see Equation 9.11 above):

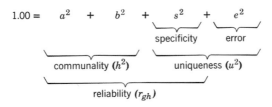

The reader should now calculate the communality, uniqueness, and reliability of the Mechanical Principles test from the data given above. (The answers are given in the Appendix on page 197.)

Problems

1. Which abilities other than the two listed in this chapter might be involved in a mechanical principles test?

2. Express z_j of Equation 9.1 as some nonlinear function of the same four factors.

3. Suppose that we choose *not* to accept the compensation hypothesis (see page 89). Can we still use Equation 9.1 as a basic assumption?

4. Modify Equation 9.1 so that it will serve as a basic assumption for Spearman's system of factor analysis (see page 95). Then what will be the appropriate equation analogous to Equation 9.8?

5. Explain verbally (without using numbers or symbols) why the specific and error factors do not contribute to the intercorrelations of the tests.

6. "Success in the Mechanical Principles test is 49% determined by the spatial factor." Should we interpret this determination in cause-effect terms?

7. Fill in the blank entries of the following table:

Test number	r_{gh}	h^2	s^2	u^2	e^2
1	.85	.70			
2	.90			.65	
3		.75	.20		
4		.85			.15
5			.40		.25
6				.40	.20

10

FURTHER MATHEMATICAL TECHNIQUES
USEFUL IN FACTOR ANALYSIS

To express the relationships of factor analysis in more concise and vivid terms, two branches of advanced mathematics have been employed, matrix algebra and vector geometry. In this chapter we shall present only a bare outline of these topics; the interested reader can learn more about them in other textbooks, for example, Thurstone (1947, pp. 1–50), Horst (1963). Matrix algebra enables one to perform many of the operations of ordinary algebra on several variables considered simultaneously. At first the new symbols may seem strange to the reader, but with some practice he will presently find himself handling the equations with almost as much facility as those of ordinary algebra.

SOME MATRIX ALGEBRA

A "matrix" is a rectangular arrangement of numbers, each of which is called an "element" of the matrix. The matrix is identified by a capital letter and its elements are represented by the corresponding lower-case letter, as is illustrated by matrix A, which appears at the top of page 106.

The subscripts j and k denote the row and column, respectively, that fix the position of the element, for example, a_{32} is the element in the third row and second column of matrix A. The "order" of a matrix is its number of rows *and* its number of columns, that is,

$m \times n$. For example, a 4×7 matrix has four rows and seven columns. A matrix with only one row is sometimes called a "row vector," and a matrix with only one column is called a "column vector."

$$\mathbf{A} = \begin{Vmatrix} a_{11} & a_{12} & a_{13} \cdots\cdots a_{1n} \\ a_{21} & a_{22} & a_{23} \cdots\cdots a_{2n} \\ a_{31} & a_{32} & a_{33} \cdots\cdots a_{3n} \\ \cdots\cdots\cdots\cdots a_{jk} \cdots\cdots \\ \cdots\cdots\cdots\cdots\cdots\cdots \\ a_{m1} & a_{m2} & a_{m3} \cdots\cdots a_{mn} \end{Vmatrix}$$

The processes of adding and subtracting matrices are quite similar to those of ordinary addition and subtraction. However, they can be performed only if the matrices are of the same order. The rule is simply to add (or subtract) the corresponding elements. Consider the following matrix addition:

$$\begin{array}{ccccc} \mathbf{A} & + & \mathbf{B} & = & \mathbf{C} \\ \begin{Vmatrix} 3 & 4 \\ 5 & 0 \\ 2 & 1 \end{Vmatrix} & + & \begin{Vmatrix} 1 & -1 \\ 2 & 2 \\ -3 & 0 \end{Vmatrix} & = & \begin{Vmatrix} (3+1) & (4-1) \\ (5+2) & (0+2) \\ (2-3) & (1+0) \end{Vmatrix} \end{array}$$

$$= \begin{Vmatrix} 4 & 3 \\ 7 & 2 \\ -1 & 1 \end{Vmatrix}$$

As an exercise the reader should perform the matrix subtraction, $\mathbf{A} - \mathbf{B} = \mathbf{D}$. (The answer is given in the Appendix p. 197). Matrix addition is "commutative", that is, $\mathbf{A} + \mathbf{B} = \mathbf{B} + \mathbf{A}$, in the same way as in ordinary algebra. At this point, the reader is probably thinking, "Of course; who would ever have doubted that!" Nevertheless, we shall soon see a situation in which an operation admissible in ordinary algebra is *not* permitted in matrix algebra.

The multiplication of matrices is a somewhat more complex matter. In the matrix multiplication, $\mathbf{AB} = \mathbf{C}$, $\mathbf{A}$ is called the premultiplier, and $\mathbf{B}$ is called the postmultiplier. Matrix multiplication is defined *if* the number of columns in the premultiplier equals the number of rows in the postmultiplier. Let us represent the order of matrices to be multiplied by enclosing each order in parentheses. The two matrices with orders (7×5) and (5×6) can be multiplied because the premultiplier has five columns and the postmultiplier has five rows. The order of the product matrix will be (7×6), that is, the number of rows in the premultiplier and the number of columns in the postmultiplier. Can we multiply matrices of orders (3×4) and (3×3)? *No*, because the number of columns in the premultiplier, four, differs from the number of rows in the postmultiplier, three.

Now we shall state the theorem that matrix multiplication, in general, is *not* commutative, that is, $\mathbf{AB} \neq \mathbf{BA}$. If we consider the first example above, we shall see that we could not perform the multiplication in the direction (5×6) by (7×5) because then six, the number of columns in the premultiplier, would differ from seven, the number of rows in the postmultiplier. Of course, in some cases the product in the reverse order will be possible, but each situation must be investigated separately.

The actual process of matrix multiplication is accomplished by calculating the "inner products" of the various rows of the premultiplier and columns of the postmultiplier. An example of the process is

$$
\underset{\mathbf{A}}{\begin{Vmatrix} 7 & 5 \\ 2 & 6 \end{Vmatrix}} \cdot \underset{\mathbf{B}}{\begin{Vmatrix} 4 & -2 \\ 9 & 3 \end{Vmatrix}} = \underset{\mathbf{C}}{\begin{Vmatrix} 7(4) + 5(9) & 7(-2) + 5(3) \\ 2(4) + 6(9) & 2(-2) + 6(3) \end{Vmatrix}}
$$

$$
= \begin{Vmatrix} 73 & 1 \\ 62 & 14 \end{Vmatrix}
$$

Let us examine in detail the calculation of c_{21}, the element in the second row and first column of the product matrix $\mathbf{C}$. We take the second row of $\mathbf{A}$, which involves the numbers 2 and 6, and the first column of $\mathbf{B}$, which involves the numbers 4 and 9. The corresponding numbers are multiplied, and then these products are added, that is, (2 times 4) plus (6 times 9), giving the numerical result of 62. Similarly, each of the other three values of $\mathbf{C}$ is obtained by selecting the corresponding row of $\mathbf{A}$ and column of $\mathbf{B}$ and calculating the inner product. At this point readers with strong visual imagery may welcome a diagram:

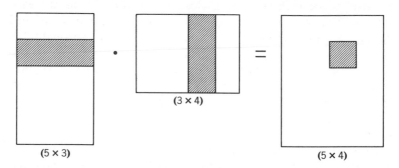

In this diagram the element indicated in the product matrix is in the second row and third column. It is obtained by multiplying the second row of the premultiplier by the third column of the postmultiplier.

Since we have been discussing whether matrix multiplication is commutative, it may be of interest to the reader to perform the multiplication **BA**, using the numbers in the matrices just given. In this case does **BA** = **AB**? (See the Appendix, page 197.)

We need one more tool before we can begin to apply matrix algebra to the equations of factor analysis. The "transpose" of a matrix is formed by interchanging its rows and columns and is denoted by affixing a prime to the capital letter labeling the matrix. For example,

$$\text{if } \mathbf{A} = \begin{Vmatrix} .9 & .0 \\ .8 & .2 \\ .0 & .8 \\ .3 & .7 \end{Vmatrix}, \quad \text{then } \mathbf{A'} = \begin{Vmatrix} .9 & .8 & .0 & .3 \\ .0 & .2 & .8 & .7 \end{Vmatrix}$$

Note that the first column of **A** contains the same numbers as the first row of **A′**, the third row of **A** has the same numbers as the third column of **A′**, etc.

Now let us return to Equation 9.8, $r_{jk} = a_j a_k + b_j b_k$. The equation is general because j and k can refer to any two tests. We can use matrix algebra to refer *simultaneously* to a large number of tests. This fundamental factor theorem can be written:

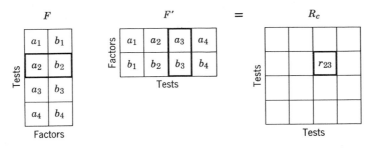

Verbally, the reduced correlation matrix (why it is "reduced" will be discussed in a moment) equals the product of a factor matrix by its own transpose.[1] Consider the correlation between test 2 and test 3. According to the fundamental theorem,

$$r_{23} = a_2 a_3 + b_2 b_3$$

Examination of the above diagram will show that this equation represents the inner product of row 2 of the factor matrix and column 3 of the transpose of the factor matrix. The reader should now select any other element of R_c and make a similar comparison.

Although our example has involved only four tests and two factors (the number of *common* factors is usually kept less than the number of tests for reasons of parsimony), this matrix equation can be generalized to any number of tests and factors. In the diagram this would mean changing the height and width of the factor matrix, but the general principle would remain the same.

Finally, let us consider the special case where $j = k$, for example,

$$r_{33} = a_3{}^2 + b_3{}^2$$

Referring the right member of this equation to the material at the end of the previous chapter (page 103), we see that r_{33} gives the *communality* of test 3:

$$r_{33} = a_3{}^2 + b_3{}^2 = h_3{}^2 = 1 - (s_3{}^2 + e_3{}^2)$$

The elements in the "principal diagonal" of R_c contain, not unity,

[1] Strictly speaking, we should refer here to the "common factor matrix" (Thurstone, pp. 78–81).

by the communalities, which in general are less than one. This is why it is called a *reduced* correlation matrix. The empirically given correlation matrix with unity in the diagonals is denoted R, without the subscript.

SOME VECTOR GEOMETRY

In the foregoing discussion we saw that the relationships of factor analysis can be expressed in a much more condensed form by using matrix algebra. However, many readers will be relieved to know that a more pictorial representation of the same relationships is also available. Roe's (1952, pp. 140–145) study of imagery of scientists indicates that, whereas some scientists (e.g., theoretical physicists) prefer to think in terms of verbal images, other scientists (e.g., experimental physicists) tend to think in terms of visual images. Fortunately, the relationships of factor analysis can be viewed alternatively by means of algebraic symbols or by a pictorial representation.

The pictorial view is accomplished by use of vector geometry. A "vector" is a line with both direction and magnitude. Vectors are often pictured by means of an arrow: ↗ The length of the line denotes the magnitude of the vector, and the head of the arrow indicates its direction. A common use of vectors is in finding the resultant of two forces in elementary physics by means of the parallelogram law.

The "projection" of one vector on another vector that originates from the same point O is obtained as follows (see Figure 10.1). From the termination of the first vector, P, drop a perpendicular to the second vector. The projection is then the vector from the point

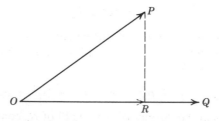

Figure 10.1 Projection of one vector on another.

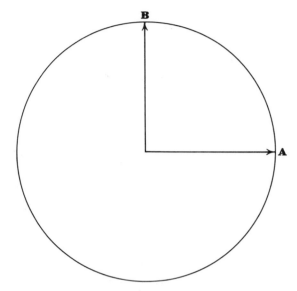

Figure 10.2 Reference vectors generating a two-space.

O to the intersection R. Thus the projection of vector **OP** on vector **OQ** is **OR**.

Two vectors at right angles to each other are said to be "orthogonal." A "unit vector" is a vector with a magnitude of unity. Two orthogonal unit vectors generate a "two-space" in the shape of a circle (see Figure 10.2). Three orthogonal unit vectors generate a three-space in the shape of a sphere. In each case, the generating vectors are "reference vectors" for the particular space. Although we cannot picture a space of dimensionality greater than three, the properties of such a "hyperspace" can be conceived of as following analogously the generalization in matrix algebra to more than two variables. In very general terms, a space of n orthogonal dimensions is called an n-space.

After this brief excursion into the rarefied atmosphere of n-space, the reader may welcome a return to consideration of variables representing, for example, psychological tests. (In the discussion below, tests will be used to exemplify the variables; however, any other variables commonly used by behavioral scientists—rating

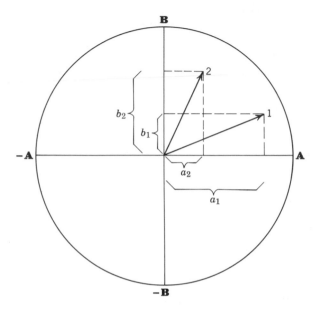

Figure 10.3　Test vectors in a two-space.

scales, demographic variables, personnel data—can be represented in the same way.)

Tests can be represented geometrically as vectors in the "common-factor space." The common-factor space is an n-space where n equals the number of common factors. For simplicity of exposition, let us again assume only two common factors. Figure 10.3 shows test vectors 1 and 2 in a two-space generated by the orthogonal reference vectors **A** and **B**. $-$**A** represents a vector with a magnitude equal to that of **A** but with an exactly opposite direction, that is, the angle between **A** and $-$**A** is 180°. $-$**B** is defined in an analogous manner.

Now, following the technique described above, let us obtain the projection of vector 1 on vector **A**. Dropping a perpendicular, we find that the magnitude of the projection is a_1. In a similar fashion, the magnitude of the projection of vector 1 on vector **B** is b_1. However, these two quantities are precisely the coordinates of the point defined by the termination of vector 1 in the rectangular

Cartesian coordinate system, which is the familiar system for graphing all sorts of everyday relationships. In fact, later we shall plot only the points in our diagrams; however, it should always be understood that the points constitute a shorthand way of picturing the test vectors. The point defined by the coordinates, a_2 and b_2, similarly locates the terminus of test vector 2.

In factor analysis, the coordinates of a point represent the factor loadings of the corresponding test vector. Thus we see that the factor loading of test 1 on factor A is precisely the projection of vector 1 on vector **A**. Although the reference vectors could be defined as being of any length, it has been found useful to conceive of them as being of unit length.

Let us next find the length of a test vector in terms of the factor loadings of the test. According to the Pythagorean theorem, the square of the hypotenuse of a right triangle equals the sum of the squares of its sides. Note in Figure 10.3 that test vector 1 is the hypotenuse of two different right triangles. The sum of the squares of the sides of *either* of these triangles is $a_1{}^2 + b_1{}^2$. Therefore the length of test vector 1 is $\sqrt{a_1{}^2 + b_1{}^2}$. Similarly, the length of test vector 2 is $\sqrt{a_2{}^2 + b_2{}^2}$. However, if the reader will now turn back to page 103, he will see that the length of a test vector thus equals the *square root* of its communality, h^2.

If there were three common factors, we would need three orthogonal reference vectors and three coordinates for the terminus of each test vector. However, the Pythagorean theorem is general for a space of any number of dimensions; thus the length of the test vector is still the square root of its communality, no matter how many terms may have to be added to obtain the communality, for example, in five-space, the length of test vector 3 would be

$$\sqrt{a_3{}^2 + b_3{}^2 + c_3{}^2 + d_3{}^2 + e_3{}^2}$$

The inner product ("scalar product") of two vectors equals the product of the magnitudes of the two vectors times the cosine of their angular separation. In factor analysis, the test vectors are drawn so that the inner product of the vectors equals the correlation between the corresponding two tests, that is,

$$r_{jk} = h_j h_k \cos \theta_{jk}$$

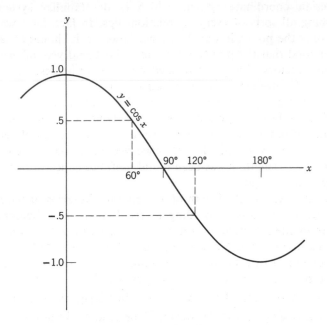

Figure 10.4 The cosine function, $y = \cos x$.

Note that the lengths of the vectors, h_j and h_k, equal the square roots of the corresponding test communalities, $h_j{}^2$ and $h_k{}^2$, as was stated above. Now let us examine the cosine function, shown in Figure 10.4 to see what sort of vectorial representation corresponds to various test correlations. Since the lengths of the test vectors are always taken as positive (or zero), the algebraic sign of the cosine corresponds to the algebraic sign of the correlation. If the tests are positively correlated, the test vectors must make an acute angle (an angle between 0° and 90°); if the tests are negatively correlated, they must make an obtuse angle (an angle between 90° and 180°). The vectors for two completely uncorrelated tests are orthogonal. Note that the reference axes are, by definition, orthogonal and therefore uncorrelated. Vectorial representations of various degrees of correlation are shown in Figure 10.5. A perfect positive correlation (+1.00) could be represented only by two vectors of unit length that exactly coincide. A perfect negative correlation

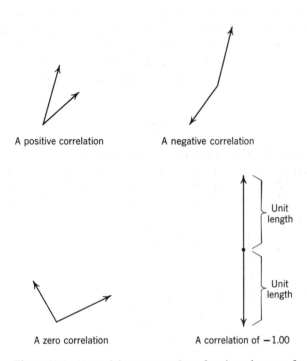

A positive correlation   A negative correlation

A zero correlation   A correlation of -1.00

Figure 10.5   Vectorial representation of various degrees of correlation.

(-1.00) would involve two vectors of unit length extending from the same origin in exactly opposite directions.

The vectors in Figure 10.5 were deliberately drawn without any framework of reference axes to emphasize the point that the relationships described in the last paragraph are independent of which set of factors one chooses to describe them by. In matrix algebra, the analogous statement is that, in general, there is more than one factor matrix $\mathbf{F}$ that will satisfy the equation, $\mathbf{FF'} = \mathbf{R}_c$. More generally speaking, there is a certain amount of arbitrariness in our choice of concepts to represent nature. Thurstone (1947, Chapter 6) cleverly illustrated this point by showing that a collection of cylinders could be parsimoniously described either (a) by using the two dimensions of tallness and thickness or (b) by using a general size dimension plus a "bipolar" dimension of short-thick versus tall-thin. Although the choice of reference axes is indeterminate on mathematical grounds, Thurstone formulated on behavioral scientific grounds a principle called "simple structure," which introduces a large (though not complete) degree of determinism into the factor problem. This principle will be described in Chapter 12.

Problems

1. Perform the following matrix multiplications:

(a) $\begin{Vmatrix} 2 & 1 & 0 \\ 0 & 1 & 2 \\ 3 & 2 & 6 \end{Vmatrix} \cdot \begin{Vmatrix} 1 & 3 \\ 1 & 0 \\ 2 & 1 \end{Vmatrix}$ (b) $\begin{Vmatrix} 2 & -1 & 0 \\ 0 & 1 & -2 \\ 3 & 2 & 6 \end{Vmatrix} \cdot \begin{Vmatrix} 1 & 3 & -5 \\ 1 & 0 & 2 \\ 2 & -1 & 4 \end{Vmatrix}$

(c) $\begin{Vmatrix} 2 & 1 & 0 \\ 0 & -1 & -2 \\ 3 & 2 & 6 \\ 9 & -1 & 0 \\ 3 & 0 & 1 \end{Vmatrix} \cdot \begin{Vmatrix} 1 & 3 \\ 1 & 0 \\ -2 & 1 \end{Vmatrix}$

(d) $\begin{Vmatrix} 4 & 9 & -3 & 2 \\ 6 & -7 & 1 & 8 \end{Vmatrix} \cdot \begin{Vmatrix} 2 & -4 \\ 5 & 0 \\ 1 & -5 \\ 0 & 3 \end{Vmatrix}$

2. Devise a method of matrix multiplication in the following two situations that avoids the necessity of writing out the transpose: (a) a matrix is *pre*multiplied by its own transpose, (b) a matrix is *post*multiplied by its own transpose.

3. A "scalar matrix" is a matrix, all of whose diagonal elements contain a constant number and all of whose other elements equal zero. What is the effect of (a) *pre*multiplying another matrix by a scalar matrix, (b) *post*multiplying another matrix by a scalar matrix?

4. Suppose that two tests contain no specific variance, that is, their communalities equal their reliabilities. The cosine of the angle between their vectors is then equivalent to which statistical index that was discussed in Chapter 7?

11

CENTROID METHOD
OF FACTOR EXTRACTION

INTRODUCTORY REMARKS

As was stated in the previous chapter, an empirically given correlation matrix, $\mathbf{R}$, can be factored into a large number of factor matrices, all of which satisfy the relationship, $\mathbf{FF'} = \mathbf{R}_c$. Which particular factor matrix we choose to deal with must depend on other considerations. In Chapter 8 five criteria for scientific theories were considered. The criteria of internal consistency and verifiability are not at issue here, and it will be assumed that the criterion of comprehensiveness has already been considered in the choice of the domain of variables that have been correlated.

This leaves the criteria of parsimony and closeness of fit to the data. The first factor analyst, Charles Spearman (1904), was much concerned with the criterion of parsimony; he postulated that ability tests could be accounted for by only one common factor (which was called a "general factor" because it was assumed to operate in *all* the tests) plus a factor specific to each test and error of measurement. However, most students of factor analysis since Spearman's time have tended to feel that Spearman attained his high degree of parsimony at the expense of goodness of fit to the data. Specifically, after the general factor had been "extracted," the "residual" values in the correlation matrix seemed too large to represent only specific and error factors. On the other hand, there would be no economy in using as many factors as there are tests.

Nevertheless, the criterion of closeness of fit suggests that the factors that are extracted should leave residuals that are as small as possible. A theoretical solution has been worked out for this problem, and the resulting factors are called "principal axes" (Harman, 1960, Chapter 9; Thurstone, 1947, Chapter 20). Some mathematical properties of this solution are described in Chapter 13 and in the Appendix. However, the computational difficulties in dealing with the principal axes are indeed formidable, even with small correlation matrices, and this solution is rarely practical unless an electronic computer is available. Since many investigators in behavioral science will undoubtedly continue to be faced with problems for which use of an electronic computer is not feasible, a considerably simpler method developed by Thurstone, called the "centroid method," will be described. In fact, the first centroid factor can be regarded as a first approximation to the first principal axis factor.

A "centroid" is a kind of multidimensional average. If the ribs of an outstretched umbrella are thought of as test vectors, the handle of the umbrella indicates the direction of the centroid. The "centroid vector" is a vector of unit length along the direction of the centroid. The projection of each test vector on this centroid vector gives the factor loading for the variable represented by the test vector. Thus, for two test vectors of equal length, the vector making the smaller angle with the centroid vector will have the greater factor loading, that is, the cosine of the angle will be larger (see page 113).

However, it will be well at this point to introduce a numerical example to give a more concrete idea of the principles involved. We shall deal with a 9×9 correlation matrix of ability tests, which is shown in Table 11.1. Since some of the problems typically involved in factor analysis are difficult to demonstrate with real empirical data unless the number of variables is quite large, the matrix consists of fictitious data. However, the reader should keep in mind that he will never be confronted with actual data in which the underlying structure is as clear-cut as in our example.

On the other hand, the titles refer to actual tests used in Thurstone's trail-blazing factor analysis of 57 tests, reported in his *Primary Mental Abilities* monograph (1938), and the correlations in Table

11.1 roughly correspond to his reported values. A short description of each test whose nature is not obvious from the title is given below.

Table 11.1 *Correlation Matrix for the Factor Analysis Problem*

	1	2	3	4	5	6	7	8	9
1. Addition	1.00	.00	.00	.54	.00	.00	.27	.18	.00
2. Cubes	.00	1.00	.00	.00	.56	.00	.08	.00	.16
3. Spelling	.00	.00	1.00	.00	.00	.56	.00	.07	.14
4. Multiplication	.54	.00	.00	1.00	.00	.00	.18	.12	.00
5. Flags	.00	.56	.00	.00	1.00	.00	.07	.00	.14
6. Vocabulary	.00	.00	.56	.00	.00	1.00	.00	.08	.16
7. Block counting	.27	.08	.00	.18	.07	.00	1.00	.06	.02
8. Arithmetic reasoning	.18	.00	.07	.12	.00	.08	.06	1.00	.02
9. Syllogisms	.00	.16	.14	.00	.14	.16	.02	.02	1.00

Cubes: In each item two cubes with various markings on the sides are presented. The subject must decide whether the second cube could possibly represent the first cube turned into a different position.

Flags: Pairs of American flags are presented. The subject must decide whether the second flag represents the same face as the first flag or whether the flag would have to be turned over to obtain the new representation.

Block Counting: In each item there is shown a pile of blocks of the same size and shape, and each is identified by a letter. The subject must write down how many other blocks each block touches.

Syllogisms: Each item involves the age relationships of three men, e.g., "Jones is younger than Brown. Brown is younger than Smith." The subject must judge whether a suggested conclusion, for example, "Therefore Smith is younger than Jones," is valid. (This particular conclusion is invalid.)

In the correlation matrix the numerical values in the cells of the "principal diagonal" (the diagonal from the upper-left to the lower-right corners of the matrix) all represent self-correlations of the variables, which are therefore unity. However, it will be recalled from our previous theoretical development (page 109) that, if specific and error factors are postulated in addition to common factors, the product of the factor matrix by its transpose equals the *reduced* correlation matrix, R_c, in which the diagonal elements contain the test communalities rather than unity.

Inasmuch as we have previously calculated communalities by summing the square of factor loadings, and inasmuch as the factor loadings themselves must be calculated from a given correlation matrix, we seem to have wandered into a blind alley. Fortunately, Thurstone (1947, Chapter 13) showed that satisfactory results are obtained when "guessed" communalities are inserted in the diagonal cells. Then, if desired, the factor loadings obtained by centroid extraction can be used to obtain newly estimated communalities, with which a more accurate set of factor loadings can be calculated, and so on.

In the "complete centroid method" new estimates are made for the diagonal cells after extraction of each factor. However, it has been found computationally more convenient to leave the diagonal cells blank on the work sheets and to handle the corresponding values in rows below the correlation matrix and "residual matrices" (see Tables 11.2 to 11.5).

EXTRACTION OF THE FIRST FACTOR

The first stage consists of calculating the first centroid loadings (see Table 11.2). The values in the row labeled s_1 represent column sums, for example, for the fourth column,

$$.54 + .00 + .00 + .00 + .00 + .18 + .12 + .00 = .84$$

If some of the column sums are negative, it is useful to "reflect" the corresponding test vectors (see below). However, in our example all the column sums are positive. A simple yet rather good estimate of each communality is the highest correlation in the column regardless of algebraic sign, that is, the highest "absolute value," see Thurstone (1947, pp. 299–300). These numbers are recorded in row D. For example, the highest absolute value in the fourth column is .54. Row E is obtained by adding the corresponding values in rows s_1 and D, for example, for the fourth column,

$$.84 + .54 = 1.38$$

The procedures of factor analysis require a large number of sequential steps, and in some cases the effect of a small computational error in one step is greatly magnified in subsequent steps.

Hence it is fortunate that checking procedures are available for most of the steps. Many of these essentially involve the First Summation Law (see page 15). Note in Table 11.2 that a sum *column* is included, the first nine values of which correspond to those in row s_1. (If the correlation matrix is large, it is useful to compute the row and column sums separately and compare them as a check against copying errors.) The sum value of 6.82 in row s_1 is the sum of all the values to its left, and the analogous situation is repeated in all the other rows of Tables 11.2 to 11.5. The row sums for rows D and E should be obtained first, and if $\sum s_1 + \sum D = \sum E$ (6.82 + 3.93 = 10.75 in our case), a check mark is written after the sum value for row E. The number 10.75 is a sum of 18 different values in rows s_1 and D, and whether we add them by rows or columns should be inconsequential.

Table 11.2 *Extraction of the First Centroid Factor*

	1	2	3	4	5	6	7	8	9	Σ
1		.00	.00	.54	.00	.00	.27	.18	.00	.99 ✓
2	.00		.00	.00	.56	.00	.08	.00	.16	.80 ✓
3	.00	.00		.00	.00	.56	.00	.07	.14	.77 ✓
4	.54	.00	.00		.00	.00	.18	.12	.00	.84 ✓
5	.00	.56	.00	.00		.00	.07	.00	.14	.77 ✓
6	.00	.00	.56	.00	.00		.00	.08	.16	.80 ✓
7	.27	.08	.00	.18	.07	.00		.06	.02	.68 ✓
8	.18	.00	.07	.12	.00	.08	.06		.02	.53 ✓
9	.00	.16	.14	.00	.14	.16	.02	.02		.64 ✓
s_1	.99	.80	.77	.84	.77	.80	.68	.53	.64	6.82 ✓
D	.54	.56	.56	.54	.56	.56	.27	.18	.16	3.93
E	1.53	1.36	1.33	1.38	1.33	1.36	.95	.71	.80	10.75 ✓
mE	.47	.41	.40	.42	.40	.41	.29	.22	.24	3.26 ✓

$$\sqrt{10.75} = 3.279$$
$$m = .3050$$

It can be shown (Thurstone, 1947, pp. 149–153) that the first centroid loadings can be computed by dividing each column sum (with the diagonal entry also included) by the square root of the grand total of these column sums. In our example, this would mean dividing 1.53, 1.36, 1.33, etc., each in turn by 3.279, which is the square root of 10.75. However, if a desk calculator is available, a faster procedure is first to calculate the reciprocal of the square root and then to lock it in as a constant multiplier, m, for example, for the first test,

$$\frac{1.53}{3.279} = \frac{1}{3.279}(1.53) = .3050(1.53) = .47$$

The resulting values, .47, .41, .40, etc., are the loadings of tests 1, 2, 3, etc., on the first centroid factor. They should be immediately checked in the following way. Their sum, 3.26, is calculated and written in the sum column. Then the multiplier, m, is applied also to the sum value of row E, that is,

$$.3050(10.75) = 3.28$$

This answer is compared with the actual sum. Here it will be noted that there is a discrepancy of two in the last figure. This arises because the factor loadings were all rounded to two decimal places. Although roundings usually tend to balance, with about as many resulting in an increase as in a decrease, the reader can expect many of his checks to involve a discrepancy of one, two, or occasionally three in the last figure. If the discrepancy is greater, he should repeat all the calculations involved in the check. When satisfactory values are obtained, a check mark is written after the actual sum. Note that it is the actual sum that we record rather than the check sum, because we shall be using it for checking future operations.

If nothing but additions and/or subtractions are involved in the check, there should be no discrepancy whatsoever. This is called an "exact check." A check involving roundings is an "approximate check."

CALCULATION OF THE FIRST FACTOR RESIDUALS

The next stage is to compute the "first factor residuals." It will be recalled (see Equation 9.9) that the correlation between two tests equals the inner product of their factor loadings:

$$r_{jk} = a_j a_k + b_j b_k + c_j c_k + \cdots \qquad (11.1)$$

Each product term of the right member of this equation represents the amount that a given factor contributes to the correlation. By subtracting the contribution of our first factor $a_j a_k$, we obtain the first factor residual:

$$r_{jk} - a_j a_k = b_j b_k + c_j c_k + \cdots \qquad (11.2)$$

This procedure can also be represented in terms of matrix algebra. Let f_1 be a column vector formed by taking only the first column of the factor matrix F. Then the first factor residual matrix W_1 is calculated by

$$W_1 = R_c - f_1 f_1' \qquad (11.3)$$

We can treat these residuals in the same way as we did the original correlations and thus extract a *second* centroid factor. However, the calculation of these residuals is a tricky process in which we can easily make mistakes in algebraic sign. Therefore a convenient routine with checks has been worked out (see Table 11.3).

At the outset, the first factor loadings from row mE of the preceding table (Table 11.2) are copied in the column to the left of the column with the row identification numbers. This column is also labeled a_1 in the new table (Table 11.3). The sum 3.26 is written below and labeled v_1. Then row k_1 is filled in; it contains the same numbers as column a_1 but with *reversed sign*. (If the matrix is a large one, a useful copying check is $\sum k_1 = -v_1$.)

Once again the diagonal cells are at first ignored; this problem is handled by row D below the table of residuals. However, several other steps must intervene. The residuals are calculated by columns; therefore the first cell to be dealt with is that in the second row and first column. The required process is to subtract from the correlation of tests 1 and 2 (.00) the product of the loadings of tests 1 and 2 on the first factor (.47 and .41, respectively). However, since the computer ordinarily would have to keep in mind three different algebraic signs, the minus sign for the subtraction itself and the signs of the two factor loadings, his task is lightened by transferring the sign of the subtraction itself to one of the factor loadings, that is,

$$.00 - (.41)(.47) = .00 + (.41)(-.47)$$

This is the reason why the loadings were recorded again in row k_1 but with reversed sign. For each cell in the new table, the computer takes the *corresponding* value from the previous table and *adds* to it the product of the a_1 and k_1 values that are in the row and column, respectively, denoting the cell. In a sense, each cell in the residual matrix is "marked" by two markers, one each from column a_1 and row k_1. Which numbers mark the cell in the seventh row and third column? The desired numbers are .29 and $-.40$, because .29 is the value in the seventh row of a_1 and $-.40$ is the value in the third column of k_1.

At first the computer should search for the numbers to be dealt with slowly and carefully, because his eyes must jump back and forth between two tables. However, he is aided in keeping his place in the *second* table by noting the entries that have already been calculated and written down. A good aid for keeping one's place in the *first* table is to place a dime directly under the value being worked with. After each calculation, the dime is moved down one cell (or else into the next column). With practice, much of the early difficulty tends to disappear; and the computer can work up some speed. As further examples, the next three values in the first column are calculated below:

$$.00 + (.40)(-.47) = -.19$$

$$.54 + (.42)(-.47) = \quad .34$$

$$.00 + (.40)(-.47) = -.19$$

After all the residual entries for the first column have been computed, they can be checked collectively. First, the s_1 values are copied from the previous table (Table 11.2 in our example). Then the k_1 value for the column is multiplied by v_1, the sum of the first factor loadings. For the first column, $-.47$ is multiplied by 3.26 to obtain -1.53. (If a desk calculator is available, a saving can be effected by locking in v_1 as a constant multiplier and also computing the $k_1 v_1$ products for all the other columns at this time.) Then the k_1 value for the column (i.e., $-.47$) is squared, which gives .22. The check value is obtained by adding the three numbers just obtained, that is,

$$.99 - 1.53 + .22 = -.32$$

Now the actual sum of the residuals is obtained and written in row s_2, that is,

$$-.19 - .19 + .34 - .19 - .19 + .13 + .08 - .11 = -.32$$

Here the check is exact, although at times there will be a discrepancy of one, two, or three in the last figure (as can be seen by comparing the already calculated values in row $s_1 + k_1v_1 + k_1{}^2$ and row s_2 of the other columns of Table 11.3). If the two numbers disagree by more, the residuals should be calculated again. When sufficient accuracy has been achieved, the residual entries of column 1 are copied into row 1. Like the correlation matrix, each matrix of residuals will be symmetrical. With large matrices, the new row should be added; then the sum is written in the sum column and checked against the number in the s_2 row. However, even if this checking procedure is not applied, the sum value from row s_2 should be copied into column $\sum$.

Now the residual for the cell in the third row and second column is calculated, that is,

$$.00 + (.40)(-.41) = -.16$$

Then the computer proceeds down the second column, that is,

$$.00 + (.42)(-.41) = -.17$$

$$.56 + (.40)(-.41) = \quad .40$$

$$.00 + (.41)(-.41) = -.17, \text{ etc.}$$

After all the residuals have been calculated for the second column, the checking procedure is again to find the sum, $s_1 + k_1v_1 + k_1{}^2$, and to compare it with the actual sum of residuals, s_2, that is,

$$.80 - 1.34 + .17 = -.37$$

$$-.19 - .16 - .17 + .40 - .17 - .04 - .09 + .06 = -.36$$

Since these two sums are sufficiently close, the remaining blank cells of row 2 are filled in, using the corresponding entries from column 2. The computer then proceeds to column 3, beginning with the cell in the fourth row. For each successive column there is one less entry to be calculated, which should produce a "goal gradient" to sustain the computer's motivation! Finally in the last column, no new residual need be calculated, but the check (i.e., $.64 - .78 + .06 = -.08$) should be completed anyway.

Table 11.3 *First Factor Residuals and Extraction of the Second Centroid Factor*

k_1	−.47	−.41	−.40	−.42	−.40	−.41	−.29	−.22	−.24	
a_1	1	2	3	4	5	6	7	8	9	Σ
.47 (1)		−.19	−.19	.34	−.19	−.19	.13	.08	−.11	−.32 √
.41 (2)	−.19		−.16	−.17	.40	−.17	−.04	−.09	.06	−.36 √
.40 (3)	−.19	−.16		−.17	−.16	.40	−.12	−.02	.04	−.38 √
.42 (4)	.34	−.17	−.17		−.17	−.17	.06	.03	−.10	−.35 √
.40 (5)	−.19	.40	−.16	−.17		−.16	−.05	−.09	.04	−.38 √
.41 (6)	−.19	−.17	.40	−.17	−.16		−.12	−.01	.06	−.36 √
.29 (7)	.13	−.04	−.12	.06	−.05	−.12		.00	−.05	−.19 √
.22 (8)	.08	−.09	−.02	.03	−.09	−.01	.00		−.03	−.13 √
.24 (9)	−.11	.06	.04	−.10	.04	.06	−.05	−.03		−.09 √
s_1	.99	.80	.77	.84	.77	.80	.68	.53	.64	6.82
$k_1 v_1$	−1.53	−1.34	−1.30	−1.37	−1.30	−1.34	−.94	−.72	−.78	
$k_1{}^2$	.22	.17	.16	.18	.16	.17	.08	.05	.06	
$s_1 + k_1 v_1 + k_1{}^2$	−.32	−.37	−.37	−.35	−.37	−.37	−.18	−.14	−.08	
s_2	−.32	−.36	−.38	−.35	−.38	−.36	−.19	−.13	−.09	−2.56
$s_2/-2 = A$	.160	.180	.190	.175	.190	.180	.095	.065	.045	1.280 √
$+3$	−.030	.020	(.190)	.005	.030	.580	−.025	.045	.085	.900 √
$+6$	−.220	−.150	(.590)	−.165	−.130	(.580)	−.145	.035	.145	.540 √
$+9$	−.330	−.090	(.630)	−.265	−.090	(.640)	−.195	.005	(.145)	.450 √
$B + 8$	−.250	−.180	(.610)	−.235	−.180	(.630)	−.195	(.005)	(.115)	.320 √
$-2B = C$	.50	.36	−1.22	.47	.36	−1.26	.39	−.01	−.23	−.64 √
D	.34	.40	−.40	.34	.40	−.40	.13	−.09	−.11	.61
$C + D = E$	.84	.76	−1.62	.81	.76	−1.66	.52	−.10	−.34	−.03 √
mE	.31	.28	−.60	.30	.28	−.61	.19	−.04	−.12	−.01 √

$v_1 = 3.26$

$\sum|E| = 7.41$ $\sqrt{7.41} = 2.722$ $m = .3674$

EXTRACTION OF THE SECOND FACTOR

Now we have a 9×9 matrix of first factor residuals, which represent the test intercorrelations with the effect of the first factor removed. What is left is presumably due to a second factor, a third factor, etc. However, we cannot immediately apply the same extraction procedure because the centroid method has the peculiarity that, for a given set of values inserted into the diagonal cells, the column *sums* of the residual matrix are all zero! (This is not evident from Table 11.3 because we did not calculate the residuals for the diagonal cells.) Nevertheless, the values that we put into the diagonal cells were merely communality estimates, and, in fact, we shall be making new communality estimates before extracting each successive new factor.

To circumvent this situation, we "reflect" some of the test vectors. We reflect in such a way as to extract a considerable amount of the variance remaining in the tests after the effect of the first centroid factor has been removed. To illustrate concretely the effect of reflecting a test vector, let us assume that the correlation between a measure of intelligence and a test of mechanical aptitude is .50. This means that the persons who do well on the mechanical test will tend to be the same persons who do well on the intelligence test. However, let us further assume that in scoring the intelligence test a clerical mistake is made such that, instead of scoring the number of correct answers, the scorer records the number of mistakes. The resulting scores will then represent a measure of "stupidity" instead of intelligence; however, the numerical value of the correlation will be the same as if the correct answers had been scored; only the algebraic sign will be changed. In other words, the correlation between the mechanical aptitude test and *stupidity* will be $-.50$, that is, the persons who score *low* on stupidity will tend to be those who score high on the mechanical aptitude test.

Now let us see how this situation is shown in our geometrical picture. In Figure 11.1 are pictured two vectors, **OM** and **ON**, which make an angle of 60°. The correlation between the tests represented by these two vectors is the product of the lengths of the two vectors and the cosine of 60°. Now let us reflect vector **OM** so that it becomes a corresponding vector of equal length but opposite direction **OM′**. The angle that **OM′** makes with **ON** is the "supple-

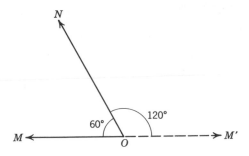

Figure 11.1 Reflection of a vector.

ment" of 60°, that is, 180° − 60°, or 120°. However, the cosine of the supplement of an angle equals the cosine of the angle itself with opposite algebraic sign. This equality can be seen graphically in Figure 10.4 of Chapter 10. The cosine of 60° is +.5, and the cosine of its supplement, 120°, is −.5. On the other hand, since reflection has not changed the lengths of the vectors, the correlation keeps the same numerical value while changing sign.

Thus the effect of reflecting a test vector is to change the sign of its correlations with all other variables. If "intelligence" correlates +.5, −.3, and +.2 with three other traits, then "stupidity" will correlate −.5, +.3, and −.2 with these same traits. This suggests that if we wish to reflect, say test 7, in our first factor residual matrix, we should change all the signs in row 7 *and* in column 7. This procedure is possible, but since we shall likely be reflecting several vectors, it would mean changing the signs of some of the residuals more than once, which would be confusing to indicate. Fortunately, a routine has been worked out that deals with the various *sums* of the residuals (which is what we shall need for extraction of the second factor, anyway) rather than with the individual residuals themselves.

A preparatory step is to divide all the entries in row s_2 of Table 11.3 by −2. To avoid cumulation of rounding errors, all the steps are carried out to one more decimal place than in the original correlations, in our case, to three decimal places. The sum value of row s_2, −2.56, should also be divided by −2. The resulting numbers are written in row A, and an exact check is provided by adding the nine entries for the variables, noting that they indeed total to the check sum, $+1.280$, and then indicating this agreement by writing a check mark after the check sum.

Our strategy is to reflect test vectors until all the column sums are positive or zero. We begin by reflecting the test whose residuals actually give the largest negative sum, which means the largest *positive* sum in row A (because row A has signs reversed from row s_2). Since in our example the largest entry in row A is .190 in the third column, we begin by reflecting test 3. (The fifth column also has an entry of .190 in row A, so the decision here is an arbitrary one.) This is accomplished by adding the numbers in the third *row of the residual matrix* to the corresponding numbers in row A. The new row is labeled $+3$. In our example, the first three operations are

$$-.19 + .160 = -.030$$
$$-.16 + .180 = +.020$$
$$.00 + .190 = +.190$$

Since there is no number written in the cell in the third column and third row of the residual matrix, the third number in row $+3$, .190, is identical to that above it in row A; however, it is enclosed in parentheses to indicate that this test has been reflected. The parentheses are retained in subsequent rows of this column, even when other tests are being reflected. The same operation is applied to the check column (i.e., $-.38 + 1.280 = .900$), and the newly calculated nine entries should total to exactly this value.

The next test to be reflected is that which gives *the largest positive value outside of parentheses*. In row $+3$ this is test 6, for which the present sum value is .580. Therefore row 6 is added to row $+3$. (Henceforth, when we speak of "adding rows" of numbers we shall mean that the entries in the corresponding columns of the rows are added individually.) The first three operations for the reflection of test 6 give

$$-.19 - .030 = -.220$$
$$-.17 + .020 = -.150$$
$$+.40 + .190 = +.590$$

Again the entries in the sum column are added to provide a check, that is, $-.36 + .900 = +.540$. Now the highest positive sum outside of parentheses is that for test 9, namely, .145. Therefore, to row $+6$

is added row 9, and then the sum check is applied. Test 8 is reflected in the same manner, and after this we notice that all the sums are either negative or enclosed within parentheses. Therefore we may stop the reflection procedure at this point.[1]

The row in which our goal is finally attained is further labeled row B. The next row, row C, is obtained by multiplying all the values in row B (including that in the sum column) by -2. This is the opposite of dividing by -2, so in effect we are "undoing" what we did in row A. The absolute values in row C are the absolute values of the sums that would have resulted if we had changed all the signs in a given row and corresponding column of the residual matrix every time we reflected a test. Row C corresponds to row s_1 below the original correlation matrix in Table 11.2.

Now we must supply new communality estimates. Again the highest *absolute* value in the particular column of the matrix is selected. However, the sign is determined by affixing the *same* sign as that in row C. For test 1 the highest residual value is .34, so .34 is written in the first column of row D. The sign is positive because .50 above it in row C is also positive. On the other hand, for test 3 the highest residual is .40, but $-.40$ is entered in row D because the number above it, -1.22, is negative. (This, in turn, is because we have reflected test 3.)

For checking purposes, the values in row D are added, giving $+.61$. Row E, the sum of rows C and D, gives the column sums of the adjusted residual matrix with communalities supplied. The loading of each test on the second centroid factor equals the value in row E divided by the square root of the sum of all the *absolute* values in row E, namely, 7.41.[2] However, again it is easier with a desk calculator first to compute the reciprocal of the square root and then to apply it as a multiplier, .3674, in turn to all the entries in row E to obtain row mE. As usual, the same operation is applied to the

---

[1] Occasionally, in order to obtain sums all of which are negative, zero, or positive within parentheses, test vectors must be reflected twice. The procedure for such cases is described by Thurstone (1947, p. 166).

[2] The reason for the seemingly arbitrary sign changes in calculation of loadings is that, for the purpose of estimation of communalities and calculation of loadings, we are assuming tests 3, 6, 8, and 9 to be reflected, but minus signs are then affixed to the loadings thus obtained to indicate that these test vectors are actually opposite in direction to the unreflected test vectors. A mathematical rationale for this procedure is given by Harman (1960, pp. 195–197).

sum column, but in this case the check is an approximate one. The numbers in row mE of Table 3 are the second centroid factor loadings.

REMAINING STEPS

Table 11.4 contains the results of the calculations for the second factor residuals and the third factor loadings. Since these are exactly analogous to the calculations for the first factor residuals and second factor loadings, which were described in detail above, only an outline of the remaining steps will be presented. In terms of matrix algebra, the calculation of the second factor residual matrix, $\mathbf{W}_2$, is represented by

$$\mathbf{W}_2 = \mathbf{W}_1 - \mathbf{f}_2\mathbf{f}_2' = \mathbf{R}_c - \mathbf{f}_1\mathbf{f}_1' - \mathbf{f}_2\mathbf{f}_2' \tag{11.4}$$

in which $\mathbf{f}_2$ is a column vector formed from the *second* column of the factor matrix, $\mathbf{F}$.

The second factor loadings are copied in column a_2, and their negatives are copied in row k_2. The value of v_2 is their sum. For checking purposes, row s_2 is copied from the previous table. Then the residuals for test 1 are calculated, beginning with the entry in the second row. To the corresponding first factor residual in Table 11.3 is added the product of the "marking" numbers from the corresponding row of column a_2 and the corresponding column of row k_2. The first three operations are

$$-.19 + (+.28)(-.31) = -.28$$

$$-.19 + (-.60)(-.31) = \quad .00$$

$$+.34 + (+.30)(-.31) = +.25$$

After all the rows of the first column have been accounted for, the check value, $s_2 + k_2v_2 + k_2{}^2$, is calculated and compared with the actual sum in row s_3. If the agreement is good, the entries of column 1 are copied into row 1. Then the residuals for the second column are calculated, checked, and copied, and so on for the other columns. Row A is again obtained by dividing the actual sums by -2. Now three vectors have to be reflected in turn, those for tests 5, 2, and 9, before the sums are all negative, zero, or positive within parentheses. After the values in row B are multiplied by -2, the communalities

Table 11.4 *Second Factor Residuals and Extraction of the Third Centroid Factor*

a_2	k_2 →	−.31	−.28	.60	−.30	−.28	.61	−.19	.04	.12	Σ
		1	2	3	4	5	6	7	8	9	
.31	1		−.28	.00	.25	−.28	.00	.07	.09	−.07	−.22 √
.28	2	−.28		.01	−.25	.32	.00	−.09	−.08	.09	−.28 √
−.60	3	.00	.01		.01	.01	.03	−.01	−.04	−.03	−.02 √
.30	4	.25	−.25	.01		−.25	.01	.00	.04	−.06	−.25 √
.28	5	−.28	.32	.01	−.25		.01	−.10	−.08	.07	−.30 √
−.61	6	.00	.00	.03	.01	.01		.01	−.03	−.01	.01 √
.19	7	.07	−.09	−.01	.00	−.10	.01		.01	−.03	−.15 √
−.04	8	.09	−.08	−.04	.04	−.08	−.03	.01		−.03	−.12 √
−.12	9	−.07	.09	−.03	−.06	.07	−.01	−.03	−.03		−.07 √
s_2		−.32	−.36	−.38	−.35	−.38	−.36	−.19	−.13	−.09	−2.56
k_2v_2		.00	.00	−.01	.00	.00	−.01	.00	.00	.00	
k_2^2		.10	.08	.36	.09	.08	.37	.04	.00	.01	
$s_2 + k_2v_2 + k_2^2$		−.22	−.28	−.03	−.26	−.30	.00	−.15	−.13	−.08	
s_3		−.22	−.28	−.02	−.25	−.30	.01	−.15	−.12	−.07	−.140 √
$s_3/-2 = A$		.110	.140	.010	.125	.150	−.005	.075	.060	.035	.700 √
$+5$		−.170	.460	.020	−.125	(.150)	.005	−.025	−.020	.105	.400 √
$+2$		−.450	(.460)	.030	−.375	(.470)	.005	−.115	−.100	.195	.120 √
$B+9$		−.520	(.550)	.000	−.435	(.540)	−.005	−.145	−.130	(.195)	.050 √
$-2B = C$		1.04	−1.10	.00	.87	−1.08	.01	.29	.26	−.39	−.10 √
D		.28	−.32	.04	.25	−.32	.03	.10	.09	−.09	.06 √
$C + D = E$		1.32	−1.42	.04	1.12	−1.40	.04	.39	.35	−.48	−.04 √
mE		.52	−.55	.02	.44	−.55	.02	.15	.14	−.19	−.02 √

$v_2 = -.01$

$\Sigma|E| = 6.56 \qquad \sqrt{6.56} = 2.561 \qquad m = .3905$

Table 11.5 *Third Factor Residuals*

k_3	−.52	.55	−.02	−.44	.55	−.02	−.15	−.14	.19	
a_3	1	2	3	4	5	6	7	8	9	Σ
.52 1		.01	−.01	.02	.01	−.01	−.01	.02	.03	.06 √
−.55 2	.01		.02	−.01	.02	−.01	−.01	.00	−.01	.03 √
.02 3	−.01	.02		.00	.02	.03	−.01	−.04	−.03	−.02 √
.44 4	.02	−.01	.00		−.01	.00	−.07	−.02	.02	−.07 √
−.55 5	.01	.02	.02	−.01		.02	−.02	.00	−.03	.01 √
.02 6	−.01	−.01	.03	.00	.02		.00	−.03	−.01	.01 √
.15 7	−.01	−.01	−.01	−.07	−.02	.00		−.01	.00	−.13 √
.14 8	.02	.00	−.04	−.02	.00	−.03	−.01		.00	−.08 √
−.19 9	.03	−.01	−.03	.02	−.03	−.01	.00	.00		−.03 √
$v_3 = .00$										
s_3	−.22	−.28	−.02	−.25	−.30	.01	−.15	−.12	−.07	−1.40
$k_3 v_3$	.00	.00	.00	.00	.00	.00	.00	.00	.00	
$k_3{}^2$	.27	.30	.00	.19	.30	.00	.02	.02	.04	
$s_3 + k_3 v_3 + k_3{}^2$	.05	.02	−.02	−.06	.00	.01	−.13	−.10	−.03	
s_4	.06	.03	−.02	−.07	.01	.01	−.13	−.08	−.03	

are ascertained and added in, and then the third centroid factor loadings are calculated.

Table 11.5 shows the calculation and checking of the third factor residuals. Note how small they are; the highest absolute value is .07. After the third factor residuals are compared with the original correlation matrix, it seems that these three centroid factors have "accounted for" most of the correlations. Therefore we stop the extraction procedure at this point.[3]

Factor extraction is continued until the residuals are "sufficiently small." The reader would undoubtedly prefer a more exact criterion than "sufficiently small residuals." Unfortunately, although many such criteria have been suggested for the centroid method, none has gained general acceptance. However, this is not the case for the more theoretically elegant (but more computationally difficult) factor solutions, such as "maximum-likelihood factor analysis," which is described briefly in Chapter 13. The following rough "rule of thumb" is offered: if all or almost all of the loadings on a factor fall between plus and minus .20, the factor probably has little explanatory value.

Problems

1. Calculate the communalities of each of the nine tests described in this chapter from the obtained factor loadings. Insert these into the diagonal cells of the original correlation matrix and compute a new set of first factor loadings. How do these compare with the original set of first factor loadings?

2. Anderson, Kunce, and Baxter (1962) obtained the intercorrelations shown below among a maze test and 13 ratings made by an industrial therapist. The subjects were 80 psychiatric patients at a VA hospital. The variables were (1) quality of work, (2) quantity of work, (3) ability to follow instructions, (4) quality of judgments, (5) ability to function without supervisor, (6) dependability, (7) ability to function under stress, (8) ability to get along with co-workers, (9) sociability, (10) ability to get along with supervisor, (11) enthusiasm for work, (12) absence of psychiatric symp-

---

[3] If it is desired that the matrix be refactored with improved communality estimates, these can be obtained by summing the squares of the three factor loadings for each test. For example, the new communality estimate for test 1 is $(.47)^2 + (.31)^2 + (.52)^2 = .59$, as compared with .54 which we used in Table 11.2.

toms, (13) employability, (14) maze performance. Extract three centroid factors from this matrix of intercorrelations:

	2	3	4	5	6	7	8	9	10	11	12	13	14
1	.59	.60	.67	.69	.55	.63	.21	.08	.35	.46	.40	.36	.21
2		.55	.45	.63	.62	.60	.19	.29	.25	.46	.41	.25	.21
3			.59	.72	.57	.61	.31	.23	.37	.32	.19	.34	.41
4				.68	.47	.54	.31	−.03	.41	.40	.32	.39	.30
5					.65	.65	.20	.06	.31	.35	.38	.38	.35
6						.66	.20	.19	.41	.49	.54	.36	.40
7							.15	.17	.35	.54	.51	.41	.39
8								.47	.74	.09	.15	.20	.18
9									.35	.24	.23	.36	.26
10										.28	.26	.34	.22
11											.59	.36	.22
12												.41	.28
13													.37

3. Below are given the tetrachoric intercorrelations among ten items measuring attitudes toward economic issues. Extract two centroid factors from this matrix. (*Note:* apply the reflection procedure *before* extraction of the first factor.)

	2	3	4	5	6	7	8	9	10
1	.12	.61	.60	.58	.51	−.39	−.02	−.47	−.52
2		−.03	.20	.25	.44	−.28	.04	−.22	−.20
3			.16	.21	.41	−.21	.19	−.18	−.42
4				.26	.52	−.51	.14	−.46	−.57
5					.64	−.16	.09	−.13	−.20
6						−.41	−.22	−.26	−.59
7							−.05	.25	.60
8								.49	.14
9									.33

12

GRAPHICAL ROTATION

OF FACTORS

It has now been shown that one can use the centroid method, described in the previous chapter, to assemble a factor matrix, **F**, in which the rows represent variables (e.g. tests) and the columns represent hypothetical factors. In the early days of factor analysis, an attempt was made to interpret the meaning of the factors in empirical terms. Factor analysis was first invented to deal with intelligence and aptitude tests, and it was found that the factors thus extracted were quite difficult to interpret. This situation led Thurstone in the early 1930's to formulate a principle called "simple structure." As applied to mental tests, this principle can be stated (Thurstone, 1947, p. 57), "In the interpretation of mind we assume that mental phenomena can be identified in terms of distinguishable functions, which do not all participate equally in everything that mind does." To illustrate the principle, Thurstone considered a hypothetical set of 20 different gymnastic stunts. He then said:

Let us suppose that some of the stunts require principally strength of the right arm, that others require principally a good sense of balance, that still others require speed of bodily movement. Several tests that require good sense of balance might not require arm strength, while those which require a strong arm might require very little bodily balance. We might then find that the correlations can be comprehended in terms of a small number of functional unities, such as sense of balance, arm strength, or speed of bodily movement. Each of the gymnastic tests might require one or several of these functional unities; *but it is not likely that every test will require every one of the functional unities* that are represented by the whole set of gymnastic tests (italics added).

In a certain sense, this postulate of simple structure is an extension of the assumption of the simplicity of nature. In Chapter 8 we discussed parsimony as one of the five basic criteria for theories in science. In factor extraction, we invoke parsimony by attempting to extract with each factor as much as possible of the total test variance and then ignoring the residuals when they become "sufficiently small." Now we shall be invoking parsimony again by "rotating"[1] the factors in such a way that the factorial composition of the tests with respect to these rotated factors is as simple as possible.

Thurstone (1947, p. 335) then suggested five more specific criteria for determining the appropriate rotations of the reference vectors to achieve simple structure for a given empirical problem. In the early 1950's several investigators independently formulated similar objective procedures for attaining simple structure as envisaged by these five criteria (see Chapter 13). However, during the preceding twenty years the empirical attempts to find simple structure had proceeded mainly by means of graphical rotations. The newer methods are sufficiently complex to preclude use by persons without access to an electronic computer, so there is a practical reason for most researchers to learn a graphical procedure of rotation. In any case, the explanation in geometrical terms aids most students considerably in understanding the issues involved in rotation.

Whichever method of factor extraction has been used, one employs the numerical values in the factor matrix as the starting point for rotation. For our example of nine aptitude tests, we now have the particular factor matrix shown in Table 12.1. (A sum row has been calculated for later checking purposes.) In our rotational procedure we shall follow Cattell's (1952, p. 193) suggestion and rechristen the factor matrix V_0, which emphasizes the fact that it is the "zero point" from which our subsequent rotations begin. The first rotated factor matrix will then be called V_1, the second rotated factor matrix, V_2, and so forth.

The first step is to plot diagrams representing the $n(n-1)/2$ pairs

[1] We shall use the word "rotate" in the sense in which the hands of a clock "rotate."

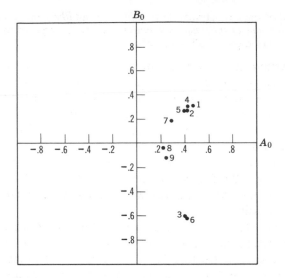

Figure 12.1   *AB* diagram for the unrotated centroid factors.

of *n* common factors.[2] In our example we have three common factors, so there are $3(3 - 1)/2$ diagrams to be plotted, that is, three diagrams. Letting *A*, *B*, and *C* represent the three factors, we shall need an *AB* diagram, an *AC* diagram, and a *BC* diagram. Each diagram will be analogous to that in Figure 10.3. in Chapter 10, but we shall not bother to draw the circle, and we shall draw only the point representing the terminus of each test vector, rather than the entire vector. The Cartesian coordinates of each point in a diagram represent the numbers in the factor matrix in the row corresponding to the particular test and in the two columns corresponding to the pair of factors being represented in the diagram. Figures 12.1, 12.2, and 12.3 represent our *AB* plot, *AC* plot, and *BC* plot, respectively. Consider the point for Test 7 in the *AC* plot. Its coordin-

[2] Each diagram represents a two-dimensional section of the *n*-dimensional space. The "streaks of points" that we shall be seeking identify "hyperplanes," which are orthogonal to the desired new reference vectors. In ordinary three-space the hyperplanes are actual planes; in two-space the hyperplanes are straight lines, which is how they appear in our two-dimensional sections. As a shorthand device, we shall henceforth refer to all of them as "planes" or "axes."

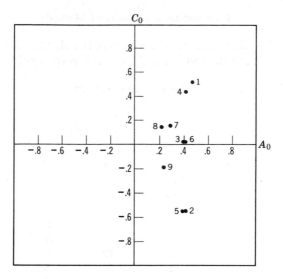

Figure 12.2 *AC* diagram for the unrotated centroid factors.

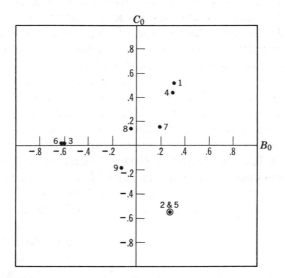

Figure 12.3 *BC* diagram for the unrotated centroid factors.

ates are .29 and .15 because the values in the A_0 and C_0 columns of our factor matrix for row 7 are .29 and .15, respectively.

Table 12.1 *Unrotated centroid factor matrix*

$$\mathbf{F} \equiv \mathbf{V}_0$$

	A_0	B_0	C_0
1	.47	.31	.52
2	.41	.28	−.55
3	.40	−.60	.02
4	.42	.30	.44
5	.40	.28	−.55
6	.41	−.61	.02
7	.29	.19	.15
8	.22	−.04	.14
9	.24	−.12	−.19
Σ	3.26	−.01	.00

If, according to the principle of simple structure, our factors are to be such that each test will not involve every one of the factors, some of the factor loadings should be zero or near zero. In fact, in graphical procedures the principle of simple structure has generally been interpreted to imply that the investigator should rotate in such a way as to maximize the number of zero or near-zero loadings. On page 113 we noted that, in the geometric representation, the loading of a test on a factor is the projection of the test vector on the corresponding reference vector. If the loading of a test on a factor is small, the corresponding point in one of our diagrams will be near to *the other* reference vector. In our example, consider the loading of Test 6 on factor C_0 (factor C before it has been rotated at all). From our factor matrix in Table 12.1, we see that the loading is .02. Note in our AC plot (Figure 12.2) that point 6 is quite close to the $\mathbf{A}_0$ vector, and note in our BC plot (Figure 12.3) that point 6 is quite close to the $\mathbf{B}_0$ vector.

If we were fortunate enough that, in plotting the tests directly from the columns of our unrotated factor matrix, we found that most of the test points were located near the reference axes (i.e., in the shape of a Christian cross), we would not need to do any rotating at all! However, unfortunately, Thurstone and others found that this situation rarely occurs with aptitude and achievement tests.[3] In fact, it is more often the case that most of the points fall rather centrally within the four quadrants of the factor plots; that is, the tests are "factorially complex" in terms of the original, unrotated factors. Therefore we rotate the reference vectors in such a way that more of the test points will fall near to the axes that are orthogonal to these vectors.

For each rotation our aim is to obtain a Λ matrix that represents a linear transformation of the original set of reference vectors to a new set of corresponding reference vectors. In our particular example, the first transformation matrix, Λ_{01}, will represent the transformation from reference vectors, A_0, B_0, and C_0, to a new set of reference vectors, A_1, B_1, and C_1. In fact, each entry in Λ_{01} represents the "direction cosine" of the angle between the two reference vectors representing the row and column of the particular entry. After drawing the new vectors, we could determine each entry in Λ_{01} by simply measuring the angle of rotation with a protractor, looking up the cosine in a table, and then writing the cosine in Λ_{01}. However, for oblique rotation it has been found more efficient and accurate to obtain the Λ matrix from two other, preceding matrices.

FIRST ROTATION

We proceed first to examine each plot to see if we can find a streak of points through which we can draw an axis radiating from the origin. In Figure 12.1, points 1, 4, 2, 5, and 7 constitute such a streak of points. Figure 12.4 is identical to Figure 12.1 except that a reference *axis* has been drawn through the points and a reference *vector*, which we shall call B_1', has been drawn *orthogonal* (at right angles) to the axis. In Figure 12.2, points 1, 4, 7, and 8 constitute a somewhat less well-defined streak of points, and in Figure 12.5 a reference axis has been drawn near to *these* points. Note that the reference vector A_1' is orthogonal to this second axis. We shall deal with A_1' first.

[3] There is now reason to believe that the main methods of factor extraction produce factors from temperament, interest, and attitude tests that are often directly interpretable without rotation. Thus the principle of simple structure might never have been formulated if psychologists had happened to analyze personality tests before ability tests!

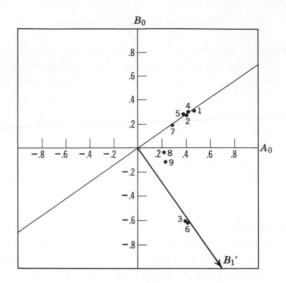

Figure 12.4 *AB* diagram for the unrotated centroid factors.

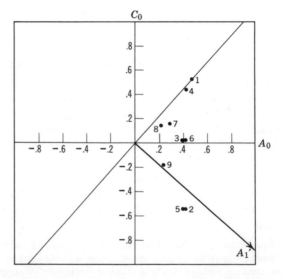

Figure 12.5 *AC* diagram for the unrotated centroid factors.

Note that A_1' has been drawn all the way to the edge of the diagram in Figure 12.5. The relation of the new reference vector to the two old reference vectors can be expressed by means of the vectorial equation,

$$A_1' = 1.00A_0 - .90C_0$$

In Figure 12.5 the coordinates of the terminus of vector A_1' (the arrow head) are 1.00 and $-.90$. Conceivably we could have chosen to call the new vector C_1' instead of A_1'; we prefer to call it A_1' simply because it is closer to A_0 than it is to C_0. In fact, we say that we have rotated vector A_0 to a new direction indicated by A_1'. It should be especially noted that, although we use the streak of points to locate a reference *axis* (or "reference plane," see the footnote on page 138), it is a reference *vector* orthogonal to it that we rotate!

Returning to the AB plot in Figure 12.4, we find that the coordinates of the terminus of the new vector are .70 and -1.00. Thus we write another vectorial equation,

$$B_1' = .70A_0 - 1.00B_0$$

The reader is probably wondering why we labeled this new vector B_1', inasmuch as it is closer to A_0 than it is to B_0. The reason is that we have already moved A_0 in the AC plane (see Figure 12.5), and in the early stages of rotation it is safer to move a vector in only one plane of rotation. Actually B_1' is close to the reflection of B_0, namely, $-B_0$.[4] Inspection of the BC plane in Figure 12.3 shows no particularly promising streak of points, so we decide to leave the C vector in its present position for this rotation, namely, C_0.

Table 12.2 shows the computational steps involved in actually performing the first rotation. The numerical values in our two vectorial equations are written in the cells of the first two *columns* of matrix S_{01}. The two entries of .00 indicate that A_1' is still orthogonal to B_0 and that B_1' is still orthogonal to C_0. The numbers in the third column of S_{01} indicate that C_1' is collinear with C_0 and orthogonal to both A_0 and B_0. In subsequent rotations we shall need

---

[4] The reader may further wonder why the new reference vector is not pointed in the opposite direction, that is, so that it is near to B_0. The reason is that this procedure would have produced many negative loadings, and most researchers think more easily in terms of positive than in terms of negative loadings.

to perform a matrix multiplication to obtain an **L** matrix corresponding to the **S** matrix. Fortunately, however, for the first rotation, the **L** and **S** matrices are identical.

Each column of L_{01} represents a "long reference vector." However, it can be seen in Figure 10.3 of Chapter 10 that the two-space containing the test vectors is a circle, that is, by definition, no test can have a communality exceeding unity. For convenience in reading from the graphs, we draw the new vector all the way to the edge of the square in which the circle is circumscribed. This procedure gives the desired *direction* of the new vector. However, we must then "normalize" the vector, that is, reduce it to unit length. To normalize a vector we multiply each of its coordinates by the reciprocal of the square root of the sum of squares of all the coordinates. The procedure is illustrated for the first rotation in Table 12.2. For the long reference vector A_1', we calculate

$$(1.00)^2 + (.00)^2 + (-.90)^2 = 1.8100$$

The square root of the sum is 1.345, and the reciprocal of 1.345 is .743. This reciprocal becomes a multiplier that is applied to each of the coordinates, 1.00, .00, and $-.90$, thus giving the values in the first column of Λ_{01}, .74, .00, and $-.67$. The latter three numbers are the cosines of the angles that the new *unit* reference vector, A_1 (without the prime), makes with the original reference vectors, A_0, B_0, and C_0. The reader can verify that, within the limits of rounding error, the sum of their squares equals unity.

The same procedure is applied to normalize the long reference vectors, B_1' and C_1', into unit reference vectors, B_1 and C_1, respectively. Since we did not rotate C_0 at all, C_1 is collinear with C_0, as is indicated by the value of 1.00 in the third row, third column of Λ_{01}.[5] For later checking purposes, we then form a sum row by adding down the columns, for example, $.07 = .74 + .00 - .67$.

The centroid process of extracting factors produces orthogonal factors (as do many of the other main methods of factor extraction). Some researchers prefer to keep the factors orthogonal during all the rotations. The rotational procedure being outlined in this chapter

---

[5] The normalization of the long vectors can also be written in terms of matrix algebra. Form a "diagonal matrix," D_1, in which the elements in the principal diagonal are the corresponding d_1 values, .743, .819, and 1.000, and *all* the other elements (the "offdiagonal elements") are zero. Then, $\Lambda_{01} = L_{01}D_1$.

involves the more general situation of "oblique factors," that is, factors that are *not* necessarily at right angles. However, the reader who prefers orthogonal factors can use exactly the same computational procedure that is being described herein; the procedure applies to both orthogonal and oblique factors.

Table 12.2 *Calculations for the First Rotation*

	$S_{01} = L_{01}$				$C_1 = \Lambda_{01}'\Lambda_{01}$		
	A_1'	B_1'	C_1'		A_1	B_1	C_1
A_0	1.00	.70	.00	A_1	1.00	.42	$-.67$
B_0	.00	-1.00	.00	B_1	.42	1.00	.00
C_0	$-.90$	.00	1.00	C_1	$-.67$	.00	1.00

	A_1'	B_1'	C_1'
Σl^2	1.8100	1.4900	1.0000
$\sqrt{\Sigma l^2}$	1.345	1.221	1.000
d_1	.743	.819	1.000

	$\Lambda_{01} = L_{01}D_1$		
	A_1	B_1	C_1
A_0	.74	.57	.00
B_0	.00	$-.82$	.00
C_0	$-.67$	.00	1.00
Σ	.07	$-.25$	1.00

	$V_1 = V_0\Lambda_{01}$		
	A_1	B_1	C_1
1	.00	.01	.52
2	.67	.00	$-.55$
3	.28	.72	.02
4	.02	$-.01$	.44
5	.66	.00	$-.55$
6	.29	.73	.02
7	.11	.01	.15
8	.07	.16	.14
9	.30	.24	$-.19$
Σ	2.40	1.86	$-.02$
Ch	2.41	1.87	.00

Our new vectors, A_1, B_1, and C_1, are not mutually orthogonal, as was the case with A_0, B_0, and C_0. It is important that we determine the cosines of the angles that do obtain between them because we shall henceforth be plotting our diagrams *as though the factors actually were orthogonal*. Since we shall therefore have no visual cues of their angular relationships, we must be careful not to "lose a factor" by rotating a pair of factors too close to each other. To help avoid such a situation, we calculate a "cosine matrix" for each rotation. For the first rotation such a matrix is designated C_1 and is calculated by premultiplying the rotation matrix Λ_{01} by its own transpose. If the reader will write out the transpose of Λ_{01} in front of the matrix itself and write down the numbers involved in the multiplications, he will find that *pre*multiplying a matrix by its transpose essentially involves multiplying (finding the inner product of) the pairs of *columns* of the matrix. This produces a cosine matrix that is "symmetric about the principal diagonal." For example, the entry in the first row and third column of C_1 is identical to the entry in the third row and first column of C_1, and each is calculated by multiplying the first and third *columns* of Λ_{01}:

$$(.74)(.00) + (.00)(.00) + (-.67)(1.00) = .00 + .00 - .67 = -.67$$

Matrix C_1 shows the cosines of the angles between the new vectors, A_1, B_1, and C_1.[6] Since the correlation between two vectors equals the product of the lengths of the vectors times the cosine of their angular separation (see page 113), and since the reference vectors are, by definition, of unit length, matrix C_1 also gives the *correlations* between the new vectors. The diagonal entries represent multiplications of each column of Λ_{01} by itself, which operation corresponds to obtaining the sum of squares of the values in each column. As was stated above, these should all be unity, within the limits of rounding error. Looking at the matter geometrically, we conclude that any vector must be collinear with itself! Therefore the angle involved should be zero, and its cosine is unity.

Although there is no absolute cutting point, it is probably well that no cosine should exceed .70 in absolute value. After our first rotation we have one value of $-.67$ (between A_1 and C_1); therefore we should try in subsequent rotations to decrease this value somewhat. Often the cosine for each pair of reference vectors is indicated directly on the diagram, as we have done in Figures 12.6, 12.7, and 12.8. (These diagrams are obtained by plotting the three possible pairs of columns of V_1, which we shall soon be calculating.) The *BC* plot still involves orthogonal factors, but now the *AB* and *AC* plots show correlated factors.

We are now ready to calculate the first set of rotated factor load-

---

[6] There is also a procedure for checking calculation of the cosine matrix. Form a sum *column* to the right of the third column of Λ_{01}. Multiplication of this sum column by each other column of Λ_{01} gives a check column for the C matrix. This should be checked against an actual sum column formed by summing the rows of the C matrix.

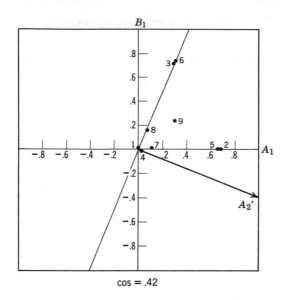

$\cos = .42$

Figure 12.6 *AB* diagram for the first rotated factors.

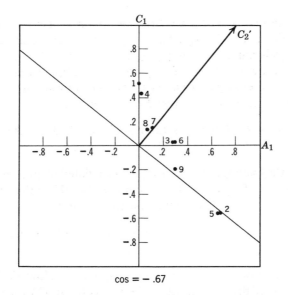

$\cos = -.67$

Figure 12.7 *AC* diagram for the first rotated factors.

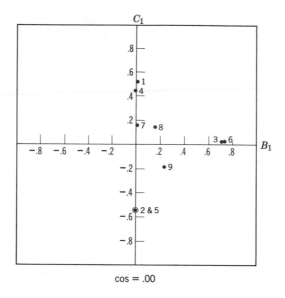

$$\cos = .00$$

Figure 12.8 *BC* diagram for the first rotated factors.

ings. In terms of matrix algebra, we obtain a new matrix, V_1, by postmultiplying V_0 by Λ_{01}. The entry in the jth row and kth column of V_1 is calculated by multiplying the jth row of V_0, the premultiplier, by the kth column of Λ_{01}, the postmultiplier (see page 108). Consider, for example, the entry in the third row and first column of V_1, that is, the loading of Test 3 on vector A_1:

$$(.40)(.74) + (-.60)(.00) + (.02)(-.67) = .2960 - .0000 - .0134$$
$$= .28$$

First, the loadings on vector A_1 are calculated by in turn multiplying each row of V_0 by the first column of Λ_{01}. Then the sum row of V_0 is *likewise* multiplied by the first column of Λ_{01}:

$$(3.26)(.74) + (-.01)(.00) + (.00)(-.67) = 2.4124 - .0000 - .0000$$
$$= 2.41$$

This value of 2.41 is entered in a *check row* below V_1. Then the actual sum of the nine values in the first column of V_1 is calculated to be 2.40. The two values agree within the limits of rounding error, so we conclude that the calculated loadings of the nine tests on vector A_1 are probably correct. Then we obtain the loadings on vector B_1 by multiplying in turn each row of V_0 by the *second* column of Λ_{01}. After checking these results, we proceed to calculate the nine loadings on vector C_1 and then to check them. Now we have completed the calculation of V_1, which is the matrix of loadings on the first set of rotated factors.

The pairs of columns of V_1 have been plotted in the diagrams of Figures 12.6, 12.7, and 12.8. Before proceeding with the second rotation, it is instructive to examine these diagrams to see if our first rotation has accomplished approximately what we want it to. In Figure 12.4 we drew a line through points 1, 4, 2, 5, and 7; this was done because we wanted these test vectors to appear in the plane orthogonal to the new *B* vector. In the new *AB* plot (Figure 12.6), note that these five test points are indeed in the plane orthogonal to B_1, although not in the same order. Similarly, in Figure 12.5 the plane orthogonal to the new *A* vector comes close to test vectors 1, 4, 7, and 8; in Figure 12.7 the corresponding points appear close to the plane orthogonal to A_1. It should not be reemphasized that, although the points serve to identify a reference plane, it is a reference vector orthogonal to it that we rotate.

SECOND ROTATION

Again we inspect the three diagrams to try to locate streaks of points. (To save space, the new reference vectors for the second rotation have been drawn directly on Figures 12.6, 12.7, and 12.8. However, at first each new set of diagrams will appear only with the axes and the points, as in Figures 12,1, 12.2, and 12.3.) On the *AB* plot a line has been drawn near to points 6, 3, and 8, and the vector orthogonal to it is designated A_2'. On the *AC* plot a line has been drawn near to points 2, 5, and 9, and the vector orthogonal to *it* is called C_2'. To indicate the transformation from the first to the second reference frames, we form a matrix S_{12} (see Table 12.3). The coordinates of the arrow head in Figure 12.6 give us the values to enter in the first column of S_{12}. The entry .00 in the third row and first column indicates that in this rotation we are not moving the *A* vector in the *AC* plane. Whenever a vector is not rotated, unity is entered in the diagonal cell and zeros are entered in the other cells of the corresponding column of the S matrix. Note in Table 12.3 that this procedure has been followed for vector B_2' in matrix S_{12}. The third column of S_{12} is filled in by noting the coordinates of the arrow head in Figure 12.7.[7]

Although it is possible to rotate directly between the successive reference frames (Deuel, 1956; Baggaley, 1960a), in the procedure that is being described in this book, each new reference frame must be referred back to the original frame determined by the particular method of factor extraction. To do so, we first calculate matrix L_{02} and then matrix Λ_{02}. These matrices show relationships between the second reference frame and the original reference frame (hence the numerical subscripts). Matrix L_{02} is calculated by postmultiplying Λ_{01} by S_{12}. Note that the second subscript of the premultiplier is identical to the first subscript of the postmultiplier and that neither appears as a subscript of the product matrix; the subscripts of the product matrix are, successively, the first subscript of the premultiplier and the second subscript of the postmultiplier. After each row of Λ_{01} is multiplied by the columns of S_{12}, we multiply the sum row by these columns to obtain three check values; for example, the third check value, 1.06, is obtained:

$$(.07)(.80) + (-.25)(.00) + (1.00)(1.00) = .0056 - .0000 + 1.0000$$
$$= 1.06$$

Then the actual sums of the calculated columns of L_{02} are obtained. The actual sum involved in our example above is

$$.59 + .00 + .46 = 1.05$$

If these actual sums are sufficiently close to the check sums, we then proceed to normalize the new long reference vectors by calculating the reciprocal of the square root of the sum of squares for each column of L_{02}. Each of the d_2 values thus obtained is applied as a multiplier to the corresponding column of L_{02}, which then gives a corresponding column of Λ_{02}. The entries in Λ_{02} show the direction cosines of the new vectors, A_2, B_2, and C_2, with reference to

[7] It is possible (though not advisable for beginners!) to rotate a vector in more than one plane of rotation at a time; see Thurstone (1947, pp. 207–210).

the *original* centroid vectors, A_0, B_0, and C_0.[8] A sum row is now formed for Λ_{02} so that the calculation of L_{03} can be checked during the third rotation.

Table 12.3   *Calculations for the Second Rotation*

	S_{12}			$C_2 = \Lambda_{02}{}'\Lambda_{02}$			
	$A_2{}'$	$B_2{}'$	$C_2{}'$		A_2	B_2	C_2
A_1	1.00	.00	.80	A_2	.99	.02	−.02
B_1	−.40	1.00	.00	B_2	.02	1.00	.45
C_1	.00	.00	1.00	C_2	−.02	.45	1.01

	$L_{02} = \Lambda_{01}S_{12}$			$V_2 = V_0\Lambda_{02}$			
	$A_2{}'$	$B_2{}'$	$C_2{}'$		A_2	B_2	C_2
A_0	.51	.57	.59	1	−.01	.01	.69
B_0	.33	−.82	.00	2	.74	.00	−.02
C_0	−.67	.00	.46	3	−.01	.72	.33
				4	.02	−.01	.60
Σ	.17	−.25	1.05	5	.73	.00	−.02
Ch	.17	−.25	1.06	6	.00	.73	.34
				7	.12	.01	.32
Σl^2	.8179	.9973	.5597	8	.00	.16	.26
$\sqrt{\Sigma l^2}$	.904	.999	.748	9	.23	.24	.07
d_2	1.106	1.001	1.337				
				Σ	1.82	1.86	2.57
				Ch	1.82	1.87	2.58

	$\Lambda_{02} = L_{02}D_2$		
	A_2	B_2	C_2
A_0	.56	.57	.79
B_0	.36	−.82	.00
C_0	−.74	.00	.62
Σ	.18	−.25	1.41

The cosine matrix for our second rotation, C_2, is shown in Table 12.3. Two of the diagonal values differ slightly from unity, but this situation is due to rounding error and should cause no concern. The other entries are generally lower (in absolute value) than the corre-

[8] These relationships can be seen vividly if the reference vectors are plotted on a blackboard sphere (Thurstone, 1947, Chapter 7). Then the cosines can be read from a specially constructed measuring scale.

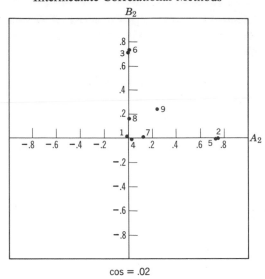

Figure 12.9 *AB* diagram for the second (and third) rotated factors.

sponding values in C_1. In rotating on the *AC* plot (Figure 12.7) we moved the *C* vector *toward* the *A* vector, thus decreasing the amount of *negative* correlation between them. Similarly, on the *AB* plot (Figure 12.6), we moved the *A* vector *away from* the *B* vector, thus decreasing the amount of *positive* correlation between *them*. The cost of these gains was the introduction of a .45 correlation between *B* and *C*; however, in general the vectors are closer to orthogonality after the second rotation than they were after the first. In rotation the researcher should concern himself with the angles between the reference vectors as well as searching for streaks of points.

We are now ready to calculate the second rotated factor matrix, V_2, by postmultiplying the original centroid factor matrix, V_0, by the second transformation matrix, Λ_{02}. The calculated values are shown in Table 12.3. Again we check by also multiplying the sum row of V_0 by the three columns of Λ_{02}. Then the three pairs of columns of V_2 are plotted in two-dimensional sections as shown in Figures 12.9, 12.10, and 12.11. It can be noted that the *AB* and *AC* plots already are close to the configuration of two arms of a Christian cross, which was our goal.

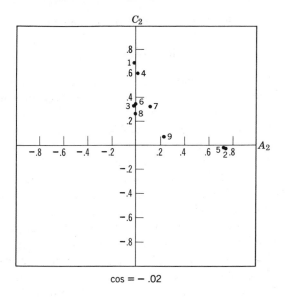

$\cos = -.02$

Figure 12.10 *AC* diagram for the second rotated factors.

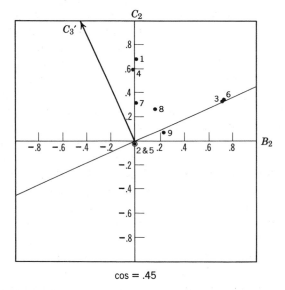

$\cos = .45$

Figure 12.11 *BC* diagram for the second rotated factors.

THIRD ROTATION

However, on the BC plot we notice a streak of points formed by Tests 6, 3, and 9. On Figure 12.11 a line has been drawn near this streak, and the long reference vector, C_3', has been drawn orthogonal to it. The C vector is the only one of the three reference vectors that we move during the third rotation. In matrix S_{23} (see Table 12.4) the A and B columns show the standard pattern indicating that these vectors are to be left in the same position for the particular rotation. The entry, $-.45$, is read from the coordinates of the arrow head in Figure 12.11. To obtain the relationships between the new long reference vectors and the original centroid vectors, L_{03} is calculated by postmultiplying Λ_{02} by S_{23}. Then these long vectors are normalized by obtaining the multipliers, d_3, and applying each to the corresponding column of L_{03}, thus giving us the three columns of Λ_{03}. The third cosine matrix, C_3, is obtained from the inner products of the columns of Λ_{03}, and we find to our delight that our three reference vectors are now virtually orthogonal! The third rotated factor matrix, V_3, is computed by postmultiplying V_0 by Λ_{03}.

Perhaps the reader has already noticed that, when a reference vector is *not* moved during a rotation, the corresponding column of the transformation matrix is identical to that of the preceding transformation matrix. For example, compare the A_3 column of Λ_{03} with the A_2 column of Λ_{02}. This means that the investigator (after acquiring some experience so that he will not become confused) can omit the corresponding column of the L matrix. Furthermore, the corresponding column of the rotated factor matrix is identical to that of the preceding rotated factor matrix, for example, compare the A_3 column of V_3 with the A_2 column of V_2. This circumstance makes theoretical sense; since we have not rotated the reference vector, the projections of the test vectors on it should remain invariant. (However, the investigator should not omit the relevant column of the Λ matrix because this is needed for obtaining the cosine matrix.)

The AC and BC plots for the third rotation appear in Figures 12.12 and 12.13; the AB plot in Figure 12.9 can serve us again because these two reference vectors were not moved during the third rotation. All three plots now show a configuration close to the desired model. Correspondingly, there are many zero or near-zero loadings

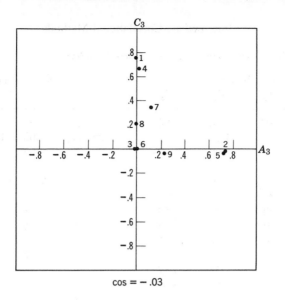

$$\cos = -.03$$

Figure 12.12 *AC* diagram for the third rotated factors.

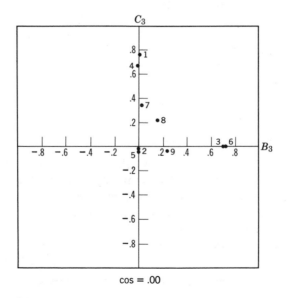

$$\cos = .00$$

Figure 12.13 *BC* diagram for the third rotated factors.

Table 12.4 *Calculations for the Third Rotation*

| | S_{23} | | | | $C_3 = \Lambda_{03}{}'\Lambda_{03}$ | | |
	A_3'	B_3'	C_3'		A_3	B_3	C_3
A_2	1.00	.00	.00	A_3	.99	.02	−.03
B_2	.00	1.00	−.45	B_3	.02	1.00	.00
C_2	.00	.00	1.00	C_3	−.03	.00	.99

| | $L_{03} = \Lambda_{02}S_{23}$ | | | | $V_3 = V_0\Lambda_{03}$ | | |
	A_3'	B_3'	C_3'		A_3	B_3	C_3
A_0	.56	.57	.53	1	−.01	.01	.76
B_0	.36	−.82	.37	2	.74	.00	−.02
C_0	−.74	.00	.62	3	−.01	.72	.00
				4	.02	−.01	.67
Σ	.18	−.25	1.52	5	.73	.00	−.03
Ch	.18	−.25	1.52	6	.00	.73	.00
				7	.12	.01	.35
Σl^2	.9908	.9973	.8022	8	.00	.16	.21
$\sqrt{\Sigma l^2}$	.995	.999	.896	9	.23	.24	−.04
d_3	1.005	1.001	1.116				
				Σ	1.82	1.86	1.90
				Ch	1.82	1.87	1.92

| | $\Lambda_{03} = L_{03}D_3$ | | |
	A_3	B_3	C_3
A_0	.56	.57	.59
B_0	.36	−.82	.41
C_0	−.74	.00	.69
Σ	.18	−.25	1.69

in V_3. At this point, however, we should repeat the warning from page 118 that this example has purposely been constructed to illustrate the principles of simple structure with a minimal number of rotations and that in real-life problems nature is not so obliging! Actually a "good simple structure" is not likely to be found when fewer than 20 variables are involved in the analysis.

INTERPRETATION OF FACTORS

We are now ready for the most interesting part of a factor analysis, interpretation of the factors. This is necessarily an inductive and somewhat subjective process. To aid us the final rotated factor matrix has been reproduced in Table 12.5 along with the titles of the nine tests. The reader should now turn back to page 119 and reread the descriptions of the tests. We shall examine each column of the factor matrix and try to imagine a theoretical construct that would involve the few tests highly loaded on the factor and that would *not* involve the several other tests. The reader can now perceive the great advantage of the simple structure criterion for interpretation of factors. Unrotated factors often tend to be loaded by half or more than half of the variables involved in the study.

Table 12.5 *Final Rotated Factor Matrix and the Artificial Factor Matrix*

Test	A_3	V_3 B_3	C_3	Artificial Factor Matrix		
1. Addition	−.01	.01	.76	.90	.00	.00
2. Cubes	.74	.00	−.02	.00	.80	.00
3. Spelling	−.01	.72	.00	.00	.00	.70
4. Multiplication	.02	−.01	.67	.60	.00	.00
5. Flags	.73	.00	−.03	.00	.70	.00
6. Vocabulary	.00	.73	.00	.00	.00	.80
7. Block Counting	.12	.01	.35	.30	.10	.00
8. Arithmetic Reasoning	.00	.16	.21	.20	.00	.10
9. Syllogisms	.23	.24	−.04	.00	.20	.20

It can readily be seen that each factor strongly involves two of the tests. Tests 2 and 5 are strongly loaded on Factor A; Tests 3 and 6 are strongly loaded on Factor B; and Tests 1 and 4 are strongly loaded on Factor C. It seems apparent from the test descriptions that Factor A is some kind of "spatial" factor, Factor B is a verbal factor, and Factor C is a numerical factor. Of special interest, however, are the small loadings of Tests 7, 8, and 9 on the factors. The loadings of Test 7 on Factor A, Test 9 on Factor B, and Test 8 on Factor C are not difficult to explain. After all, the Block Counting test uses geometric figures for content, the Syllogisms test uses words, and the Arithmetic Reasoning test uses numbers. However, an arithmetic reasoning test (as opposed to a test involving only computations, that is, where the problem has already been "set up") also uses verbal content. This tends to make plausible the small loading of Test 8 on Factor B[9]. Block *counting* necessarily involves numbers; hence the small loading of Test 7 on Factor C. Most interesting of all is the loading of the Syllogisms test on the spatial factor. Many examinees who introspect while performing on this particular test report that they are aided in solving these problems by imagining a spatial placement of the three names. In the example cited on page 119, a spatial placement could be imagined in which Smith is on top, Jones is on the bottom, and Brown is in the middle. Then it is easy to "see" that Smith cannot be below (i.e., younger than) Jones. Thus a psychometric investigator should not depend completely on his own analysis of what a test should involve. Particularly in reasoning-type problems, the human organism seems to be particularly flexible in that, finding that his usual techniques of problem solution do not work, he will try any method he can think of, no matter how bizarre!

At this point, we shall "let the cat out of the bag" by remarking that the correlation matrix with which we started our analysis (see page 119) was artificially constructed by postmultiplying the factor matrix shown in Table 12.5 by its own transpose (see page 109). The reader should now compare our final rotated factor matrix, V_3, with this matrix. Although the numbers are not identical, the same general *pattern* of loadings is visible in the two matrices. (The order of the columns is not important, for we interpret each column of the rotated factor matrix independently.) Thus it has been demonstrated that it is possible by the methods of factor extraction and rotation outlined above to recover a factor matrix that was artificially constructed to involve a "simple structure."

Problems

1. If we were rotating eight common factors, how many diagrams would be needed for each rotation?

2. Draw a set of orthogonal reference vectors on a sheet of graph paper. Then draw a new set of *unit* vectors that represent a rotation of 30° in the counterclockwise direction from each of the original vectors. (Thus the new vectors are also orthogonal.) Measure the projections of the new vectors on the old vectors, and write these values in a 2×2 transformation

---

[9] Guilford's analyses (Guilford et al., 1954) suggest that arithmetic reasoning tests also load highly on a "general reasoning factor."

matrix. Which trigonometric functions of the angle of rotation do these projections represent?

3. Below are given, for a problem involving 10 variables and 3 factors, the V_0, Λ_{02}, and S_{23} matrices. For the third rotation, calculate the L_{03}, Λ_{03}, C_3, and V_3 matrices.

	V_0				Λ_{02}		
	A_0	B_0	C_0		A_2	B_2	C_2
1	.37	−.36	−.32	A_0	.82	.00	.00
2	.20	.54	−.20	B_0	−.56	.86	−.56
3	.44	−.64	−.24	C_0	−.05	.51	.83
4	.50	−.40	−.25				
5	.72	−.19	.31				
6	.74	−.11	.26			S_{23}	
7	.37	.42	.50		A_3'	B_3'	C_3'
8	.18	.44	.56	A_2	1.00	.00	.54
9	.56	.37	.26	B_2	.36	1.00	.00
10	.51	−.13	.17	C_2	.00	.00	−1.00

4. Bell (1955) intercorrelated 7 demographic variables over 570 census tracts in the Los Angeles area and computed the factor loadings shown below. He then applied the transformation matrix also shown below. Calculate his rotated factor loadings.

Centroid factor matrix

	A_0	B_0	C_0
Occupation	.89	.08	−.23
Education	.78	.51	.09
Rent	.69	.39	−.36
Fertility	.91	−.19	.09
Women in the labor force	.65	−.56	−.18
Single-family dwelling units	.48	−.64	.06
Subordinate ethnic groups	.46	.45	.44

Transformation matrix

	A_1	B_1	C_1
A_0	.28	.41	.14
B_0	.35	−.79	.18
C_0	− 89	.46	.98

13

FRONTIERS
IN FACTOR ANALYSIS

In the previous two chapters the most frequently used method of factor extraction and of factor rotation have each been described. In the present chapter a brief description will be given of some alternative methods. In addition, some topics of special interest in factor analysis will be discussed. The purpose is to give the reader who wishes to pursue the factor analytic approach more thoroughly some leads and references.

OTHER METHODS OF FACTOR EXTRACTION

A relatively simple method of factor extraction is the *diagonal method* (Thurstone, 1947, Chapter 4). In this method the first reference vector is chosen so as to be collinear with one of the test vectors. Then the second reference vector is placed orthogonal to the first reference vector and in the plane spanned by two of the test vectors; the third reference vector is placed orthogonal to the first two, and so forth. Although the calculations are rather simple, the diagonal method has the limitation that the successive choices of tests on which to pivot is rather arbitrary, and thus the process of communality estimation is hazardous.

Another method that is computationally simpler than the centroid method is the *multiple-group method* (Thurstone, 1947, pp. 170–175). In this method all the factors are extracted simultaneously, so ordinarily only one set of residuals is calculated. The investigator selects several groups of variables in each of which the variables show high intercorrelations, and then he obtains a centroid for each group. The relationships between the group centroids are then ascertained. An immediately apparent limitation of this method is that the variables that the investigator is using must show some fairly tight clusters in terms of intercorrelations. Since factor analysis is often used in situations where the researcher has relatively little advance knowledge of the domain (see Chapter 8), this requirement may be difficult to fulfill. Also the method of communality estimation is not as efficient as in the "complete centroid method."

In recent years two other factor extraction techniques involving "iterative" procedures have been used extensively, that is, a set of operations is repeated until some criterion of convergence is reached. Therefore, except in problems involving less than, say, ten variables, these methods require use of an electronic computer. The *principal-axes method* was invented early in this century by Pearson and later rediscovered by Hotelling (1933) and Kelley (1935). The essential feature of the method is that each factor successively extracts as much variance as possible from the variables, that is, the residuals are as small as possible after each factor is extracted. This is a very desirable feature of a method of factor extraction because, in a sense, it provides the most "complete" factoring of the correlation matrix. Kelley's procedure, which deals with all the factors simultaneously, has proved to be more practical for programming electronic computers. However, Hotelling's procedure, which extracts one factor at a time, is usually more feasible for those without access to an electronic computer. Furthermore, it often turns out that the first few factors are all that are of either statistical or practical significance anyway. A brief outline of Hotelling's procedure is given on page 202 of the Appendix. Parenthetically, it is interesting to note that Thurstone (1947, pp. 473–480) developed still another procedure for calculation of the principal axes and that he regarded the centroid method as a temporary approximation to the principal axes (1947, pp. 149, 509).

Building on earlier work by Lawley, Rao (1955) developed a *maximum-likelihood method* of factor extraction (also called "canonical factor analysis"). In this method the correlation between the observed and hypothetical variables is maximized. The great advantage of this method is that, after extraction of each factor, a statistical test is available to determine whether the residuals represent more than random sampling variation.[1] Thus the investigator does not need to exercise his personal judgment about when the residuals are "sufficiently small" (see page 134)! However, the complexity of this method makes it even less feasible for desk calculators than the principal-axes method.

OTHER METHODS OF FACTOR ROTATION

The major objection to the graphical method has been its subjectivity. Different researchers may draw rather different conclusions about the factorial composition of the same correlation matrix (e.g., Couch and Keniston, 1961, versus Edwards and Walker, 1961). Therefore, over the past few decades, several attempts were made to develop "analytic" methods, that is, methods by which every computer would obtain identical results. Some of these suggested rotational methods were "semianalytic" in that a group of variables must first be selected subjectively, but after this decision all calculations are automatic. Thurstone himself developed some of them (1947, Chapter 17; 1954).

Then in the early 1950's three groups of researchers independently formulated completely analytic rotational methods that turned out to be closely related (Carroll, 1953; Neuhaus and Wrigley, 1954; Saunders, 1961). At about the same time Ferguson (1954) developed the same point of view from a logical consideration of the concept of parsimony. The four formulations are equivalent under orthogonal rotation. Since one of these approaches involves maximization of the factor loadings raised to the fourth power, the term "quartimax criterion" has been used in describing all of them. The aim is to obtain rotated matrices with a maximal tendency to have both large and small loadings.

Kaiser (1958), a student of Wrigley, then proposed a modification.

---

[1] Kaiser (1960, pp. 144–146) has suggested, on grounds *other than* those of statistical significance, that all the factors of an observed correlation matrix be considered that involve "latent roots" of greater than unity.

He pointed out that the quartimax criterion tends to simplify the *rows* of the factor matrix—the variables—and that it often produces a general factor. Kaiser formulated a "varimax criterion" that simplifies the *columns* of the factor matrix—the factors themselves. A further modification called the "normal varimax criterion" seems to be emerging as the most popular analytic method of rotation. Kaiser showed that this method gives a solution that tends to be invariant under changes in the composition of the test battery, thus accomplishing Thurstone's original aim in developing the concept of simple structure (1947, p. 361). Yet again, unfortunately, the computations are so complex that an electronic computer is requisite for use of the method. Hence the graphical method described in Chapter 12 will undoubtedly continue for several years to be of practical use in many problems.

In concluding this section, we should remark that the methods of rotation are independent of the methods of factor extraction, for example, principal axes factors could be rotated graphically, or by the quartimax criterion, or by the varimax criterion. Furthermore, it may often be desirable to perform further graphical rotations after an analytic rotation has been initially performed on a factor matrix (Cattell and Dickman, 1962).

CHOICE OF VARIABLES IN A FACTOR ANALYSIS

In many problems facing behavioral scientists, the researcher finds himself with many more variables than he can possibly factor analyze with existing computational apparatus. Hence, he desires to select a smaller group of variables. On which bases should he make his selection? In this section we shall try to outline some general principles that may be of aid in selecting variables for a factor analysis. This problem has previously been discussed by Guilford (1952) in an article entitled "When Not to Factor Analyze"; however, the point of view of the present author is not as pessimistic!

First, the investigator should try to avoid putting into a factor analysis variables that are "dependent." At least two types of dependence can be theoretically distinguished, although they tend to covary in practice. We shall say that "mathematical dependence" exists whenever there is a simple mathematical relationship between two variables. A frequent example of mathematical dependence is the inclusion of a total score in correlational analysis along with its component part scores, for example, the Wechsler Full-scale IQ as well as the Verbal IQ and Performance IQ. If the number of part scores is small, this procedure will usually generate a factor strongly involving only these particular scores, because the full-scale IQ is necessarily correlated with the other two IQ scores.

Another instance of mathematical dependence occurs when some of the items of a test are scored on more than one variable, for example, in the Strong Vocational Interest Blank and the Minnesota Multiphasic Personality Inventory. As with total and part scores, this situation often produces factors that largely involve the particular items, especially if the degree of overlap is considerable.

A special instance of mathematical dependence is use of "ipsative scores." As generally interpreted, these are scores for a person expressed relative to his own average (and sometimes also his variability) over a series of traits or occasions. When the scoring system of a test is such that, if a person scores high on some traits he must score low on other traits, then the scores are ipsative. Often in such tests the examinee is confronted with "forced-choice items," such as in the Kuder Preference Record and the Edwards Personal Preference Schedule. Guilford advises that ipsative scores should not be factor analyzed at all! The present author believes that this admonition is too restrictive and that much useful information has been derived from analyses of tests like the Kuder and the Edwards. However, it is certainly true that one must be considerably more cautious in interpreting factors from ipsative variables, especially when the number of variables thus analyzed is small. It must be kept in mind that it is mathematically necessary that a high proportion of the correlations between ipsative variables be negative.

If two scores are derived from the same physical performance, even though they do not show a direct mathematical relationship, they are probably "experimentally dependent." An example is the taking of both speed and accuracy scores from a single performance. Thus in any testing situation in which more than one score is taken, there will be extraneous sources of variance that tend to make the measures show spuriously high correlations. In this case we are dealing with *correlated* errors of measurement rather than *random* errors of measurement (see page 75).

Particularly in investigations of personality, a researcher will often administer five or more pencil-and-paper tests, each of which yields several scores. In planning a factor analysis, he should select only two or three variables from each test so that he can avoid the appearance of factors, each of which represents only the scores from a single testing instrument. If one of his tests involves a total score and its component parts, he should select either only the total score or only some of its parts, but not both!

Granting that some of the scores from a particular test should be eliminated, how should the investigator make this choice? Here he can be guided by some of the same principles that are relevant in multiple correlation (see Chapter 5). Scores should be selected that show relatively little correlation with the other scores from the *same* testing instrument but (if possible) show high correlations with the scores from *other* testing instruments. This procedure tends to generate factors that cut across testing instruments and are therefore more likely to aid, for example, in the development of sociological constructs rather than "mere mathematical artifacts." Campbell and Fiske (1959) treated a closely related topic in their discussion of the "multitrait-multimethod matrix."

Further reduction of the number of variables in a factor analysis can be made after the computations are begun. Variables that show very low intercorrelations with all the other variables (say, between $+.15$ and $-.15$) should be eliminated because they will contribute little to definition of the factors. Similarly, after the process of factor extraction has been accomplished, variables whose communalities are quite low can be eliminated for the same reason (Thurstone, 1947, pp. 334–335).

Q TECHNIQUE AND OTHER VARIANTS

All the foregoing discussion has assumed that we are correlating *between stimuli* (*e.g., tests*) *over persons*. In the 1930's Burt and Stephenson considered the possibility of correlating *between persons over stimuli*. This approach has come to be called "*Q* technique" as opposed to the more traditional "*R* technique." Stephenson (1953), in particular, has claimed many unique advantages for *Q* technique and in fact has attempted to build an entire philosophy of behavioral science from it. Cattell (1952, p. 109) added the time variable and drew a "covariation chart" from which six different "techniques" can be derived. Coan (1961) extended the system even further to include 24 different techniques, but it seems likely that only Q technique and P technique will find much application in behavioral science.

It has been claimed that Q technique produces factors of personality that are different in nature from those produced by R technique (Block, 1955; Broverman, 1961). Although these arguments seem plausible, more empirical evidence is needed on the problem. Part of the difference seems to depend on whether the scores that are correlated are ipsative scores. The term "person" has been interpreted broadly to include different aspects of a single person, for example, the client's "real self" versus his "ideal self," as in the work of Rogers and his students (Rogers and Dymond, 1954). A practical advantage of using Q instead of R is that it is often easier to obtain a large number of tests (or test items) than a large number of persons for research purposes. However, this point indicates a corresponding disadvantage of Q technique, namely, in any tests of statistical inference, generalization must be to a universe of content rather than to a population of persons (Cattell, 1952, p. 102). Furthermore, whereas for constitution of a population a person is an indivisible unit easily defined, there is no correspondingly unambiguous unit for constitution of a universe of content. A third disadvantage is that a factor that loads, say, John, Joe, and Bill, is not easy to interpret unless we turn back to the tests or stimuli, whereas a factor that loads certain tests can usually be interpreted without further reference to the specific persons who took the tests. However, we can hardly agree with Beck (1953) and Stephenson in their arguments for Q technique that R technique constitutes "psychology without a subject."

In P technique, the correlation is *between stimuli over time*. Thus it is similar to the study of time series by economists (Anderson, 1963). Probably the most direct application of P technique in behavioral science is to physiological variables. As was discussed in Chapter 6 in connection with temporal reliability, we expect these variables to change over hours, days, or months, whereas psychological traits, by definition, are more stable. Another application of P technique is in the study of demographic variables over time (Cattell and Adelson, 1951).

CONCLUDING REMARKS

In our discussion of construct validity in Chapter 6, we claimed that factor analysis is probably the most elegant method presently available for finding out what a variable "really" measures. The reader has undoubtedly concluded by this time that factor analysis is not as exact a scientific procedure as many used in the physical sciences. It finds its greatest utility in the borderline areas of science (Thurstone, 1947, pp. 56–57). It seems particularly well suited to some of the less exact areas of behavioral science, for example, social psychology as opposed to experimental psychology. Furthermore, these remarks apply to correlational techniques in general. It is hoped that this book will inspire many readers who have little interest in mathematics for its own sake to learn some of the correlational methods so that they can more efficiently attack the challenging problems in the area of behavioral science. Readers who have a knowledge of calculus may wish to consider more advanced aspects of multivariate analysis, for example in books by Harman (1960) and Rao (1952).

Problems

1. Which areas of test content are most favorable for application of the multiple-group method of factor extraction?

2. Explain how a factor could have statistical significance but not practical significance.

3. Why is a rotational method that tends to produce a general factor inconvenient for the purposes of personnel guidance and classification?

4. Why would it be undesirable to correlate IQ scores with scores on the "educational quotient" ("educational age" as measured by an achievement test divided by chronological age)?

5. If, in a column of a factor matrix, there are loadings of substantial magnitude and with both positive and negative algebraic sign, the factor is called "bipolar." Why do ipsative variables tend to produce bipolar factors?

6. In recent years there has been much discussion of response styles (Messick, 1962). Is experimental dependence involved in response styles, and if so, how?

7. If the perceptions of a single person by himself and by his family and friends were correlated and factor analyzed, which kinds of factorial structure would you expect if the person were (a) "well integrated," (b) neurotic, (c) schizophrenic, (d) characterized as having a "multiple personality"?

8. Would it be fruitful to factor analyze post-mortem ratings of famous persons, like Beethoven, Newton, and Shakespeare? If so, which "technique" should be applied?

9. Discuss the problem of experimental dependence in relation to P technique.

10. In which areas of sociology, anthropology, education, and social work does the nonexperimental approach seem more feasible than the experimental approach (see also Chapter 1)?

REFERENCES

Aitken, A. C. The evaluation of a certain triple-product matrix. *Proc. Roy. Soc. Edinburgh*, 1937, **57**, 172–181.

Alexander, S., and Husek, T. R. The anxiety differential: initial steps in the development of a measure of situational anxiety. *Educ. psychol. Measmt*, 1962, **22**, 325–348.

Anastasi, Anne. *Psychological Testing* (2nd ed.). New York: Macmillan, 1961.

Anderson, T. W. The use of factor analysis in the statistical analysis of multiple time series. *Psychometrika*, 1963, **28**, 1–25.

Anderson, Wayne, Kunce, Joseph, and Baxter, John. Maze score and job performance in psychiatric patients. *J. counsel. Psychol.*, 1962, **9**, 173–175.

Baggaley, A. R. The relation between scores obtained by Harvard freshmen on the Kuder Preference Record and their fields of concentration. *J. educ. Psychol.*, 1947, **38**, 421–427.

Baggaley, A. R. Matrix formulation of Deuel's rotational method. *Psychometrika*, 1960a, **25**, 207–209.

Baggaley, A. R. Some remarks on scales of measurement and related topics. *J. gen. Psychol.*, 1960b, **62**, 141–145.

Bayley, Nancy. Consistency and variability in the growth of intelligence from birth to eighteen. *J. genet. Psychol.*, 1949, **75**, 165–196.

Bechtoldt, H. P. Construct validity: a critique. *Amer. Psychologist*, 1959, **14**, 619–629. (This paper was presented orally at an APA convention under the title mentioned in the text.)

Beck, S. J. The science of personality: nomothetic or idiographic? *Psychol. Rev.*, 1953, **60**, 353–359.

Becker, W. C. A comparison of the factor structure and other properties of the 16 PF and the Guilford-Martin personality inventories. *Educ. psychol. Measmt*, 1961, **21**, 393–404.

Bell, Wendell. Economic, family, and ethnic status: an empirical test. *Amer. sociol. Rev.*, 1955, **20**, 45–52.

Block, Jack. The difference between *Q* and *R*. *Psychol. Rev.*, 1955, **52**, 356–358.

Block, Jack. The equivalence of measures and the correction for attenuation. *Psychol. Bull.*, 1963, **60**, 152–156.

Brogden, H. E. Efficiency of classification as a function of number of jobs, per cent rejected, and the validity and intercorrelation of job performance estimates. *Educ. psychol. Measmt*, 1959, **19**, 181–190.

Broverman, D. M. Effects of score transformations in Q and R factor analysis techniques. *Psychol. Rev.*, 1961, **68**, 68–80.

Brown, C. W., and Ghiselli, E. E. *Scientific Method in Psychology*. New York: McGraw-Hill, 1955.

Brunswik, Egon. *Perception and the Representative Design of Psychological Experiments*. Berkeley: University of California Press, 1956.

Bryan, J. G. The generalized discriminant function: mathematical foundation and computational routine. *Harvard educ. Rev.*, 1951, **21**, 90–95.

Burt, Cyril. *The Factors of Mind*. New York: Macmillan, 1941.

Campbell, D. T. Factors relevant to the validity of experiments in social settings. *Psychol. Bull.*, 1957, **54**, 297–312.

Campbell, D. T., and Fiske, D. W. Convergent and discriminant validation by the multitrait-multimethod matrix. *Psychol. Bull.*, 1959, **56**, 81–105.

Carnap, Rudolf. Testibility and meaning. *Phil. Sci.*, 1936, **3**, 419–471; 1937, **4**, 1–40.

Carroll, J. B. An analytic solution for approximating simple structure in factor analysis. *Psychometrika*, 1953, **18**, 23–38.

Cattell, R. B. *Factor Analysis*. New York: Harper, 1952.

Cattell, R. B. *Personality and Motivation Structure and Measurement*. Yonkers-on-Hudson: World Book, 1957.

Cattell, R. B., and Adelson, Marvin. The dimensions of social change in the U.S.A. as determined by *P*-technique. *Social Forces*, 1951, **30**, 190–201.

Cattell, R. B., and Dickman, Kern. A dynamic model of physical influences demonstrating the necessity of oblique simple structure. *Psychol. Bull.*, 1962, **59**, 389–400.

Coan, R. W. Basic forms of covariation and concomitance designs. *Psychol. Bull.*, 1961, **58**, 317–324.

Comrey, A. L., and Levonian, E. A comparison of three point coefficients in factor analyses of MMPI items. *Educ. psychol. Measmt*, 1958, **18**, 739–755.

Couch, Arthur, and Keniston, Kenneth. Agreeing response set and social desirability. *J. abnorm. soc. Psychol.*, 1961, **62**, 175–179.

Cronbach, L. J. Coefficient alpha and the internal structure of tests. *Psychometrika*, 1951, **16**, 297–334.

Cronbach, L. J. The two disciplines of scientific psychology. *Amer. Psychologist*, 1957, **12**, 671–684.

Cronbach, L. J. *Essentials of Psychological Testing* (2nd ed.). New York: Harper, 1960.

Cronbach, L. J., and Gleser, Goldine. *Psychological Tests and Personnel Decisions*. Urbana: University of Illinois Press, 1957.

Cronbach, L. J., and Meehl, P. E. Construct validity in psychological tests. *Psychol. Bull.*, 1955, **52**, 281–302.

Deuel, P. D. A nomogram for factor analysis. *Psychometrika*, 1956, **21**, 291–294.

Ebel, R. L. Estimation of the reliability of ratings. *Psychometrika*, 1951, **16**, 407–424.

Ebel, R. L. Must all tests be valid? *Amer. Psychologist*, 1961, **16**, 640–647.

Edwards, A. L. *Techniques of Attitude Scale Construction*. New York: Appleton-Century-Crofts, 1957.

Edwards, A. L. *Experimental Design in Psychological Research* (2nd ed.). New York: Holt-Rinehart-Winston, 1960.

Edwards, A. L., and Walker, J. N. Social desirability and agreement response set. *J. abnorm. soc. Psychol.*, 1961, **62**, 180–183.

Ellis, Albert. An operational reformulation of some basic principles of psychoanalysis. *Psychoanal. Rev.*, 1956, **43**, 163–180.

Ezekiel, Mordecai, and Fox, K. A. *Methods of Correlation and Regression Analysis* (3rd ed.). New York: Wiley, 1959.

Ferguson, G. A. A note on the Kuder-Richardson formula. *Educ. psychol. Measmt*, 1951, **11**, 612–615.

Ferguson, G. A. The concept of parsimony in factor analysis. *Psychometrika*, 1954, **19**, 281–290.

Flanagan, J. C. The critical incident technique. *Psychol. Bull.*, 1954, 51, 327–358.

Francis, R. G. *The Rhetoric of Science*. Minneapolis: University of Minnesota Press, 1961.

Frank, Philipp. *Modern Science and Its Philosophy*. Cambridge: Harvard University Press, 1949.

Franz, Gretchen, Davis, J. A., and Garcia, Dolores. Prediction of grades from pre-admissions indices in Georgia tax supported colleges. *Educ. psychol. Measmt*, 1958, **18**, 841–844.

Freud, Sigmund. *Three Essays on the Theory of Sexuality*. New York: Hillary, 1905.

Freud, Sigmund. *Beyond the Pleasure Principle*. New York: Liveright, 1920.

Freud, Sigmund. *Civilization and Its Discontents*. New York: Hillary, 1930.

Glanzer, Murray, and Glaser, Robert. Techniques for the study of group structure and behavior: II. Empirical studies of the effects of structure in small groups. *Psychol. Bull.*, 1961, **58**, 1–27.

Guilford, J. P. When not to factor analyze. *Psychol. Bull.*, 1952, **49**, 26–37.

Guilford, J. P. *Fundamental Statistics in Psychology and Education* (3rd ed.). New York: McGraw-Hill, 1956.

Guilford, J. P., Christensen, P. R., Kettner, N. W., Green, R. F., and Hertzka, A. F. A factor-analytic study of Navy reasoning tests with the Air Force Aircrew Classification Battery. *Educ. psychol. Measmt*, 1954, **14**, 301–325.

Gulliksen, Harold. *Theory of Mental Tests*. New York: Wiley, 1950.

Guttman, Louis. A special review of Harold Gulliksen, *Theory of Mental Tests*. *Psychometrika*, 1953, **18**, 123–130.

Hall, C. S., and Lindzey, G. *Theories of Personality*. New York: Wiley, 1957.

Hall, R. C. Occupational group contrasts in terms of the Differential Aptitude Tests: an application of multiple discriminant analysis. *Educ. psychol. Measmt*, 1957, **17**, 556–567.

Hansen, M. H., Hurwitz, W. N., and Madow, W. G. *Sample Survey Methods and Theory*. Vol. 1. New York: Wiley, 1953.

Harman, H. H. *Modern Factor Analysis*. Chicago: University of Chicago Press, 1960.

Heer, D. M. The marital status of second-generation Americans. *Amer. sociol. Rev.*, 1961, **26**, 233–241.

Heilbrun, A. B., Jr. Prediction of first year college drop-out, using ACL need scales. *J. counsel. Psychol.*, 1962, **9**, 58–63.

Henrysson, Sten. *Applicability of Factor Analysis in the Behavioral Sciences*. Stockholm: Almquist-Wiksell, 1957.

Hilgard, E. R. *Theories of Learning* (2nd ed.). New York: Appleton-Century-Crofts, 1956.

Hilgard, E. R., and Marquis, D. G. *Conditioning and Learning*. New York: Appleton-Century, 1940.

Horst, Paul. Optimal estimates of multiple criteria with restrictions on the covariance matrix of estimated criteria. *Psychol. Rep.*, 1960, **6**, 427–444.

Horst, Paul. *Matrix Algebra for Social Scientists*. Holt-Rinehart-Winston, 1963.

Hotelling, Harold. Analysis of a complex of statistical variables into principal components. *J. educ. Psychol.*, 1933, **24**, 417–441, 498–520.

Kaiser, H. F. The varimax criterion for analytic rotation in factor analysis. *Psychometrika*, 1958, **23**, 187–200.

Kaiser, H. F. The application of electronic computers to factor analysis. *Educ. psychol. Measmt*, 1960, **20**, 141–151.

Kelley, T. L. *Essential Traits of Mental Life*. Cambridge: Harvard University Press, 1935.

Kuder, G. F., and Richardson, M. W. The theory of the estimation of test reliability. *Psychometrika*, 1937, **2**, 151–160.

Lewis, Don. *Quantitative Methods in Psychology*. New York: McGraw-Hill, 1960.

Lewis, J. W. Utilizing the stepwise multiple regression procedure in selecting predictor variables by sex group. *Educ. psychol. Measmt*, 1962, **22**, 401–404.

Lord, F. M. Cutting scores and errors of measurement. *Psychometrika*, 1962, **27**, 19–30.

MacCorquodale, K., and Meehl, P. E. On a distinction between hypothetical constructs and intervening variables. *Psychol. Rev.*, 1948, **55**, 95–107.

McDougall, William. *An Introduction to Social Psychology*. Boston: John W. Luce, 1908.

McNemar, Quinn. *Psychological Statistics* (3rd ed.). New York: Wiley, 1962.

Maxwell, A. E. Canonical variate analysis when the variables are dichotomous. *Educ. psychol. Measmt*, 1961, **21**, 259–271.

Meehl, P. E., and Hathaway, S. R. The *K* factor as a suppressor variable in the MMPI. *J. appl. Psychol.*, 1946, **30**, 525–564.

Messick, Samuel. Response style and content measures from personality inventories. *Educ. psychol. Measmt*, 1962, **22**, 41–56.

Michael, W. B., Jones, R. A., Gaddis, L. W., and Kaiser, H. F. Abacs for determination of a correlation coefficient corrected for restriction of range. *Psychometrika*, 1962, **27**, 197–202.

Neuhaus, J. O., and Wrigley, C. The quartimax method. *Brit. J. statist. Psychol.*, 1954, **7**, 81–91.

Nunnally, J. C. *Tests and Measurements*. New York: McGraw-Hill, 1959.

Nunnally, J. C. The place of statistics in psychology. *Educ. psychol. Measmt,* 1960, **20,** 641–650.

Ogburn, W. F., and Talbot, Nell. A measurement of the factors in the Presidential election of 1928. *Social Forces,* 1929, **8,** 175–183.

Pubols, B. H., Jr. Incentive magnitude, learning, and performance in animals. *Psychol. Bull.,* 1960, **57,** 89–115.

Rao, C. R. *Advanced Statistical Methods in Biometric Research.* New York: Wiley, 1952.

Rao, C. R. Estimation and tests of significance in factor analysis. *Psychometrika,* 1955, **20,** 93–111.

Roe, Anne. *The Making of a Scientist.* New York: Dodd-Mead, 1952.

Rogers, C. R., and Dymond, Rosalind (Eds.). *Psychotherapy and Personality Change.* Chicago: University of Chicago Press, 1954.

Saunders, D. R. The rationale for an "oblimax" method of transformation in factor analysis. *Psychometrika,* 1961, **26,** 317–324.

Siegel, Sidney. *Nonparametric Statistics for the Behavioral Sciences.* New York: McGraw-Hill, 1956.

Snedecor, G. W. *Statistical Methods Applied to Experiments in Agriculture and Biology* (4th ed.). Ames: University of Iowa Press, 1946.

Spearman, Charles. The proof and measurement of association between two things. *Amer. J. Psychol.,* 1904, **15,** 72–101. (See abridged version in Jenkins, J. J., and Paterson, D. G. (Eds.), *Studies in Individual Differences.* New York: Appleton-Century-Crofts, 1961.)

Spearman, Charles. "General intelligence," objectively determined and measured. *Amer. J. Psychol.,* 1904, **15,** 201–293.

Stephenson, William. *The Study of Behavior.* Chicago: University of Chicago Press, 1953.

Taylor, Janet. A personality scale of manifest anxiety. *J. abnorm. soc. Psychol.,* 1953, **48,** 1953, 285–290.

Thorndike, R. L. Reliability. In E. F. Lindquist (Ed.), *Educational Measurement.* Washington, D.C.; American Council on Education, 1951, pp. 560–620.

Thorndike, R. L., and Hagen, Elizabeth. *Measurement and Evaluation in Psychology and Education* (2nd ed.). New York: Wiley, 1961.

Thurstone, L. L. *Primary Mental Abilities.* Chicago: University of Chicago Press, 1938.

Thurstone, L. L. *Multiple-factor Analysis.* Chicago: University of Chicago Press, 1947.

Thurstone, L. L. An analytical method for simple structure. *Psychometrika,* 1954, **19,** 173–182.

Tiffin, J., and McCormick, E. J. *Industrial Psychology* (4th ed.). Englewood Cliffs: Prentice-Hall, 1958.

Tryon, R. C. Reliability and behavior domain validity: reformulation and historical critique. *Psychol. Bull.,* 1957, **54,** 229–249.

Tucker, L. R. The objective definition of simple structure in linear factor analysis. *Psychometrika,* 1955, **20,** 209–225.

Underwood, B. J. *Psychological Research.* New York: Appleton-Century-Crofts, 1957.

Underwood, B. J., Duncan, C. P., Taylor, Janet, and Cotton, J. W. *Elementary Statistics.* New York: Appleton-Century-Crofts, 1954.

Watson, J. B. *Behaviorism* (2nd ed.). New York: Norton, 1930.

Wert, J. E., Neidt, C. O., and Ahmann, J. S. *Statistical Methods in Educational and Psychological Research.* New York: Appleton-Century-Crofts, 1954.

Wilson, R. C., Guilford, J. P., Christensen, P. R., and Lewis, D. J. A factor-analytic study of creative-thinking abilities. *Psychometrika,* 1954, **19**, 297–311.

APPENDIX ONE

TABLE A. Squares and square roots of numbers from 1 to 1000*

Number	Square	Square root	Number	Square	Square root
1	1	1.0000	41	16 81	6.4031
2	4	1.4142	42	17 64	6.4807
3	9	1.7321	43	18 49	6.5574
4	16	2.0000	44	19 36	6.6332
5	25	2.2361	45	20 25	6.7082
6	36	2.4495	46	21 16	6.7823
7	49	2.6458	47	22 09	6.8557
8	64	2.8284	48	23 04	6.9282
9	81	3.0000	49	24 01	7.0000
10	1 00	3.1623	50	25 00	7.0711
11	1 21	3.3166	51	26 01	7.1414
12	1 44	3.4641	52	27 04	7.2111
13	1 69	3.6056	53	28 09	7.2801
14	1 96	3.7417	54	29 16	7.3485
15	2 25	3.8730	55	30 25	7.4162
16	2 56	4.0000	56	31 36	7.4833
17	2 89	4.1231	57	32 49	7.5498
18	3 24	4.2426	58	33 64	7.6158
19	3 61	4.3589	59	34 81	7.6811
20	4 00	4.4721	60	36 00	7.7460
21	4 41	4.5826	61	37 21	7.8102
22	4 84	4.6904	62	38 44	7.8740
23	5 29	4.7958	63	39 69	7.9373
24	5 76	4.8990	64	40 96	8.0000
25	6 25	5.0000	65	42 25	8.0623
26	6 76	5.0990	66	43 56	8.1240
27	7 29	5.1962	67	44 89	8.1854
28	7 84	5.2915	68	46 24	8.2462
29	8 41	5.3852	69	47 61	8.3066
30	9 00	5.4772	70	49 00	8.3666
31	9 61	5.5678	71	50 41	8.4261
32	10 24	5.6569	72	51 84	8.4853
33	10 89	5.7446	73	53 29	8.5440
34	11 56	5.8310	74	54 76	8.6023
35	12 25	5.9161	75	56 25	8.6603
36	12 96	6.0000	76	57 76	8.7178
37	13 69	6.0828	77	59 29	8.7750
38	14 44	6.1644	78	60 84	8.8318
39	15 21	6.2450	79	62 41	8.8882
40	16 00	6.3246	80	64 00	8.9443

* From Sorenson. *Statistics for Students of Psychology and Education.*   New York: McGraw-Hill. 1936.

TABLE A—*continued*

Number	Square	Square root	Number	Square	Square root
81	65 61	9.0000	121	1 46 41	11.0000
82	67 24	9.0554	122	1 48 84	11.0454
83	68 89	9.1104	123	1 51 29	11.0905
84	70 56	9.1652	124	1 53 76	11.1355
85	72 25	9.2195	125	1 56 25	11.1803
86	73 96	9.2736	126	1 58 76	11.2250
87	75 69	9.3274	127	1 61 29	11.2694
88	77 44	9.3808	128	1 63 84	11.3137
89	79 21	9.4340	129	1 66 41	11.3578
90	81 00	9.4868	130	1 69 00	11.4018
91	82 81	9.5394	131	1 71 61	11.4455
92	84 64	9.5917	132	1 74 24	11.4891
93	86 49	9.6437	133	1 76 89	11.5326
94	88 36	9.6954	134	1 79 56	11.5758
95	90 25	9.7468	135	1 82 25	11.6190
96	92 16	9.7980	136	1 84 96	11.6619
97	94 09	9.8489	137	1 87 69	11.7047
98	96 04	9.8995	138	1 90 44	11.7473
99	98 01	9.9499	139	1 93 21	11.7898
100	1 00 00	10.0000	140	1 96 00	11.8322
101	1 02 01	10.0499	141	1 98 81	11.8743
102	1 04 04	10.0995	142	2 01 64	11.9164
103	1 06 09	10.1489	143	2 04 49	11.9583
104	1 08 16	10.1980	144	2 07 36	12.0000
105	1 10 25	10.2470	145	2 10 25	12.0416
106	1 12 36	10.2956	146	2 13 16	12.0830
107	1 14 49	10.3441	147	2 16 09	12.1244
108	1 16 64	10.3923	148	2 19 04	12.1655
109	1 18 81	10.4403	149	2 22 01	12.2066
110	1 21 00	10.4881	150	2 25 00	12.2474
111	1 23 21	10.5357	151	2 28 01	12.2882
112	1 25 44	10.5830	152	2 31 04	12.3288
113	1 27 69	10.6301	153	2 34 09	12.3693
114	1 29 96	10.6771	154	2 37 16	12.4097
115	1 32 25	10.7238	155	2 40 25	12.4499
116	1 34 56	10.7703	156	2 43 36	12.4900
117	1 36 89	10.8167	157	2 46 49	12.5300
118	1 39 24	10.8628	158	2 49 64	12.5698
119	1 41 61	10.9087	159	2 52 81	12.6095
120	1 44 00	10.9545	160	2 56 00	12.6491

* From Sorenson. *Statistics for Students of Psychology and Education.* New York: McGraw-Hill, 1936.

TABLE A—*continued*

Number	Square	Square root	Number	Square	Square root
161	2 59 21	12.6886	201	4 04 01	14.1774
162	2 62 44	12.7279	202	4 08 04	14.2127
163	2 65 69	12.7671	203	4 12 09	14.2478
164	2 68 96	12.8062	204	4 16 16	14.2829
165	2 72 25	12.8452	205	4 20 25	14.3178
166	2 75 56	12.8841	206	4 24 36	14.3527
167	2 78 89	12.9228	207	4 28 49	14.3875
168	2 82 24	12.9615	208	4 32 64	14.4222
169	2 85 61	13.0000	209	4 36 81	14.4568
170	2 89 00	13.0384	210	4 41 00	14.4914
171	2 92 41	13.0767	211	4 45 21	14.5258
172	2 95 84	13.1149	212	4 49 44	14.5602
173	2 99 29	13.1529	213	4 53 69	14.5945
174	3 02 76	13.1909	214	4 57 96	14.6287
175	3 06 25	13.2288	215	4 62 25	14.6629
176	3 09 76	13.2665	216	4 66 56	14.6969
177	3 13 29	13.3041	217	4 70 89	14.7309
178	3 16 84	13.3417	218	4 75 24	14.7648
179	3 20 41	13.3791	219	4 79 61	14.7986
180	3 24 00	13.4164	220	4 84 00	14.8324
181	3 27 61	13.4536	221	4 88 41	14.8661
182	3 31 24	13.4907	222	4 92 84	14.8997
183	3 34 89	13.5277	223	4 97 29	14.9332
184	3 38 56	13.5647	224	5 01 76	14.9666
185	3 42 25	13.6015	225	5 06 25	15.0000
186	3 45 96	13.6382	226	5 10 76	15.0333
187	3 49 69	13.6748	227	5 15 29	15.0665
188	3 53 44	13.7113	228	5 19 84	15.0997
189	3 57 21	13.7477	229	5 24 41	15.1327
190	3 61 00	13.7840	230	5 29 00	15.1658
191	3 64 81	13.8203	231	5 33 61	15.1987
192	3 68 64	13.8564	232	5 38 24	15.2315
193	3 72 49	13.8924	233	5 42 89	15.2643
194	3 76 36	13.9284	234	5 47 56	15.2971
195	3 80 25	13.9642	235	5 52 25	15.3297
196	3 84 16	14.0000	236	5 56 96	15.3623
197	3 88 09	14.0357	237	5 61 69	15.3948
198	3 92 04	14.0712	238	5 66 44	15.4272
199	3 96 01	14.1067	239	5 71 21	15.4596
200	4 00 00	14.1421	240	5 76 00	15.4919

* From Sorenson. *Statistics for Students of Psychology and Education.* New York: McGraw-Hill, 1936.

TABLE A—*continued*

Number	Square	Square root	Number	Square	Square root
241	5 80 81	15.5242	281	7 89 61	16.7631
242	5 85 64	15.5563	282	7 95 24	16.7929
243	5 90 49	15.5885	283	8 00 89	16.8226
244	5 95 36	15.6205	284	8 06 56	16.8523
245	6 00 25	15.6525	285	8 12 25	16.8819
246	6 05 16	15.6844	286	8 17 96	16.9115
247	6 10 09	15.7162	287	8 23 69	16.9411
248	6 15 04	15.7480	288	8 29 44	16.9706
249	6 20 01	15.7797	289	8 35 21	17.0000
250	6 25 00	15.8114	290	8 41 00	17.0294
251	6 30 01	15.8430	291	8 46 81	17.0587
252	6 35 04	15.8745	292	8 52 64	17.0880
253	6 40 09	15.9060	293	8 58 49	17.1172
254	6 45 16	15.9374	294	8 64 36	17.1464
255	6 50 25	15.9687	295	8 70 25	17.1756
256	6 55 36	16.0000	296	8 76 16	17.2047
257	6 60 49	16.0312	297	8 82 09	17.2337
258	6 65 64	16.0624	298	8 88 04	17.2627
259	6 70 81	16.0935	299	8 94 01	17.2916
260	6 76 00	16.1245	300	9 00 00	17.3205
261	6 81 21	16.1555	301	9 06 01	17.3494
262	6 86 44	16.1864	302	9 12 04	17.3781
263	6 91 69	16.2173	303	9 18 09	17.4069
264	6 96 96	16.2481	304	9 24 16	17.4356
265	7 02 25	16.2788	305	9 30 25	17.4642
266	7 07 56	16.3095	306	9 36 36	17.4929
267	7 12 89	16.3401	307	9 42 49	17.5214
268	7 18 24	16.3707	308	9 48 64	17.5499
269	7 23 61	16.4012	309	9 54 81	17.5784
270	7 29 00	16.4317	310	9 61 00	17.6068
271	7 34 41	16.4621	311	9 67 21	17.6352
272	7 39 84	16.4924	312	9 73 44	17.6635
273	7 45 29	16.5227	313	9 79 69	17.6918
274	7 50 76	16.5529	314	9 85 96	17.7200
275	7 56 25	16.5831	315	9 92 25	17.7482
276	7 61 76	16.6132	316	9 98 56	17.7764
277	7 67 29	16.6433	317	10 04 89	17.8045
278	7 72 84	16.6733	318	10 11 24	17.8326
279	7 78 41	16.7033	319	10 17 61	17.8606
280	7 84 00	16.7332	320	10 24 00	17.8885

* From Sorenson. *Statistics for Students of Psychology and Education.* New York: McGraw-Hill, 1936.

TABLE A—*continued*

Number	Square	Square root	Number	Square	Square root
321	10 30 41	17.9165	361	13 03 21	19.0000
322	10 36 84	17.9444	362	13 10 44	19.0263
323	10 43 29	17.9722	363	13 17 69	19.0526
324	10 49 76	18.0000	364	13 24 96	19.0788
325	10 56 25	18.0278	365	13 32 25	19.1050
326	10 62 76	18.0555	366	13 39 56	19.1311
327	10 69 29	18.0831	367	13 46 89	19.1572
328	10 75 84	18.1108	368	13 54 24	19.1833
329	10 82 41	18.1384	369	13 61 61	19.2094
330	10 89 00	18.1659	370	13 69 00	19.2354
331	10 95 61	18.1934	371	13 76 41	19.2614
332	11 02 24	18.2209	372	13 83 84	19.2873
333	11 08 89	18.2483	373	13 91 29	19.3132
334	11 15 56	18.2757	374	13 98 76	19.3391
335	11 22 25	18.3030	375	14 06 25	19.3649
336	11 28 96	18.3303	376	14 13 76	19.3907
337	11 35 69	18.3576	377	14 21 29	19.4165
338	11 42 44	18.3848	378	14 28 84	19.4422
339	11 49 21	18.4120	379	14 36 41	19.4679
340	11 56 00	18.4391	380	14 44 00	19.4936
341	11 62 81	18.4662	381	14 51 61	19.5192
342	11 69 64	18.4932	382	14 59 24	19.5448
343	11 76 49	18.5203	383	14 66 89	19.5704
344	11 83 36	18.5472	384	14 74 56	19.5959
345	11 90 25	18.5742	385	14 82 25	19.6214
346	11 97 16	18.6011	386	14 89 96	19.6469
347	12 04 09	18.6279	387	14 97 69	19.6723
348	12 11 04	18.6548	388	15 05 44	19.6977
349	12 18 01	18.6815	389	15 13 21	19.7231
350	12 25 00	18.7083	390	15 21 00	19.7484
351	12 32 01	18.7350	391	15 28 81	19.7737
352	12 39 04	18.7617	392	15 36 64	19.7990
353	12 46 09	18.7883	393	15 44 49	19.8242
354	12 53 16	18.8149	394	15 52 36	19.8494
355	12 60 25	18.8414	395	15 60 25	19.8746
356	12 67 36	18.8680	396	15 68 16	19.8997
357	12 74 49	18.8944	397	15 76 09	19.9249
358	12 81 64	18.9209	398	15 84 04	19.9499
359	12 88 81	18.9473	399	15 92 01	19.9750
360	12 96 00	18.9737	400	16 00 00	20.0000

* From Sorenson. *Statistics for Students of Psychology and Education.* New York: McGraw-Hill, 1936.

TABLE A—*continued*

Number	Square	Square root	Number	Square	Square root
401	16 08 01	20.0250	441	19 44 81	21.0000
402	16 16 04	20.0499	442	19 53 64	21.0238
403	16 24 09	20.0749	443	19 62 49	21.0476
404	16 32 16	20.0998	444	19 71 36	21.0713
405	16 40 25	20.1246	445	19 80 25	21.0950
406	16 48 36	20.1494	446	19 89 16	21.1187
407	16 56 49	20.1742	447	19 98 09	21.1424
408	16 64 64	20.1990	448	20 07 04	21.1660
409	16 72 81	20.2237	449	20 16 01	21.1896
410	16 81 00	20.2485	450	20 25 00	21.2132
411	16 89 21	20.2731	451	20 34 01	21.2368
412	16 97 44	20.2978	452	20 43 04	21.2603
413	17 05 69	20.3224	453	20 52 09	21.2838
414	17 13 96	20.3470	454	20 61 16	21.3073
415	17 22 25	20.3715	455	20 70 25	21.3307
416	17 30 56	20.3961	456	20 79 36	21.3542
417	17 38 89	20.4206	457	20 88 49	21.3776
418	17 47 24	20.4450	458	20 97 64	21.4009
419	17 55 61	20.4695	459	21 06 81	21.4243
420	17 64 00	20.4939	460	21 16 00	21.4476
421	17 72 41	20.5183	461	21 25 21	21.4709
422	17 80 84	20.5426	462	21 34 44	21.4947
423	17 89 29	20.5670	463	21 43 69	21.5174
424	17 97 76	20.5913	464	21 52 96	21.5407
425	18 06 25	20.6155	465	21 62 25	21.5639
426	18 14 76	20.6398	466	21 71 56	21.5870
427	18 23 29	20.6640	467	21 80 89	21.6102
428	18 31 84	20.6882	468	21 90 24	21.6333
429	18 40 41	20.7123	469	21 99 61	21.6564
430	18 49 00	20.7364	470	22 09 00	21.6795
431	18 57 61	20.7605	471	22 18 41	21.7025
432	18 66 24	20.7846	472	22 27 84	21.7256
433	18 74 89	20.8087	473	22 37 29	21.7486
434	18 83 56	20.8327	474	22 46 76	21.7715
435	18 92 25	20.8567	475	22 56 25	21.7945
436	19 00 96	20.8806	476	22 65 76	21.8174
437	19 09 69	20.9045	477	22 75 29	21.8403
438	19 18 44	20.9284	478	22 84 84	21.8632
439	19 27 21	20.9523	479	22 94 41	21.8861
440	19 36 00	20.9762	480	23 04 00	21.9089

* From Sorenson. *Statistics for Students of Psychology and Education.* New York: McGraw-Hill, 1936.

TABLE A—*continued*

Number	Square	Square root	Number	Square	Square root
481	23 13 61	21.9317	521	27 14 41	22.8254
482	23 23 24	21.9545	522	27 24 84	22.8473
483	23 32 89	21.9773	523	27 35 29	22.8692
484	23 42 56	22.0000	524	27 45 76	22.8910
485	23 52 25	22.0227	525	27 56 25	22.9129
486	23 61 96	22.0454	526	27 66 76	22.9347
487	23 71 69	22.0681	527	27 77 29	22.9565
488	23 81 44	22.0907	528	27 87 84	22.9783
489	23 91 21	22.1133	529	27 98 41	23.0000
490	24 01 00	22.1359	530	28 09 00	23.0217
491	24 10 81	22.1585	531	28 19 61	23.0434
492	24 20 64	22.1811	532	28 30 24	23.0651
493	24 30 49	22.2036	533	28 40 89	23.0868
494	24 40 36	22.2261	534	28 51 56	23.1084
495	24 50 25	22.2486	535	28 62 25	23.1301
496	24 60 16	22.2711	536	28 72 96	23.1517
497	24 70 09	22.2935	537	28 83 69	23.1733
498	24 80 04	22.3159	538	28 94 44	23.1948
499	24 90 01	22.3383	539	29 05 21	23.2164
500	25 00 00	22.3607	540	29 16 00	23.2379
501	25 10 01	22.3830	541	29 26 81	23.2594
502	25 20 04	22.4054	542	29 37 64	23.2809
503	25 30 09	22.4277	543	29 48 49	23.3024
504	25 40 16	22.4499	544	29 59 36	23.3238
505	25 50 25	22.4722	545	29 70 25	23.3452
506	25 60 36	22.4944	546	29 81 16	23.3666
507	25 70 49	22.5167	547	29 92 09	23.3880
508	25 80 64	22.5389	548	30 03 04	23.4094
509	25 90 81	22.5610	549	30 14 01	23.4307
510	26 01 00	22.5832	550	30 25 00	23.4521
511	26 11 21	22.6053	551	30 36 01	23.4734
512	26 21 44	22.6274	552	30 47 04	23.4947
513	26 31 69	22.6495	553	30 58 09	23.5160
514	26 41 96	22.6716	554	30 69 16	23.5372
515	26 52 25	22.6936	555	30 80 25	23.5584
516	26 62 56	22.7156	556	30 91 36	23.5797
517	26 72 89	22.7376	557	31 02 49	23.6008
518	26 83 24	22.7596	558	31 13 64	23.6220
519	26 93 61	22.7816	559	31 24 81	23.6432
520	27 04 00	22.8035	560	31 36 00	23.6643

* From Sorenson.   *Statistics for Students of Psychology and Education.*   New York: McGraw-Hill, 1936.

TABLE A—*continued*

Number	Square	Square root	Number	Square	Square root
561	31 47 21	23.6854	601	36 12 01	24.5153
562	31 58 44	23.7065	602	36 24 04	24.5357
563	31 69 69	23.7276	603	36 36 09	24.5561
564	31 80 96	23.7487	604	36 48 16	24.5764
565	31 92 25	23.7697	605	36 60 25	24.5967
566	32 03 56	23.7908	606	36 72 36	24.6171
567	32 14 89	23.8118	607	36 84 49	24.6374
568	32 26 24	23.8328	608	36 96 64	24.6577
569	32 37 61	23.8537	609	37 08 81	24.6779
570	32 49 00	23.8747	610	37 21 00	24.6982
571	32 60 41	23.8956	611	37 33 21	24.7184
572	32 71 84	23.9165	612	37 45 44	24.7385
573	32 83 29	23.9374	613	37 57 69	24.7588
574	32 94 76	23.9583	614	37 69 96	24.7790
575	33 06 25	23.9792	615	37 82 25	24.7992
576	33 17 76	24.0000	616	37 94 56	24.8193
577	33 29 29	24.0208	617	38 06 89	24.8395
578	33 40 84	24.0416	618	38 19 24	24.8596
579	33 52 41	24.0624	619	38 31 61	24.8797
580	33 64 00	24.0832	620	38 44 00	24.8998
581	33 75 61	24.1039	621	38 56 41	24.9199
582	33 87 24	24.1247	622	38 68 84	24.9399
583	33 98 89	24.1454	623	38 81 29	24.9600
584	34 10 56	24.1661	624	38 93 76	24.9800
585	34 22 25	24.1868	625	39 06 25	25.0000
586	34 33 96	24.2074	626	39 18 76	25.0200
587	34 45 69	24.2281	627	39 31 29	25.0400
588	34 57 44	24.2487	628	39 43 84	25.0599
589	34 69 21	24.2693	629	39 56 41	25.0799
590	34 81 00	24.2899	630	39 69 00	25.0998
591	34 92 81	24.3105	631	39 81 61	25.1197
592	35 04 64	24.3311	632	39 94 24	25.1396
593	35 16 49	24.3516	633	40 06 89	25.1595
594	35 28 36	24.3721	634	40 19 56	25.1794
595	35 40 25	24.3926	635	40 32 25	25.1992
596	35 52 16	24.4131	636	40 44 96	25.2190
597	35 64 09	24.4336	637	40 57 69	25.2389
598	35 76 04	24.4540	638	40 70 44	25.2587
599	35 88 01	24.4745	639	40 83 21	25.2784
600	36 00 00	24.4949	640	40 96 00	25.2982

* From Sorenson. *Statistics for Students of Psychology and Education.* New York: McGraw-Hill, 1936.

TABLE A—*continued*

Number	Square	Square root	Number	Square	Square root
641	41 08 81	25.3180	681	46 37 61	26.0960
642	41 21 64	25.3377	682	46 51 24	26.1151
643	41 34 49	25.3574	683	46 64 89	26.1343
644	41 47 36	25.3772	684	46 78 56	26.1534
645	41 60 25	25.3969	685	46 92 25	26.1725
646	41 73 16	25.4165	686	47 05 96	26.1916
647	41 86 09	25.4362	687	47 19 69	26.2107
648	41 99 04	25.4558	688	47 33 44	26.2298
649	42 12 01	25.4755	689	47 47 21	26.2488
650	42 25 00	25.4951	690	47 61 00	26.2679
651	42 38 01	25.5147	691	47 74 81	26.2869
652	42 51 04	25.5343	692	47 88 64	26.3059
653	42 64 09	25.5539	693	48 02 49	26.3249
654	42 77 16	25.5734	694	48 16 36	26.3439
655	42 90 25	25.5930	695	48 30 25	26.3629
656	43 03 36	25.6125	696	48 44 16	26.3818
657	43 16 49	25.6320	697	48 58 09	26.4008
658	43 29 64	25.6515	698	48 72 04	26.4197
659	43 42 81	25.6710	699	48 86 01	26.4386
660	43 56 00	25.6905	700	49 00 00	26.4575
661	43 69 21	25.7099	701	49 14 01	26.4764
662	43 82 44	25.7294	702	49 28 04	26.4953
663	43 95 69	25.7488	703	49 42 09	26.5141
664	44 08 96	25.7682	704	49 56 16	26.5330
665	44 22 25	25.7876	705	49 70 25	26.5518
666	44 35 56	25.8070	706	49 84 36	26.5707
667	44 48 89	25.8263	707	49 98 49	26.5895
668	44 62 24	25.8457	708	50 12 64	26.6083
669	44 75 61	25.8650	709	50 26 81	26.6271
670	44 89 00	25.8844	710	50 41 00	26.6458
671	45 02 41	25.9037	711	50 55 21	26.6646
672	45 15 84	25.9230	712	50 69 44	26.6833
673	45 29 29	25.9422	713	50 83 69	26.7021
674	45 42 76	25.9615	714	50 97 96	26.7208
675	45 56 25	25.9808	715	51 12 25	26.7395
676	45 69 76	26.0000	716	51 26 56	26.7582
677	45 83 29	26.0192	717	51 40 89	26.7769
678	45 96 84	26.0384	718	51 55 24	26.7955
679	46 10 41	26.0576	719	51 69 61	26.8142
680	46 24 00	26.0768	720	51 84 00	26.8328

* From Sorenson. *Statistics for Students of Psychology and Education.* New York: McGraw-Hill, 1936.

TABLE A—*continued*

Number	Square	Square root	Number	Square	Square root
721	51 98 41	26.8514	761	57 91 21	27.5862
722	52 12 84	26.8701	762	58 06 44	27.6043
723	52 27 29	26.8887	763	58 21 69	27.6225
724	52 41 76	26.9072	764	58 36 96	27.6405
725	52 56 25	26.9258	765	58 52 25	27.6586
726	52 70 76	26.9444	766	58 67 56	27.6767
727	52 85 29	26.9629	767	58 82 89	27.6948
728	52 99 84	26.9815	768	58 98 24	27.7128
729	53 14 41	27.0000	769	59 13 61	27.7308
730	53 29 00	27.0185	770	59 29 00	27.7489
731	53 43 61	27.0370	771	59 44 41	27.7669
732	53 58 24	27.0555	772	59 59 84	27.7849
733	53 72 89	27.0740	773	59 75 29	27.8029
734	53 87 56	27.0924	774	59 90 76	27.8209
735	54 02 25	27.1109	775	60 06 25	27.8388
736	54 16 96	27.1293	776	60 21 76	27.8568
737	54 31 69	27.1477	777	60 37 29	27.8747
738	54 46 44	27.1662	778	60 52 84	27.8927
739	54 61 27	27.1846	779	60 68 41	27.9106
740	54 76 00	27.2029	780	60 84 00	27.9285
741	54 90 81	27.2213	781	60 99 61	27.9464
742	55 05 64	27.2397	782	61 15 24	27.9643
743	55 20 49	27.2580	783	61 30 89	27.9821
744	55 35 36	27.2764	784	61 46 56	28.0000
745	55 50 25	27.2947	785	61 62 25	28.0179
746	55 65 16	27.3130	786	61 77 96	28.0357
747	55 80 09	27.3313	787	61 93 69	28.0535
748	55 95 04	27.3496	788	62 09 44	28.0713
749	56 10 01	27.3679	789	62 25 21	28.0891
750	56 25 00	27.3861	790	62 41 00	28.1069
751	56 40 01	27.4044	791	62 56 81	28.1247
752	56 55 04	27.4226	792	62 72 64	28.1425
753	56 70 09	27.4408	793	62 88 49	28.1603
754	56 85 16	27.4591	794	63 04 36	28.1780
755	57 00 25	27.4773	795	63 20 25	28.1957
756	57 15 36	27.4955	796	63 36 16	28.2135
757	57 30 49	27.5136	797	63 52 09	28.2312
758	57 45 64	27.5318	798	63 68 04	28.2489
759	57 60 81	27.5500	799	63 84 01	28.2666
760	57 76 00	27.5681	800	64 00 00	28.2843

* From Sorenson. *Statistics for Students of Psychology and Education.* New York: McGraw-Hill, 1936.

TABLE A—*continued*

Number	Square	Square root	Number	Square	Square root
801	64 16 01	28.3019	841	70 72 81	29.0000
802	64 32 04	28.3196	842	70 89 64	29.0172
803	64 48 09	28.3373	843	71 06 49	29.0345
804	64 64 16	28.3049	844	71 23 36	29.0517
805	64 80 25	28.3725	845	71 40 25	29.0689
806	64 96 36	28.3901	846	71 57 16	29.0861
807	65 12 49	28.4077	847	71 74 09	29.1033
808	65 28 64	28.4253	848	71 91 04	29.1204
809	65 44 81	28.4429	849	72 08 01	29.1376
810	65 61 00	28.4605	850	72 25 00	29.1548
811	65 77 21	28.4781	851	72 42 01	29.1719
812	65 93 44	28.4956	852	72 59 04	29.1890
813	66 09 69	28.5132	853	72 76 09	29.2062
814	66 25 96	28.5307	854	72 93 16	29.2233
815	66 42 25	28.5482	855	73 10 25	29.2404
816	66 58 56	28.5657	856	73 27 36	29.2575
817	66 74 89	28.5832	857	73 44 49	29.2746
818	66 91 24	28.6007	858	73 61 64	29.2916
819	67 07 61	28.6082	859	73 78 81	29.3087
820	67 24 00	28.6356	860	73 96 00	29.3258
821	67 40 41	28.6531	861	74 13 21	29.3428
822	67 56 84	28.6705	862	74 30 44	29.3598
823	67 73 29	28.6880	863	74 47 69	29.3769
824	67 89 76	28.7054	864	74 64 96	29.3939
825	68 06 25	28.7228	865	74 82 25	29.4109
826	68 22 76	28.7402	866	74 99 56	29.4279
827	68 39 29	28.7576	867	75 16 89	29.4449
828	68 55 84	28.7750	868	75 34 24	29.4618
829	68 72 41	28.7924	869	75 51 61	29.4788
830	68 89 00	28.8097	870	75 69 00	29.4958
831	69 05 61	28.8271	871	75 86 41	29.5127
832	69 22 24	28.8444	872	76 03 84	29.5296
833	69 38 89	28.8617	873	76 21 29	29.5466
834	69 55 56	28.8791	874	76 38 76	29.5635
835	69 72 25	28.8964	875	76 56 25	29.5804
836	69 88 96	28.9137	876	76 73 76	29.5973
837	70 05 69	28.9310	877	76 91 29	29.6142
838	70 22 44	28.9482	878	77 08 84	29.6311
839	70 39 21	28.9655	879	77 26 41	29.6479
840	70 56 00	28.9828	880	77 44 00	29.6648

* From Sorenson. *Statistics for Students of Psychology and Education.* New York: McGraw-Hill 1936.

TABLE A—*continued*

Number	Square	Square root	Number	Square	Square root
881	77 61 61	29.6816	921	84 82 41	30.3480
882	77 79 24	29.6985	922	85 00 84	30.3645
883	77 96 89	29.7153	923	85 19 29	30.3809
884	78 14 56	29.7321	924	85 37 76	30.3974
885	78 32 25	29.7489	925	85 56 25	30.4138
886	78 49 96	29.7658	926	85 74 76	30.4302
887	78 67 69	29.7825	927	85 93 29	30.4467
888	78 85 44	29.7993	928	86 11 84	30.4631
889	79 03 21	29.8161	929	86 30 41	30.4795
890	79 21 00	29.8329	930	86 49 00	30.4959
891	79 38 81	29.8496	931	86 67 61	30.5123
892	79 56 64	29.8664	932	86 86 24	30.5287
893	79 74 49	29.8831	933	87 04 89	30.5450
894	79 92 36	29.8998	934	87 23 56	30.5614
895	80 10 25	29.9166	935	87 42 25	30.5778
896	80 28 16	29.9333	936	87 60 96	30.5941
897	80 46 09	29.9500	937	87 79 69	30.6105
898	80 64 04	29.9666	938	87 98 44	30.6268
899	80 82 01	29.9833	939	88 17 21	30.6431
900	81 00 00	30.0000	940	88 36 00	30.6594
901	81 18 01	30.0167	941	88 54 81	30.6757
902	81 36 04	30.0333	942	88 73 64	30.6920
903	81 54 09	30.0500	943	88 92 49	30.7083
904	81 72 16	30.0666	944	89 11 36	30.7246
905	81 90 25	30.0832	945	89 30 25	30.7409
906	82 08 36	30.0998	946	89 49 16	30.7571
907	82 26 49	30.1164	947	89 68 09	30.7734
908	82 44 64	30.1330	948	89 87 04	30.7896
909	82 62 81	30.1496	949	90 06 01	30.8058
910	82 81 00	30.1662	950	90 25 00	30.8221
911	82 99 21	30.1828	951	90 44 01	30.8383
912	83 17 44	30.1993	952	90 63 04	30.8545
913	83 35 69	30.2159	953	90 82 09	30.8707
914	83 53 96	30.2324	954	91 01 16	30.8869
915	83 72 25	30.2490	955	91 20 25	30.9031
916	83 90 56	30.2655	956	91 39 36	30.9192
917	84 08 89	30.2820	957	91 58 49	30.9354
918	84 27 24	30.2985	958	91 77 64	30.9516
919	84 45 61	30.3150	959	91 96 81	30.9677
920	84 64 00	30.3315	960	92 16 00	30.9839

* From Sorenson. *Statistics for Students of Psychology and Education.* New York: McGraw-Hill, 1936.

TABLE A—*continued*

Number	Square	Square root	Number	Square	Square root
961	92 35 21	31.0000	981	96 23 61	31.3209
962	92 54 44	31.0161	982	96 43 24	31.3369
963	92 73 69	31.0322	983	96 62 89	31.3528
964	92 92 96	31.0483	984	96 82 56	31.3688
965	93 12 25	31.0644	985	97 02 25	31.3847
966	93 31 56	31.0805	986	97 21 96	31.4006
967	93 50 89	31.0966	987	97 41 69	31.4166
968	93 70 24	31.1127	988	97 61 44	31.4325
969	93 89 61	31.1288	989	97 81 21	31.4484
970	94 09 00	31.1448	990	98 01 00	31.4643
971	94 28 41	31.1609	991	98 20 81	31.4802
972	94 47 84	31.1769	992	98 40 64	31.4960
973	94 67 29	31.1929	993	98 60 49	31.5119
974	94 86 76	31.2090	994	98 80 36	31.5278
975	95 06 25	31.2250	995	99 00 25	31.5436
976	95 25 76	31.2410	996	99 20 16	31.5595
977	95 45 29	31.2570	997	99 40 09	31.5753
978	95 64 84	31.2730	998	99 60 04	31.5911
979	95 84 41	31.2890	999	99 80 01	31.6070
980	96 04 00	31.3050	1000	100 00 00	31.6228

* From Sorenson. *Statistics for Students of Psychology and Education.* New York: McGraw-Hill, 1936.

TABLE B. Coefficients of correlation and t ratios significant at the .05 level (roman type) and at the .01 level (boldface type) for varying degrees of freedom*

Degrees of freedom	Number of variables									t
	2	3	4	5	6	7	9	13	25	
1	.997 / **1.000**	.999 / **1.000**	.999 / **1.000**	.999 / **1.000**	1.000 / **1.000**	1.000 / **1.000**	1.000 / **1.000**	1.000 / **1.000**	1.000 / **1.000**	12.706 / **63.657**
2	.950 / **.990**	.975 / **.995**	.983 / **.997**	.987 / **.998**	.990 / **.998**	.992 / **.998**	.994 / **.999**	.996 / **.999**	.998 / **1.000**	4.303 / **9.925**
3	.878 / **.959**	.930 / **.976**	.950 / **.983**	.961 / **.987**	.968 / **.990**	.973 / **.991**	.979 / **.993**	.986 / **.995**	.993 / **.998**	3.182 / **5.841**
4	.811 / **.917**	.881 / **.949**	.912 / **.962**	.930 / **.970**	.942 / **.975**	.950 / **.979**	.961 / **.984**	.973 / **.989**	.986 / **.994**	2.776 / **4.604**
5	.754 / **.874**	.836 / **.917**	.874 / **.937**	.898 / **.949**	.914 / **.957**	.925 / **.963**	.941 / **.971**	.958 / **.980**	.978 / **.989**	2.571 / **4.032**
6	.707 / **.834**	.795 / **.886**	.839 / **.911**	.867 / **.927**	.886 / **.938**	.900 / **.946**	.920 / **.957**	.943 / **.969**	.969 / **.983**	2.447 / **3.707**
7	.666 / **.798**	.758 / **.855**	.807 / **.885**	.838 / **.904**	.860 / **.918**	.876 / **.928**	.900 / **.942**	.927 / **.958**	.960 / **.977**	2.365 / **3.499**
8	.632 / **.765**	.726 / **.827**	.777 / **.860**	.811 / **.882**	.835 / **.898**	.854 / **.909**	.880 / **.926**	.912 / **.946**	.950 / **.970**	2.306 / **3.355**
9	.602 / **.735**	.697 / **.800**	.750 / **.836**	.786 / **.861**	.812 / **.878**	.832 / **.891**	.861 / **.911**	.897 / **.934**	.941 / **.963**	2.262 / **3.250**
10	.576 / **.708**	.671 / **.776**	.726 / **.814**	.763 / **.840**	.790 / **.859**	.812 / **.874**	.843 / **.895**	.882 / **.922**	.932 / **.955**	2.228 / **3.169**
11	.553 / **.684**	.648 / **.753**	.703 / **.793**	.741 / **.821**	.770 / **.841**	.792 / **.857**	.826 / **.880**	.868 / **.910**	.922 / **.948**	2.201 / **3.106**
12	.532 / **.661**	.627 / **.732**	.683 / **.773**	.722 / **.802**	.751 / **.824**	.774 / **.841**	.809 / **.866**	.854 / **.898**	.913 / **.940**	2.179 / **3.055**
13	.514 / **.641**	.608 / **.712**	.664 / **.755**	.703 / **.785**	.733 / **.807**	.757 / **.825**	.794 / **.852**	.840 / **.886**	.904 / **.932**	2.160 / **3.012**
14	.497 / **.623**	.590 / **.694**	.646 / **.737**	.686 / **.768**	.717 / **.792**	.741 / **.810**	.779 / **.838**	.828 / **.875**	.895 / **.924**	2.145 / **2.977**
15	.482 / **.606**	.574 / **.677**	.630 / **.721**	.670 / **.752**	.701 / **.776**	.726 / **.796**	.765 / **.825**	.815 / **.864**	.886 / **.917**	2.131 / **2.947**
16	.468 / **.590**	.559 / **.662**	.615 / **.706**	.655 / **.738**	.686 / **.762**	.712 / **.782**	.751 / **.813**	.803 / **.853**	.878 / **.909**	2.120 / **2.921**
17	.456 / **.575**	.545 / **.647**	.601 / **.691**	.641 / **.724**	.673 / **.749**	.698 / **.769**	.738 / **.800**	.792 / **.842**	.869 / **.902**	2.110 / **2.898**
18	.444 / **.561**	.532 / **.633**	.587 / **.678**	.628 / **.710**	.660 / **.736**	.686 / **.756**	.726 / **.789**	.781 / **.832**	.861 / **.894**	2.101 / **2.878**
19	.433 / **.549**	.520 / **.620**	.575 / **.665**	.615 / **.698**	.647 / **.723**	.674 / **.744**	.714 / **.778**	.770 / **.822**	.853 / **.887**	2.093 / **2.861**
20	.423 / **.537**	.509 / **.608**	.563 / **.652**	.604 / **.685**	.636 / **.712**	.662 / **.733**	.703 / **.767**	.760 / **.812**	.845 / **.880**	2.086 / **2.845**
21	.413 / **.526**	.498 / **.596**	.552 / **.641**	.592 / **.674**	.624 / **.700**	.651 / **.722**	.693 / **.756**	.750 / **.803**	.837 / **.873**	2.080 / **2.831**
22	.404 / **.515**	.488 / **.585**	.542 / **.630**	.582 / **.663**	.614 / **.690**	.640 / **.712**	.682 / **.746**	.740 / **.794**	.830 / **.866**	2.074 / **2.819**
23	.396 / **.505**	.479 / **.574**	.532 / **.619**	.572 / **.652**	.604 / **.679**	.630 / **.701**	.673 / **.736**	.731 / **.785**	.823 / **.859**	2.069 / **2.807**

* Adapted from Wallace, H. A., and Snedecor, G. W. *Correlation and Machine Calculation*, 1931, by courtesy of the authors.

TABLE B.—*continued*

Degrees of freedom	Number of variables									*t*
	2	3	4	5	6	7	9	13	25	
24	.388 **.496**	.470 **.565**	.523 **.609**	.562 **.642**	.594 **.669**	.621 **.692**	.663 **.727**	.722 **.776**	.815 **.852**	2.064 **2.797**
25	.381 **.487**	.462 **.555**	.514 **.600**	.553 **.633**	.585 **.660**	.612 **.682**	.654 **.718**	.714 **.768**	.808 **.846**	2.060 **2.787**
26	.374 **.478**	.454 **.546**	.506 **.590**	.545 **.624**	.576 **.651**	.603 **.673**	.645 **.709**	.706 **.760**	.802 **.839**	2.056 **2.779**
27	.367 **.470**	.446 **.538**	.498 **.582**	.536 **.615**	.568 **.642**	.594 **.664**	.637 **.701**	.698 **.752**	.795 **.833**	2.052 **2.771**
28	.361 **.463**	.439 **.530**	.490 **.573**	.529 **.606**	.560 **.634**	.586 **.656**	.629 **.692**	.690 **.744**	.788 **.827**	2.048 **2.763**
29	.355 **.456**	.432 **.522**	.482 **.565**	.521 **.598**	.552 **.625**	.579 **.648**	.621 **.685**	.682 **.737**	.782 **.821**	2.045 **2.756**
30	.349 **.449**	.426 **.514**	.476 **.558**	.514 **.591**	.545 **.618**	.571 **.640**	.614 **.677**	.675 **.729**	.776 **.815**	2.042 **2.750**
35	.325 **.418**	.397 **.481**	.445 **.523**	.482 **.556**	.512 **.582**	.538 **.605**	.580 **.642**	.642 **.696**	.746 **.786**	2.030 **2.724**
40	.304 **.393**	.373 **.454**	.419 **.494**	.455 **.526**	.484 **.552**	.509 **.575**	.551 **.612**	.613 **.667**	.720 **.761**	2.021 **2.704**
45	.288 **.372**	.353 **.430**	.397 **.470**	.432 **.501**	.460 **.527**	.485 **.549**	.526 **.586**	.587 **.640**	.696 **.737**	2.014 **2.690**
50	.273 **.354**	.336 **.410**	.379 **.449**	.412 **.479**	.440 **.504**	.464 **.526**	.504 **.562**	.565 **.617**	.674 **.715**	2.008 **2.678**
60	.250 **.325**	.308 **.377**	.348 **.414**	.380 **.442**	.406 **.466**	.429 **.488**	.467 **.523**	.526 **.577**	.636 **.677**	2.000 **2.660**
70	.233 **.302**	.286 **.351**	.324 **.386**	.354 **.413**	.379 **.436**	.401 **.456**	.438 **.491**	.495 **.544**	.604 **.644**	1.994 **2.648**
80	.217 **.283**	.269 **.330**	.304 **.362**	.332 **.389**	.356 **.411**	.377 **.431**	.413 **.464**	.469 **.516**	.576 **.615**	1.990 **2.638**
90	.205 **.267**	.254 **.312**	.288 **.343**	.315 **.368**	.338 **.390**	.358 **.409**	.392 **.441**	.446 **.492**	.552 **.590**	1.987 **2.632**
100	.195 **.254**	.241 **.297**	.274 **.327**	.300 **.351**	.322 **.372**	.341 **.330**	.374 **.421**	.426 **.470**	.530 **.568**	1.984 **2.626**
125	.174 **.228**	.216 **.266**	.246 **.294**	.269 **.316**	.290 **.335**	.307 **.352**	.338 **.381**	.387 **.428**	.485 **.521**	1.979 **2.616**
150	.159 **.208**	.198 **.244**	.225 **.270**	.247 **.290**	.266 **.308**	.282 **.324**	.310 **.351**	.356 **.395**	.450 **.484**	1.976 **2.609**
200	.138 **.181**	.172 **.212**	.196 **.234**	.215 **.253**	.231 **.269**	.246 **.283**	.271 **.307**	.312 **.347**	.398 **.430**	1.972 **2.601**
300	.113 **.148**	.141 **.174**	.160 **.192**	.176 **.208**	.190 **.221**	.202 **.233**	.223 **.253**	.258 **.287**	.332 **.359**	1.968 **2.592**
400	.098 **.128**	.122 **.151**	.139 **.167**	.153 **.180**	.165 **.192**	.176 **.202**	.194 **.220**	.225 **.250**	.291 **.315**	1.966 **2.588**
500	.088 **.115**	.109 **.135**	.124 **.150**	.137 **.162**	.148 **.172**	.157 **.182**	.174 **.198**	.202 **.225**	.262 **.284**	1.965 **2.586**
1000	.062 **.081**	.077 **.096**	.088 **.106**	.097 **.115**	.105 **.122**	.112 **.129**	.124 **.141**	.144 **.160**	.188 **.204**	1.962 **2.581**
∞										1.960 **2.576**

**TABLE C. Values of ρ (rank-order correlation coefficient) at the 5%
and 1% levels of significance**

N	5%	1%
5	1.000	—
6	.886	1.000
7	.786	.929
8	.738	.881
9	.683	.833
10	.648	.794
12	.591	.777
14	.544	.715
16	.506	.665
18	.475	.625
20	.450	.591
22	.428	.562
24	.409	.537
26	.392	.515
28	.377	.496
30	.364	.478

* Computed from Olds, E. G., Distribution of the sum of squares of rank
differences for small numbers of individuals, *Ann. Math. Statist.*, 1938, 9,
133–148, and, The 5% significance levels for sums of squares of rank
differences and a correction, *Ann. Math. Statist.*, 1949, 20, 117–118, by
permission of the author and the Institute of Mathematical Statistics.

TABLE D. Functions of p, q, z, and y, where p and q are proportions (p + q = 1.00) and z and y are constants of the unit normal distribution curve*

p (or q)	A pq	B √pq	C pq/y	D √pq/y	E p/y	F y/p	G zy/p	H y	I zy/q	J y/q	K q/y	L √p/q	M √q/p	q (or p)
.99	.0099	.0995−	.3715	3.733	37.15−	.02692	−.06262	.02665	6.2002	2.665	.3752	9.950	.1005	.01
.98	.0196	.1400	.4048	2.892	20.24	.04941	−.1015	.04842	4.9719	2.421	.4131	7.000	.1429	.02
.97	.0291	.1706	.4277	2.507	14.26	.07015	−.1319	.06804	4.2657	2.268	.4409	5.686	.1759	.03
.96	.0384	.1960	.4456	2.274	11.14	.08976	−.1571	.08617	3.7717	2.154	.4642	4.899	.2041	.04
.95	.0475	.2179	.4605	2.113	9.211	.1086	−.1786	.1031	3.3928	2.063	.4848	4.359	.2294	.05
.94	.0564	.2375−	.4735	1.994	7.891	.1267	−.1970	.1191	3.0868	1.985	.5037	3.958	.2526	.06
.93	.0651	.2551	.4848	1.900	6.926	.1444	−.2131	.1343	2.8307	1.918	.5213	3.645	.2743	.07
.92	.0736	.2713	.4951	1.825	6.188	.1616	−.2271	.1487	2.6110	1.858	.5381	3.391	.2949	.08
.91	.0819	.2862	.5043	1.762	5.604	.1785	−.2393	.1624	2.4191	1.804	.5542	3.180	.3145	.09
.90	.0900	.3000	.5128	1.709	5.128	.1950	−.2499	.1755	2.2491	1.755	.5698	3.000	.3333	.10
.89	.0979	.3129	.5206	1.664	4.733	.2113	−.2591	.1880	2.0966	1.709	.5850	2.844	.3516	.11
.88	.1056	.3250	.5279	1.625	4.399	.2273	−.2671	.2000	1.9587	1.667	.5999	2.708	.3693	.12
.87	.1131	.3363	.5346	1.590	4.112	.2432	−.2739	.2115	1.8330	1.627	.6145	2.587	.3865	.13
.86	.1204	.3470	.5409	1.559	3.864	.2588	−.2796	.2226	1.7175	1.590	.6290	2.478	.4035	.14
.85	.1275	.3571	.5468	1.532	3.646	.2743	−.2843	.2332	1.6110	1.554	.6433	2.380	.4201	.15
.84	.1344	.3666	.5524	1.507	3.452	.2896	−.2880	.2433	1.5123	1.521	.6576	2.291	.4365	.16
.83	.1411	.3756	.5576	1.484	3.280	.3049	−.2909	.2531	1.4203	1.489	.6718	2.210	.4525	.17
.82	.1476	.3842	.5625	1.464	3.125	.3200	−.2929	.2624	1.3344	1.458	.6860	2.134	.4685	.18
.81	.1539	.3923	.5671	1.446	2.985	.3350	−.2941	.2714	1.2538	1.428	.7002	2.065	.4844	.19
.80	.1600	.4000	.5715	1.429	2.858	.3500	−.2946	.2800	1.1781	1.400	.7144	2.000	.5000	.20
.79	.1659	.4073	.5756	1.413	2.741	.3648	−.2942	.2882	1.1067	1.372	.7287	1.940	.5156	.21
.78	.1716	.4142	.5796	1.399	2.634	.3796	−.2931	.2961	1.0393	1.346	.7430	1.883	.5311	.22
.77	.1771	.4208	.5832	1.386	2.536	.3943	−.2913	.3036	.9754	1.320	.7575	1.830	.5465	.23
.76	.1824	.4271	.5867	1.374	2.445	.4090	−.2889	.3109	.9149	1.295	.7720	1.780	.5620	.24
.75	.1875	.4330	.5900	1.363	2.360	.4237	−.2858	.3178	.8573	1.271	.7867	1.732	.5774	.25

* When p is less than .50, interchange p and q, as the headings of the first and last columns indicate.

p (or q)	A pq	B $\sqrt{pq}$	C pq/y	D $\sqrt{pq}/y$	E p/y	F y/p	G zxy/p	H y	I zxy/q	J y/q	K q/y	L $\sqrt{p/q}$	M $\sqrt{q/p}$	q (or p)
.74	.1924	.4386	.5931	1.352	2.281	.4384	−.2820	.3244	.8026	1.248	.8016	1.687	.5928	.26
.73	.1971	.4440	.5961	1.343	2.208	.4529	−.2775	.3306	.7504	1.225	.8166	1.644	.6082	.27
.72	.2016	.4490	.5989	1.334	2.139	.4675	−.2725	.3366	.7006	1.202	.8318	1.604	.6236	.28
.71	.2059	.4538	.6015	1.326	2.074	.4822	−.2668	.3423	.6532	1.180	.8472	1.565	.6391	.29
.70	.2100	.4583	.6040	1.318	2.013	.4967	−.2605	.3477	.6078	1.159	.8628	1.528	.6547	.30
.69	.2139	.4625−	.6063	1.311	1.956	.5113	−.2535	.3528	.5643	1.138	.8787	1.492	.6703	.31
.68	.2176	.4665−	.6085	1.304	1.902	.5259	−.2460	.3576	.5227	1.118	.8949	1.458	.6860	.32
.67	.2211	.4702	.6106	1.298	1.850	.5405	−.2378	.3621	.4828	1.097	.9112	1.425	.7018	.33
.66	.2244	.4737	.6124	1.293	1.801	.5552	−.2290	.3664	.4445	1.078	.9279	1.393	.7178	.34
.65	.2275	.4770	.6142	1.288	1.755	.5698	−.2196	.3704	.4078	1.058	.9449	1.363	.7338	.35
.64	.2304	.4800	.6158	1.283	1.711	.5845	−.2095	.3741	.3725	1.039	.9623	1.333	.7500	.36
.63	.2331	.4828	.6174	1.279	1.669	.5993	−.1989	.3776	.3387	1.020	.9800	1.305	.7663	.37
.62	.2356	.4854	.6188	1.275	1.628	.6141	−.1876	.3808	.3061	1.002	.9980	1.277	.7829	.38
.61	.2379	.4877	.6200	1.271	1.590	.6290	−.1757	.3837	.2748	.9938	1.016	1.251	.7996	.39
.60	.2400	.4899	.6212	1.268	1.553	.6439	−.1631	.3863	.2447	.9659	1.035	1.225	.8165	.40
.59	.2419	.4918	.6223	1.265	1.518	.6589	−.1499	.3888	.2158	.9482	1.055	1.200	.8336	.41
.58	.2436	.4936	.6232	1.263	1.484	.6739	−.1361	.3909	.1879	.9307	1.074	1.175	.8510	.42
.57	.2451	.4951	.6240	1.260	1.451	.6891	−.1215	.3928	.1611	.9134	1.095	1.151	.8686	.43
.56	.2464	.4964	.6247	1.259	1.420	.7043	−.1063	.3944	.1353	.8964	1.116	1.128	.8864	.44
.55	.2475	.4975−	.6253	1.257	1.390	.7196	−.09043	.3958	.1105	.8796	1.137	1.106	.9045	.45
.54	.2484	.4984	.6258	1.256	1.360	.7351	−.07382	.3969	.0867	.8629	1.159	1.083	.9229	.46
.53	.2491	.4991	.6262	1.255	1.332	.7506	−.05650	.3978	.0637	.8464	1.181	1.062	.9417	.47
.52	.2496	.4996	.6264	1.254	1.305	.7662	−.03843	.3984	.0416	.8301	1.205	1.041	.9608	.48
.51	.2499	.4999	.6266	1.253	1.279	.7820	−.01960	.3988	.0204	.8139	1.229	1.020	.9802	.49
.50	.2500	.5000	.6267	1.253	1.253	.7979	−.00000	.3989	.0000	.7979	1.253	1.000	1.0000	.50

From Guilford, J. P. *Fundamental Statistics in Psychology and Education*. New York; McGraw-Hill, 1956.

TABLE E. Pearson's Q_3 estimates of r_t for various values of BC/AD*

r_t	BC/AD	r_t	BC/AD	r_t	BC/AD
.00	1.00	.35	2.49–2.55	.70	8.50–8.90
.01	1.01–1.03	.36	2.56–2.63	.71	8.91–9.35
.02	1.04–1.06	.37	2.64–2.71	.72	9.36–9.82
.03	1.07–1.08	.38	2.72–2.79	.73	9.83–10.33
.04	1.09–1.11	.39	2.80–2.87	.74	10.34–10.90
.05	1.12–1.14	.40	2.88–2.96	.75	10.91–11.51
.06	1.15–1.17	.41	2.97–3.05	.76	11.52–12.16
.07	1.18–1.20	.42	3.06–3.14	.77	12.17–12.89
.08	1.21–1.23	.43	3.15–3.24	.78	12.90–13.70
.09	1.24–1.27	.44	3.25–3.34	.79	13.71–14.58
.10	1.28–1.30	.45	3.35–3.45	.80	14.59–15.57
.11	1.31–1.33	.46	3.46–3.56	.81	15.58–16.65
.12	1.34–1.37	.47	3.57–3.68	.82	16.66–17.88
.13	1.38–1.40	.48	3.69–3.80	.83	17.89–19.28
.14	1.41–1.44	.49	3.81–3.92	.84	19.29–20.85
.15	1.45–1.48	.50	3.93–4.06	.85	20.86–22.68
.16	1.49–1.52	.51	4.07–4.20	.86	22.69–24.76
.17	1.53–1.56	.52	4.21–4.34	.87	24.77–27.22
.18	1.57–1.60	.53	4.35–4.49	.88	27.23–30.09
.19	1.61–1.64	.54	4.50–4.66	.89	30.10–33.60
.20	1.65–1.69	.55	4.67–4.82	.90	33.61–37.79
.21	1.70–1.73	.56	4.83–4.99	.91	37.80–43.06
.22	1.74–1.78	.57	5.00–5.18	.92	43.07–49.83
.23	1.79–1.83	.58	5.19–5.38	.93	49.84–58.79
.24	1.84–1.88	.59	5.39–5.59	.94	58.80–70.95
.25	1.89–1.93	.60	5.60–5.80	.95	70.96–89.01
.26	1.94–1.98	.61	5.81–6.03	.96	89.02–117.54
.27	1.99–2.04	.62	6.04–6.28	.97	117.55–169.67
.28	2.05–2.10	.63	6.29–6.54	.98	169.68–293.12
.29	2.11–2.15	.64	6.55–6.81	.99	293.13–923.97
.30	2.16–2.22	.65	6.82–7.10	1.00	923.98
.31	2.23–2.28	.66	7.11–7.42		
.32	2.29–2.34	.67	7.43–7.75		
.33	2.35–2.41	.68	7.76–8.11		
.34	2.42–2.48	.69	8.12–8.49		

* From Davidoff, M. D., and Goheen, H. W. A table for the rapid determination of the tetrachoric correlation coefficient. *Psychometrika*, 1953, **18**, 115–121.

TABLE F. Corrected split-halves reliability coefficients based on the Spearman-Brown formula

Uncorrected Value	Corrected Value	Uncorrected Value	Corrected Value
.01	.02	.36	.53
.02	.04	.37	.54
.03	.06	.38	.55
.04	.08	.39	.56
.05	.10	.40	.57
.06	.11		
.07	.13	.41	.58
.08	.15	.42	.59
.09	.16	.43	.60
.10	.18	.44	.61
		.45	.62
.11	.20	.46	.63
.12	.21	.47	.64
.13	.23	.48	.65
.14	.24	.49	.66
.15	.26	.50	.67
.16	.28		
.17	.29	.51	.68
.18	.30	.52	.68
.19	.32	.53	.69
.20	.33	.54	.70
		.55	.71
.21	.35	.56	.72
.22	.36	.57	.73
.23	.37	.58	.73
.24	.39	.59	.74
.25	.40	.60	.75
.26	.41		
.27	.42	.61	.76
.28	.44	.62	.76
.29	.45	.63	.77
.30	.46	.64	.78
		.65	.79
.31	.47	.66	.80
.32	.48	.67	.80
.33	.50	.68	.81
.34	.51	.69	.82
.35	.52	.70	.82

TABLE F.—*continued*

Uncorrected Value	Corrected Value	Uncorrected Value	Corrected Value
.71	.83	.86	.92
.72	.84	.87	.93
.73	.84	.88	.94
.74	.85	.89	.94
.75	.86	.90	.95
.76	.86	.91	.95
.77	.87	.92	.96
.78	.88	.93	.96
.79	.88	.94	.97
.80	.89	.95	.97
.81	.90	.96	.98
.82	.90	.97	.98
.83	.91	.98	.99
.84	.91	.99	.99
.85	.92	1.00	1.00

APPENDIX TWO

ANSWERS TO PROBLEMS GIVEN IN THE TEXT

Chapter 9, page 103: For the Mechanical Principles test, $h^2 = .74$, $u^2 = .26$, and $r_{gh} = .84$.

Chapter 10, page 106:

$$\mathbf{D} = \begin{Vmatrix} 2 & 5 \\ 3 & -2 \\ 5 & 1 \end{Vmatrix}$$

Chapter 10, page 108:

$$\mathbf{BA} = \begin{Vmatrix} 24 & 8 \\ 69 & 63 \end{Vmatrix}$$

APPENDIX THREE

DERIVATIONS AND MORE ADVANCED MATERIAL

1. *Proof that the Regression Line for* z *Scores Passes Through the Origin* (see page 36):

We shall deal with deviation scores,

$$x \equiv X - M_X \text{ and } y \equiv Y - M_Y$$

It can be shown that each set of deviation scores is balanced around its mean, that is,

$$\sum x = 0 \text{ and } \sum y = 0$$

The predicted deviation score is given by the linear equation,

$$\hat{y} = a + bx$$

(The a and b values of this equation are not necessarily equal to those in Equation 5.10 of Chapter 5 for the two-variable problem because that equation deals with *raw* scores.)

Let Q represent the sum of squares of deviations of the observed y values from the predicted y values:

$$Q \equiv \sum (y - \hat{y})^2$$

Now we substitute the expression for y from above and square:

$$Q = \sum (y - a - bx)^2$$
$$Q = \sum (y^2 + a^2 + b^2 x^2 - 2ay - 2bxy + 2abx)$$

The summation sign is distributed to the terms, and the constants are brought outside the summation signs, giving

$$Q = \sum y^2 + Na^2 + b^2 \sum x^2 - 2a \sum y - 2b \sum xy + 2ab \sum x$$

($\sum a^2 = Na^2$ because of the Third Summation Law; see Chapter 2.)

Assuming that a sample of x and y values has been observed, all the quantities behind summation signs become constants, and a and b become variables (see page 39). Now we partially differentiate Q with respect to a and set equal to zero, giving

$$\frac{\partial Q}{\partial a} = 0 + 2Na + 0 - 2\sum y - 0 + 2b\sum x = 0$$

$$2Na - 2\sum y + 2b\sum x = 0$$

Since both $\sum x$ and $\sum y$ equal zero,

$$2Na = 0$$

Since a sample of persons has been measured, N cannot equal zero, so a must equal zero. Therefore the regression line for deviation scores must pass through the origin. Since the transformation from deviation scores to z scores involves only multiplication by a constant (namely, the reciprocal of the standard deviation), the regression line for z scores must also pass through the origin.

2. *Derivation of the Simultaneous Equations for Multiple Correlation with Three Variables* (see page 43)

The predicted z_0 score is a linear combination of z_1 and z_2 scores:

$$\hat{z}_0 = \beta_1 z_1 + \beta_2 z_2$$

Let P represent the sum of squares of deviations of the observed z_0 values from the predicted z_0 values:

$$P \equiv \sum(z_0 - \hat{z}_0)^2$$

Substituting, squaring, distributing, and taking out constants, we have

$$P = \sum(z_0 - \beta_1 z_1 - \beta_2 z_2)^2$$

$$P = \sum(z_0^2 + \beta_1^2 z_1^2 + \beta_2^2 z_2^2 - 2\beta_1 z_0 z_1 - 2\beta_2 z_0 z_2 + 2\beta_1\beta_2 z_1 z_2)$$

$$P = \sum z_0^2 + \beta_1^2\sum z_1^2 + \beta_2^2\sum z_2^2 - 2\beta_1\sum z_0 z_1 - 2\beta_2\sum z_0 z_2 + 2\beta_1\beta_2\sum z_1 z_2$$

Differentiating P partially with respect to β_1 and setting equal to zero, we have

$$2\beta_1\sum z_1^2 - 2\sum z_0 z_1 + 2\beta_2\sum z_1 z_2 = 0$$

Differentiating P partially with respect to β_2 and setting equal to zero, we have

$$2\beta_2\sum z_2^2 - 2\sum z_0 z_2 + 2\beta_1\sum z_1 z_2 = 0$$

Dividing each of these equations by $2N$ gives

$$\begin{bmatrix} \beta_1(\sum z_1^2/N) - (\sum z_0 z_1/N) + \beta_2(\sum z_1 z_2/N) = 0 \\ \beta_2(\sum z_2^2/N) - (\sum z_0 z_2/N) + \beta_1(\sum z_1 z_2/N) = 0 \end{bmatrix}$$

The factors in parentheses are either correlations or else the mean of squared standard scores (which are equivalent to unity; see page 41). Thus we can simplify:

$$\begin{bmatrix} \beta_1 - r_{01} + r_{12}\beta_2 = 0 \\ \beta_2 - r_{02} + r_{12}\beta_1 = 0 \end{bmatrix}$$

Rearranging terms, we have a system of equations that is analogous to Equation 4.22 of Chapter 4:

$$\begin{bmatrix} \beta_1 + r_{12}\beta_2 = r_{01} \\ r_{12}\beta_1 + \beta_2 = r_{02} \end{bmatrix}$$

3. *The Significance Test for the Multiple Correlation Coefficient as a Variance-Ratio Test* (see page 57)

The nonpredicted variance, $(1 - R^2)\sigma_0^2$, and the predicted variance, $R^2\sigma_0^2$, can each be considered to be an estimate of the population variance. However, for this purpose we must divide each of the corresponding "sums of squares," which are $(1 - R^2)N\sigma_0^2$ and $R^2 N\sigma_0^2$, respectively, by the corresponding degrees of freedom, which are $N - m - 1$ and m (where m is the number of predictor variables), respectively (McNemar, 1962, pp. 281–284). The variance ratio, F, is formed as the second estimate divided by the first estimate:

$$F = \frac{R^2 N\sigma_0^2/m}{(1 - R^2)N\sigma_0^2/N - m - 1} = \frac{R^2(N - m - 1)}{(1 - R^2)m}$$

This equation can be solved for R, giving

$$R = \sqrt{Fm/Fm + N - m - 1}$$

The entries in Table B can be calculated by this formula from the corresponding entries in a variance-ratio table. However, note that the "number of variables" in Table B is $m + 1$, using our present notation!

4. A Variance-Ratio Test for the Addition of a New Predictor Variable to an Existing Battery of Predictors (see page 57)

Let R be the multiple correlation involving m predictors and R_+ be the multiple correlation involving $m + 1$ predictors. The following quotient should be referred to an F table with d.f. $= 1$ for the "greater mean square" and d.f. $= N - m - 2$ for the "lesser mean square":

$$F = \frac{(R_+{}^2 - R^2)(N - m - 2)}{1 - R_+{}^2}$$

5. Definition of the Inverse of a Matrix

The identity matrix $\mathbf{I}$ defines a special class of square matrices. All the elements in its principal diagonal have a value of unity, and all its other elements have a value of zero, for example,

$$\mathbf{I} = \begin{Vmatrix} 1 & 0 & 0 \\ 0 & 1 & 0 \\ 0 & 0 & 1 \end{Vmatrix}$$

If the determinant of a square matrix $\mathbf{A}$ does not vanish, there exists another unique square matrix $\mathbf{A}^{-1}$ called the "inverse" or "reciprocal" of $\mathbf{A}$. The inverse matrix is defined by the relationship,

$$\mathbf{A}\mathbf{A}^{-1} = \mathbf{I}$$

Although the definition of the inverse matrix is thus a rather simple one, its calculation is usually quite tedious. A procedure that is particularly efficient for use with automatic desk calculators is given by Cattell (1952, pp. 226–229).

6. *Multiple Correlation Expressed in Terms of Matrix Algebra* (see page 44)

Let $\mathbf{R}$ be a square matrix giving the intercorrelations of a set of predictor variables, let $\boldsymbol{\beta}$ be a column vector of β coefficients, and let $\mathbf{r_0}$ be a column vector of validity coefficients. Then Equation 4.22 of Chapter 4 can be expressed thus in terms of matrix algebra:

$$
\begin{matrix} \mathbf{R} \end{matrix}
\begin{Vmatrix}
1 & r_{12} & r_{13} \cdot \cdot r_{1m} \\
r_{21} & 1 & r_{23} \cdot \cdot r_{2m} \\
\cdot & \cdot & \cdot \cdot \cdot \cdot \cdot \cdot \\
\cdot & \cdot & \cdot \cdot \cdot \cdot \cdot \cdot \\
r_{m1} & r_{m2} & r_{m3} \cdot \cdot \ \ 1
\end{Vmatrix}
\cdot
\begin{matrix} \boldsymbol{\beta} \end{matrix}
\begin{Vmatrix}
\beta_1 \\ \beta_2 \\ \cdot \\ \cdot \\ \beta_m
\end{Vmatrix}
=
\begin{matrix} = \ \ \ \mathbf{r_0} \end{matrix}
\begin{Vmatrix}
r_{01} \\ r_{02} \\ \cdot \\ \cdot \\ r_{0m}
\end{Vmatrix}
$$

By a process that is analogous in ordinary algebra to dividing both sides of the equation by $\mathbf{R}$, we can obtain

$$\boldsymbol{\beta} = \mathbf{R}^{-1}\mathbf{r_0}$$

This equation indicates that, to obtain the β weights for a given set of data, we can postmultiply *the inverse of* the matrix of intercorrelations by the column vector of validity coefficients. This expression is particularly useful if we are dealing with more than one criterion variable but a single set of predictor variables. In this case, after the inverse of $\mathbf{R}$ has been calculated, it is a relatively simple matter to obtain the set of β weights to be used in predicting each new criterion.

7. *Brief Description of the Principal Axes Method of Factor Extraction* (see page 161)

For any symmetric matrix $\mathbf{A}$ there is a matrix $\mathbf{U}$ whose rows and columns are all normal and whose inner products are all zero:

$$\mathbf{A} = \mathbf{U}\boldsymbol{\Lambda}\mathbf{U}'$$

$\mathbf{U}$ is a matrix of "latent vectors," and $\boldsymbol{\Lambda}$ is a matrix whose entries in the principal diagonal are "latent roots" and whose other entries are all zero. (Note that this $\boldsymbol{\Lambda}$ matrix is *not* the same as Thurstone's transformation matrix!) $\Lambda^{1/2}$ is a matrix whose entries are the square roots of the entries in Λ. The principal axes factor matrix can be obtained by postmultiplying U by $\Lambda^{1/2}$.

In Hotelling's method of extracting principal axes factors, one obtains as a first approximation the column totals of the correlation matrix. (At this point the values are proportional to the first centroid factor loadings.) Then the column totals are "scaled" by dividing by the largest column total. The scaled column totals can be considered to be a row vector, which is then postmultiplied by the correlation matrix. This gives a second approximation, which is similarly scaled. Then another postmultiplication is performed, and the cycle is repeated until a scaled row vector is equal to the preceding scaled row vector to any desired degree of accuracy. Then multiplication by a constant factor gives the first principal axis factor loadings. The first factor residuals are calculated by the same process that is described in Chapter 11. Then the second principal axis factor can be extracted from this residual matrix, and so forth.

AUTHOR INDEX

SUBJECT INDEX